Measuring Marke

103 Key Metrics Eve
Marketer Needs

	DATE DUE		
July 5/12			

Measuring Marketing
103 Key Metrics Every Marketer Needs

John Davis

John Wiley & Sons (Asia) Pte Ltd

Other Wiley Editorial Offices
John Wiley & Sons, Inc., 111 River Street, Hoboken, NJ 07030, USA
John Wiley & Sons Ltd, The Atrium, Southern Gate, Chichester PO19 8Q, England
John Wiley & Sons (Canada) Ltd, 5353 Dundas Street West, Suite 400, Toronto, Ontario, Canada
John Wiley & Sons Australia Ltd, M9B 6HB, 42 McDougall Street, Milton, Queensland 4064, Australia
Wiley-VCH, Bosch Strasse 12, D-69469 Weinheim, Germany

Library of Congress Cataloging-in-Publication Data:
ISBN-13: 978-0-470-82132-9
ISBN-10: 0-470-82132-9

Typeset in 11/13 point, Palatino by ChungKing Data Systems
Printed in Singapore by Saik Wah Press Pte Ltd
10 9 8 7 6 5 4 3 2

Contents

To Barb, Kate, Chris and Bridget…

You make everything worthwhile.

Acknowledgments

The past few years have seen surging interest in measuring marketing performance from senior management and marketing managers. The challenge for management is knowing what to measure and how to measure it. Starting from an initial set of over 200 measures (and there are many others beyond this), 103 measures made the cut. It was not an easy decision because so many of the measures not included are useful, but usually in very specific, even unique, marketing situations.

Several people and organizations need to be thanked for their support during the writing of this book. Nick Wallwork, the John Wiley & Sons publisher, is a spark of supportive inspiration. Nick's team, including Janis, CJ, Pauline and Louise are a dynamic group that eagerly supported this project, in addition to others, on which I am working. Brickwork Consultancy provided research support for several metrics. Steinar Cramer was an editing marvel, helping with readability, ensuring narrative consistency and finessing subtle details. Many colleagues at Singapore Management University were supportive throughout: Annie Koh, Associate Dean of the Lee Kong Chian School of Business (LKCSB) and Dean of Executive Education at Singapore Management University (SMU), has been an enthusiastic cheerleader since day one; David Montgomery, former Dean of the Lee Kong Chian School of Business and the Sebastian S. Kresge Professor of Marketing Strategy, Emeritus at Stanford University Graduate School of Business has relentlessly hammered home the message of rigor with relevance; Jin Han, Area Coordinator for Marketing, leads SMU's marketing faculty and it is a pleasure to work with both him and so many talented colleagues. They are an exceptional group. Shashank Nigam, a bright and energetic undergraduate at Singapore Management University, deserves special recognition for his research support while also taking a full academic load, traveling around the world presenting papers at international competitions (winning, too!) and maintaining an unfailingly optimistic disposition under intense pressure. He is a future business leader to watch.

Most importantly, my family somehow allowed me to have a year of weekends and late nights devoted to working on this book. The love and support they showed is immeasurable—no marketing formula can capture that.

Introduction

The measurement of marketing has become one of the most important business needs today as companies face increasing pressures to demonstrate financial returns across the organization from shareholders, investors, senior managers and boards of directors.

A common question asked by senior managers is "what measure can I use to determine if my company's marketing is effective?" The answer is that there is no single measure that accomplishes this. Companies develop with their own unique organizational DNA, including vision, strategies, corporate culture, hiring practices, products and customers. No two companies are identical, even when competing in the same markets with similar products. Relying on industry benchmarks is useful as a starting point, but benchmarks hide the biases arising from competitors that have vastly different cost structures, distribution networks, compensation practices and even company personalities.

To effectively measure marketing, company management must begin by understanding the context of their business situation. Figure 1 outlines the relationship between the company and its customers. Since a key determinant of business success is acquiring customers, managers must understand this relationship.

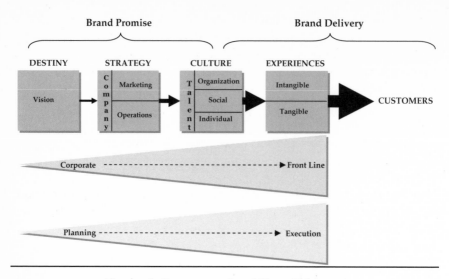

Figure 1: Components of Brand Value

Source: John Davis and Brand New View, INC.

As the diagram illustrates, business leaders must have a clear sense of corporate destiny, or vision, which guides the company for the long term. The vision provides direction for the business and a strategy that articulates the goals and objectives of every area of the company. The vision is then translated into operating and marketing strategies, each aligned with the company strategy but tailored to reflect their roles in the organization. When the vision and strategy are effectively combined, this has a positive influence on the development of the company's culture, starting with the hiring practices, which, in turn, translate into individual and organizational roles and practices. An important element of culture is the social structure of the firm, which describes the unwritten rules that guide acceptable behavior inside the company, affecting how decisions are made formally and informally. These first three areas—destiny, strategy and culture—comprise the company's promise to the market (i.e. this is who we are, this is what we stand for, this is what we are known for and this is how we behave). The final area, experiences, is concerned with how the company delivers its offerings to the market. More than products and services, companies are increasingly discovering the importance of providing value-added experiences that connect to customers at multiple points in the market (products, locations, advertising, web, events, entertainment, design, service…). This final stage represents the company's effort to deliver on the promises made.

Below this chain of events are the connections between the vision-setters and the customer-facing implementers. It is clear that the further a company progresses along this path toward the customer, the more important the front-line staff becomes to delivering on the promises made by senior management. As shown, the business effort shifts from senior management planning to front-line execution.

Each point along the way is both an opportunity to reinforce the company's offerings, or a potential point of failure between the brand promise and brand delivery. For example, the relationship between marketing and operations at the strategy stage is paramount to effective execution. If their respective strategic efforts are aligned with the company strategy, then the chance for successful delivery increases significantly.

For marketers, the implications are clear because their role is no longer functional or tactical, but strategic. From customer targeting to product development to integrated marketing communications, each is dependent on a consistent implementation of strategy. For non-marketers, understanding the importance of organizational alignment throughout means that execution must be accomplished with full knowledge of the company's and marketing's promises to the market.

When the business-customer relationship is viewed from this perspective, the inadequacy of a single measure of marketing performance becomes clear. When discussing the measurement of marketing performance, are we asking about strategy? Or customer relationship development? Or advertising? Or products? Or retail experiences?

The question grows more complex when lifecycle stages are introduced as in Figure 2.

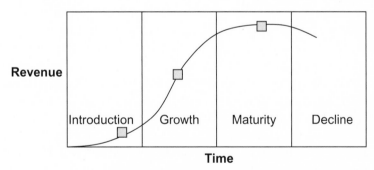

Figure 2: Traditional Product Lifecycle

Each stage of the classic lifecycle curve (known as the "S" curve for its shape) has different implications for marketing programs and, consequently, marketing measures. For example, the introduction stage of a new product or a new company is an uncertain time at best. Market acceptance is unknown, yet expense has been incurred to produce a product. However, without marketing to announce the product to the market, it will fail for lack of awareness, no matter how innovative or clever the design. The company's objective is to generate revenues, since survival is most important. Aggressive advertising to build awareness and educate the market plus volume-oriented sales programs to attract customers may be the best combination of activities.

Assuming the company is fortunate enough to enter the growth stage, the marketer will want to build momentum by modifying the marketing communications message, perhaps emphasizing the product's unique value versus that of emerging competitors and reducing or eliminating the educational aspects of their message (since the product is now known). Finally, as our fictional firm enters the maturity stage, the customers' needs have changed as has the required marketing communication. Customers who have been loyal to the company throughout the lifecycle want to know why they should continue supporting its products, so a one-to-one relationship-oriented marketing campaign is developed, with entirely different goals and expectations.

Several events are occurring in this scenario:

- The launch of a new product to an uncertain market

- The development of marketing and sales efforts to build early awareness

- The rapid growth of the product's acceptance and the concurrent demands on expanded production, distribution, and product and customer support that this implies

- Refined marketing communications that reinforce the product's unique value compared to the competition

- The maturing of the customer base toward a loyalty-based relationship

Again, no single marketing measure will succinctly or accurately capture and measure these activities. There must be multiple measures, reflecting different marketing approaches, changing lifecycle stages and a maturing customer audience. Marketers and senior managers must understand this if there is to be useful measurement of marketing activities.

How the Book is Organized

This book reviews 103 different marketing measures organized within three primary themes with sub-segments:

1. Marketing Planning and Customers
   a. Objectives
   b. Forecasts
   c. Markets
   d. Segments and Customers

2. The Offering

   a. Products and New Products

   b. Prices

   c. Advertising

   d. Sales Promotion

   e. Direct Marketing

   f. Internet Marketing

   g. Brands

   h. Retail

3. Sales Force

   a. Sales Force Size

   b. Sales Force Quotas

   c. Sales Variance Analysis

   d. Sales Force Compensation

Each measure is described according to three categories:

1. Measurement Need: the basis for the measure

2. Solution: the formula or framework, with an example

3. Impact on Decision Making: the potential impact for the company and the marketing effort

Finally, this book is designed as a reference for marketing and sales management. But the measures are important for managers across the organization since few company decisions have a contained impact. The more that senior management and emerging managers understand about the complexity of measuring marketing, the greater their appreciation and understanding of marketers, which can only benefit organizations.

I

MARKETING PLANNING AND CUSTOMERS

Marketers have an array of challenges, responsibilities, demands and expectations to perform their jobs successfully. The days of marketers focusing mostly on creativity and communications programs, such as advertising and public relations, have been rendered obsolete by the needs of a more sophisticated, globalizing business world. Marketers have a strategic role in most organizations that guides companies toward achieving long-term objectives. Success is predicated on quickly synthesizing volumes of data, understanding rapidly changing markets and their underlying dynamics, building complex business and customer relationships, and doing all of this profitably. Their marketing plan must align with the overall corporate business strategy while also providing specific information about customer needs (and how those needs will be addressed) and the probable impact to the company if the plan succeeds.

The measures discussed in this section are:

Objectives

- Revenue
- Gross profit
- Value to volume ratio
- Net profit
- Earnings-based value
- Return on sales
- Return on assets
- Return on equity
- Marketing cost per unit
- Program/non-program ratio
- Program/payroll ratio
- Net sales contribution
- Time-driven activity-based costing

Forecasts

- Causal forecast
- Time series analysis

Markets

- Market growth
- Market share
- Market demand
- Market penetration

Customers and Segments

- Segment profitability
- Customer profitability
- Share of customer
- Customer acquisition costs
- Cost per lead
- Break-even analysis
- Customer equity and lifetime value analysis
- Consumer franchise
- Retention rate
- Churn rate
- New customer gains
- Customer losses
- Return on customer

Planning Objectives

To start, marketers must know how well their companies are doing by understanding common financial measures. Each measure derives its result from the performance of a marketing-related activity, whether that is customer development, product, price, place, or promotion. When developing a marketing plan, marketers must understand the connection between their pricing strategy for a new product and the ultimate influence on revenue, for example. Furthermore, marketers add weight to their plans if they forecast alternative scenarios and demonstrate the potential financial implications of different product and pricing choices.

The objective measures described within this section provide marketers with a sensible and simple review of key financial measures and why they are relevant to the marketer's work. As with all of the measures in this book, they are not sequential (although some are organized that way). Instead, they are a reference of key measures beneficial to the overall progress of the marketing effort.

Markets, Customers and Segments

The measures in this section are grouped into two sub-themes:

1. Markets

2. Customers and Segments

A key expectation of marketers and their responsibilities is to clearly analyze and describe the markets they are targeting and the customers within. It is incumbent on marketers that they evaluate and defend why they believe the markets they wish to enter are attractive. Senior management is likely to ask:

- Is the market opportunity large enough to justify the financial and resource commitments marketers are recommending?

- Is the market growing at an attractive rate?

- Can the company build leading and/or defensible share of market?

- Does each of the segments offer attractive profit potential?

The role of marketing is to help the company grow by attracting and retaining customers in the context of the company's core competencies, as described in the introduction. Figure 3 depicts the steps marketers take to develop their customer base.

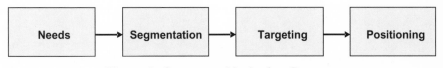

Figure 3: Customer Marketing Process

Needs

Successful customer development requires that marketers begin with research to identify and understand needs that exist in the market. This initial research will enable marketers to determine if the needs can be met by their company based on its competencies. There are two common types of needs that research helps uncover:

1. Articulated:

> These needs are clearly described by customers to the marketer, such as, "I would like this car to have leather seats". The customer is able to easily convey their needs based on existing experiences with products. Understanding articulated needs helps companies improve existing features, extend product lines or offer value-added enhancements, such as VIP service.

2. Latent:

> Identifying latent needs can reveal entirely new opportunities through new products and new markets. Innovation is an important ingredient in successfully tapping into latent needs. The challenge for marketers is that latent needs are hidden and unknown. They are much harder to identify since customers have difficulty imagining true innovation versus offering the incremental improvements described by articulated needs. In their book, *Blue Ocean Strategy*, authors W. Chan Kim and Renée Mauborgne discuss "The Four Actions Framework"[1], which provides guidance for companies seeking wholly new opportunities outside conventional strategic planning approaches. Among the companies they cite, Cirque du Soleil stands out as a company that created an entirely new market and customer base: those seeking a unique entertainment blend of live music, theatre, art and acrobatics mixed with select circus themes (*sans* animals!) to create an unparalleled experience. Guy Laliberté, founder of Cirque du Soleil, did not conduct the classic marketer's retinue of focus groups, surveys, test markets or even ROI to develop the company and its products. It simply *happened*. In a similar fashion, the original Polaroid camera developed by Edwin Land was not the result of extensive market research or consumer testing. No consumers approached him to articulate that instant photography was what they needed, other than his daughter casually telling him that it took too long to develop film. That is hardly a scientific sample. But when Polaroid cameras came out, they revolutionized photography, despite the lack of evidence to support such a significant innovation.

The marketer's effort to identify and understand is a critical step to developing a sustainable customer base, since it directly influences how a company's products (or services) are developed and communicated to maximize their appeal to the target audience.

Segmentation

The next step is identifying segments comprised of groups of customers that share a common set of characteristics, including similar needs. The absence of such segments, or highly fragmented, hard to service customers in challenging locations, suggests the lack of a viable market, and the marketer should therefore abandon further planning on that specific product or project.

Market segmentation differs slightly between consumer and business markets. Market segments are evaluated on the basis of Figure 4.

Demographic	**Geographic**
Psychographic	**Product Use**

Figure 4: Segmentation Choices

Source: Corey, E.R. *Marketing Strategy—An Overview.* Boston, MA; Harvard Business School Publishing, 1999.

- Demographic:

  - Demographic segmentation data for consumers has information about the most common variables found in census surveys, including age, sex, income, and ethnicity. Demographic segmentation does differ slightly around the world, with the U.S. and Europe having the most complete data. Asia is a vast region with countries from India in the west to Japan and China in the north, and Malaysia, Indonesia and Singapore in the south. Each country collects census data differently (some not at all), so finding accurate information is a marketer's central challenge. Demographics are generic, offering little or no insight into shared needs or behaviors.

  - Business demographic segmentation focuses on company size, industry and/or specialization, and location.

- Geographic:

  - Consumer geographic data describes population, climate and region or country. It can be useful to marketers seeking to reach customers who share location-based characteristics (i.e. cold weather or water-based activities).

- o Business geographic data is similar to consumer geographic data and also considers location clusters, which are high concentrations of operations due to population, physical boundaries (mountains) and even some economic/political characteristics (legal, capital markets, educational infrastructure), since countries are still geographically defined.

- • Psychographic:

  - o Consumer psychographic information focuses on lifestyle, behaviors and interests. It is more qualitative than just demographic (i.e. "people aged 15-24") and geographic (i.e."4.5 million people live in Singapore's tropical climate") since it focuses on how customers live and behave. Consumer marketers, in particular, like psychographics since they identify many emotional qualities that can be tapped into for marketing campaigns.

  - o Business psychographics are concerned with the behaviors, internal status, and portfolio (authority) of the customer and their buying team. This is described by the 5 Ambassadors model in the introduction section of the Sales Force theme (see p.327).

- • Product Use:

  - o Consumer product use segmentation focuses on how target customers will use the product (or service). For example, Stanley is a toolmaker that targets its products toward construction professionals and do-it-yourself consumers working on home improvement projects.

  - o Business product use is similar, but in a company-to-company context. For example, Oracle sells database software to companies in many industries. The product is used to help all companies organize, retrieve and analyze customer, product, competitor and company data. Any company with the need to organize its data would be a potential customer.

Targeting

After identifying segments with common characteristics, marketers identify or target those segments that are the most attractive financially, in terms of size and growth prospects, and that match the company's core competencies well. Philip Kotler describes five approaches to targeting[2] (adapted from Derek F. Abell[3]), as shown in Figure 5.

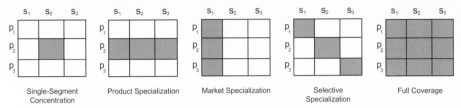

Figure 5: Target Market Selection Patterns

(S = segments, P = products)

Source: Adapted from Kotler, P., Swee, H. A., Siew, M. L., Tan, C. T. *Marketing Management: An Asian Perspective*. Singapore: Prentice Hall Pearson Education Asia Ptd Ltd, 2003.

Single-segment concentration: All product and marketing efforts are directed to one segment. Firms with limited resources often find this approach to be the most effective since it minimizes the risk of the company spreading its product and marketing dollars across too many product and market needs. Start-ups in the introductory phase of their lifecycle would find this approach useful since they do not have the resources to reach multiple markets simultaneously. Alternatively, firms specializing in a very specific area, such as bio-tech solutions for various cancers, may also choose this, since they do not need, or care about reaching, non-cancer segments.

Product specialization: Management concentrates on marketing a single product to multiple segments. Pixar has developed a reputation for top-quality films using proprietary computer animation. Its films appeal to a wide range of market segments, from kids to adults, and even across cultures. Pixar does not make washing machines, food or nose-hair trimmers. It simply concentrates on computer-animated films.

Market specialization: Market specialization is concerned with offering multiple products to specific customers (unlike a specific product to multiple customers, as we saw in product specialization) who have particular needs or interest. LVMH (the French luxury goods giant) does not spend time, money or product development efforts trying to reach budget consumers. Its area of expertise is consumers who love luxury products, and LVMH offers over 50 well-known luxury brands (including Louis Vuitton, Givenchy, Krug, Donna Karan and Christian Dior).

Selective specialization: The company believes it can successfully sell different products in multiple, even unrelated markets simultaneously. The marketing challenge grows because the markets a company chooses and the products offered can escalate from controlled selectivity to uncontrolled chaos, spreading marketing investments too thin. It is tempting for rapidly growing companies to expand into new markets quickly and to diversify their product offerings, both to appeal to markets and to spread risk. Mars, a privately-owned, U.S.-based firm best known for its snack foods, including

Mars Bars (the same candy bar is called "Milky Way" in the U.S.), Snickers and M&M's. Additionally, Mars competes successfully in the pet care, main meal foods, and branded beverages businesses. These businesses comprise the extent of Mars' selective specialization. Unlike Procter & Gamble, Mars is not in dozens of different consumer products categories. In each instance, Mars is a market leader in a specialized area.

Full market coverage: The company concentrates on offering the broadest product offering to the widest possible range of consumers. Toyota and General Motors (GM) both provide full market coverage, offering automobiles to everyone from entry-level buyers to luxury consumers. GM's products range from the low-end Saturn to the high-end Cadillac. Toyota's coverage includes the Echo at the entry level and Lexus at the luxury level. GM has not done nearly as well with this strategy in recent decades as Toyota. Firms attempting such an approach must have substantial resources.[4]

Positioning

Positioning is how marketers influence customers' perceptions of a product or service. With the growth of marketing vehicles such as new media, the Internet and mobile communications, there are multiple entry points through which to influence target customers, but added complexity as well. Perceptions are not created overnight. They take a combination of direct customer experience with the product, word of mouth, and years of market acceptance and use. There are four primary positioning themes a company can pursue as illustrated in Figure 6.

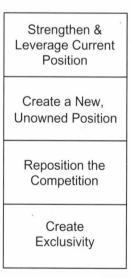

Figure 6: Positioning Choices

Strengthen and leverage current position

Companies that own a market-leading position focus on reminding the market of this leadership through advertising that touts their status. Measuring this status is not precise, however. While traditional measures like dollar sales or units sold can convey market position, they are not always the best approach to the market. Customers increasingly want to know why this information is relevant to them. For example, GM is the world's largest company by revenues (US$193 billion in 2005), but their size has not proven to be persuasive to customers since their market share has been declining for years. Conversely, companies that own a unique niche, even if they are not market-leading as measured by dollars or units, can leverage this to reinforce their reputation and carve out a distinct identity. Joie de Vivre Hospitality, based in San Francisco, is a boutique hotel company with 30 properties in northern California. They are not the biggest hotelier in the market, but they have a highly regarded reputation as the most innovative and idiosyncratic hotel company. Joie de Vivre has garnered critical acclaim from travel guides, including Conde Nast's Gold List, plus earned coverage from leading business publications around the world.

Create a new, unowned position

This is a worthy and challenging positioning objective. Those who succeed are often remembered for being first to market, even if they are not first in market share. Amazon ("earth's biggest bookstore"[5]), Starbucks (Howard Schultz, founder and Chairman, calls Starbucks"the third place"[6], after home and work), Mars' Milky Way candy bars ("if only all good things could last this long"[7]), and the Boeing 747 (the world's first jumbo jet[8]) each created new, unowned positions.

Reposition the competition

Apple Computer has attempted to do this by convincing PC/Windows users to switch to the Mac platform, through a campaign called "Switch". In it, regular consumers are shown on film describing why they switched to Apple. Apple is positioning their Mac operating system as a higher quality alternative to Microsoft, despite Windows' market dominance as measured by operating system market share.

Create exclusivity

Exclusivity attracts customers because it suggests that something is utterly unique and/or for the privileged few. It is a way of creating a perception that says, "this is not for everybody, only for you." Exclusivity can be powerful. Frequent flyer programs have evolved into marketing necessities for airlines. With more people traveling and becoming frequent flyer members, categories of flyers have been created, with the most exclusive flyers, designated as Platinum or VIPs, receiving benefits other frequent flyers do not get (unless they dramatically increase their air travel).

Summary

The frameworks discussed in this introduction are part of a marketer's normal activities. Measuring these activities is vital to understanding if the marketing effort succeeded or not. The measures within this book will help marketers understand the strengths and weaknesses of their planning, the impact on their company, and the opportunities to pursue versus those that should be abandoned.

Endnotes

1 Kim, W.C. and Mauborgne, R. *Blue Ocean Strategy*. Harvard Business School Press, 2005: p.28.

2 Abell, D.F. *Defining the Business: The Starting Point of Strategic Planning*. Englewood Cliffs, NJ: Prentice-Hall, 1980: Chap. 8 pp.192-96.

3 Kotler, P., Swee H.A., Siew, M.L., Tan, C.T. *Marketing Management: An Asian Perspective*. Prentice-Hall Pearson Education, Inc. Pte Ltd., 2003: pp.288f.

4 Davis, J. *Magic Numbers for Consumer Marketing*. John Wiley & Sons (Asia) Pte Ltd., 2005: pp.23-30.

5 1997 Annual Report http://media.corporate-ir.net/media_files/irol/97/97664/reports/123197_10k.pdf, p.4

6 Serwer, A."Hot Starbucks to Go: It's a new American institution. Its stores are everywhere. Doubters say it can't get much bigger. But Howard Schultz is setting up his company for more growth—in coffee and beyond". *FORTUNE Magazine*, Monday, January 12, 2004. http://money.cnn.com/magazines/fortune/fortune_archive/2004/01/26/358850/index.htm

7 http://www.milkywaybar.com/,http://www.mury.k12.ut.us/mhs/ecommerce2/DW%20Project%201%20Spring%202003/DW_PROJECT1%20LAS/index.htm

8 http://seattlepi.nwsource.com/business/246741_air02.html

Revenue

Measurement Need

Companies need to measure whether there is financial gain from the production and sale of products and services.

Solution

Revenue is the total income from sales of products and services. It is represented by the following:

$$R = P \times Q_t$$

Where

R = revenue

P = price of products or services

Q_t = quantity in time period t

Price refers to the actual price received for all products and services sold, not a projected price. Quantity is simply the number of units sold. If a marketer is selling services, then revenue may be calculated by multiplying the hours worked by the amount billed each hour. Or, revenue may be counted based on an agreed fixed fee for a contracted amount of time. An advertising agency, for example, bids based on a combination of the client's advertising budget and the communications objectives the client is trying to accomplish.

Impact on Decision Making

From a marketing standpoint, revenue is the first indicator, and often a lead driver, of performance measurement. When launching a new product, forecasting revenues and, upon post-launch review, measuring them, provides a guideline for assessing success. As simple as it sounds, revenue is included in this book because it comprises two ingredients vital to marketing: price and quantity; in other words, how much and how many. When marketers start considering the factors that influence price and quantity, they begin to understand more about the business.

Revenue is, of course, merely a starting point and marketers must resist the temptation to focus only on top-line growth, because their financial colleagues are going to be concerned with bottom-line results and how much it cost to earn those revenues. Therefore, marketers must be concerned with costs as well. Revenue must be evaluated in the context of the total performance of the business and, for comparison, the market and the business' key competitors. Furthermore, understanding revenue ought to inspire management to consider more carefully its sources (customers, products, price, competitors, market conditions) and how it can leverage its current level of business into additional growth.

Source

Davis, J. *Magic Numbers for Consumer Marketing*. Singapore: John Wiley & Sons (Asia) Pte Ltd., 2005: pp.55-56.

Gross Profit

Measurement Need

A high gross profit suggests that a company is efficient, well-run and has its costs under control. Operations costs are controlled through internal programs designed to ensure they remain within certain limits. Marketing costs are more difficult to control since the expenditures usually go toward marketing programs and communications that have unpredictable longer-term impact. Marketers may be tempted to grow market share through low prices that drive revenue, but profitability will be sacrificed as a result. Marketers have a responsibility to know whether their efforts contribute to gross profit.

Solution

Gross profit is a company's total revenue minus the costs it incurred when producing the product that generated the revenue. More simply, it is total sales less total costs (or cost of goods sold—COGS), and it is represented by the following:

$$P_g = R - C$$

Where

P_g = gross profit

R = revenue

C = costs

To illustrate, take a look at these figures from Yahoo! for the years 2001-2003 in Table 1.

Table 1: Income Statement Summary for Yahoo! Inc.

PERIOD ENDING	31-Dec-03	31-Dec-02	31-Dec-01
Total Revenue	**US$3,574,517**	**US$1,625,097**	**US$953,067**
Cost of Revenue	US$1,298,559	US$358,103	US$162,881
Gross Profit	**US$2,275,958**	**US$1,266,994**	**US$790,186**

Source: Adapted from Yahoo! Finance. *Income Statement Summary for Yahoo! Inc.*

Here is the gross profit for Kimberly Clark, a consumer products company with well-known brands in paper products, health and hygiene:

Table 2: Income Statement Summary for Kimberly-Clark Corp.

PERIOD ENDING	31-Dec-04	31-Dec-03	31-Dec-02
Total Revenue	**US$15,083,200**	**U$14,348,000**	**US$13,566,300**
Cost of Revenue	US$10,014,700	US$9,448,100	US$8,750,700
Gross Profit	**US$5,068,500**	**US$4,899,900**	**US$4,815,600**

Source: Adapted from Yahoo! Finance. *Income Statement Summary for Kimberly-Clark Corp.*

Based on gross profit, both companies are doing well. From here, marketers would want to understand more about the performance of the company and whether their efforts are having a positive impact.

Impact on Decision Making

Gross profit by itself doesn't tell marketers much about the overall performance of their company or product line, except to suggest whether its performance is generally positive, or cause for concern. From the two examples used above, however, marketers can glean positive trends for both companies. As an investor, that would be a good start. As a marketer, it hopefully indicates that there is momentum in the market and that, as a "caretaker" of the company's marketing success, they ought to ensure their marketing efforts continue to build share, brand equity and long-term customer loyalty as profitably as possible.

Gross profit is calculated before accounting for operating expenses including: SGA (selling, general and administrative), R&D (research and development) and non-recurring expenses. Therefore, a company could have a positive performance trend with gross profit increasing each year, but the operating expenses might have increased substantially during that time (perhaps to pay for the effort to grow revenues and gross profit), which would severely affect net profit or net income. Marketers want to know and understand these numbers because they may suggest areas where their marketing expenses are growing too quickly, not quickly enough or are being improperly directed. Gross profit is found in the income statement and follows the total sales minus cost of sales figures.

Sources

Shim, J.K., Siegel, J.G., Simon, A.J. *The Vest Pocket MBA*. Prentice-Hall, Inc., 1986: p.18.

Davis, J. *Magic Numbers for Consumer Marketing*. Singapore: John Wiley & Sons (Asia) Pte Ltd., 2005: pp.57-59.

Value to Volume Ratio

3

Measurement Need

When measuring market share, marketers understand that the result indicates the percentage of business their company (or product category) has relative to its competitors. A key question is determining how *efficient* the marketing efforts are compared to the competition.

Solution[1]

The value to volume ratio measures the firm's estimated share of total market gross profits (either for the company overall or a specific product) compared to the firm's share of the total dollar volume sold in the market or the product category:

$$VVR = \frac{\%P_{gm}}{\%V_m}$$

Where

VVR = value to volume ratio

$\%P_{gm}$ = estimated percentage share of total market gross profits

$\%V_m$ = percentage share of market total dollar volume

In 2004, Airbus and Boeing were the two dominant commercial aircraft manufacturers. Their financial performances were as shown in Table 3.

Table 3: Revenue and Profit Comparison of Airbus and Boeing

	Airbus[2]	Boeing
Revenues	US$25.11 billion	US$21 billion
Gross Profits	US$2.39 billion	US$750 million

To simplify this example, we will assume Airbus and Boeing were the only two competitors in the market. Boeing's VVR was:

$$VVR = \frac{0.239}{0.455}$$

$$= 0.525 \text{ or } 52.5\%$$

Boeing's $\%P_{gm}$ of 0.239 was calculated by dividing its gross profit of $750 million by the combined gross profit of both airlines ($3.14 billion = $2.39 billion + $750 million):

$$\frac{\$0.75 \text{ b}}{\$3.14 \text{ b}}$$

$$= 0.239$$

Note: Boeing's $\%V_m$ of 0.455 was calculated by dividing its gross revenues of $21 billion by the combined revenues of both airlines ($46.11 billion = $25.11 billion + $21 billion):

$$\frac{\$21 \text{ b}}{\$46.11 \text{ b}}$$

$$= 0.455$$

Now let's look at Airbus's VVR:

$$VVR = \frac{0.761}{0.545}$$

$$= 1.40 \text{ or } 140\%$$

Note: Airbus's $\%P_{gm}$ of 0.761 was calculated by dividing its gross profit of $2.39 billion by the combined gross profit of both airlines, just as we did for Boeing

$$\frac{\$2.39 \text{ b}}{\$3.14 \text{ b}}$$

$$= 0.761$$

Airbus's $\%V_m$ of 0.545 was calculated by dividing its gross revenues of $25.11 billion by the combined revenues of both airlines:

$$\frac{\$25.11 \text{ b}}{\$46.11 \text{ b}}$$

$$= 0.545$$

Impact on Decision Making

Boeing's ratio is 52.5% while Airbus's is 140%. Figures below 100% signal several possible concerns: costs are too high, prices are too low, or both. Conversely, Airbus appears to be highly effective at leveraging its investment.

For any company, VVR is a useful metric as the calculation provides an early guide on areas of the company that need improvement or that are being effectively utilized. Marketers can use the data to adjust the marketing program accordingly. If the VVR is below 100%, then marketing needs to review pricing, improve perceived value and also consider changing the product to conform more closely to market needs. If the ratio is higher than 100%, it likely indicates a marketing leading position, so marketing has an opportunity to capitalize on the company's efficient performance by touting its success.

Endnotes

1 LaPointe, P. *Marketing by the Dashboard Light.* Patrick LaPointe in cooperaton with the Association of National Advertisers, 2005.

2 Airbus' figures were calculated using 2004's report results in Euros, converted to dollars based on an average 2004 euro-dollar exchange rate over four quarters as described in http://www.hwwa.de/publikationen/Discussion_Paper/2005/321.pdf.

Sources

Boeing: http://www.boeing.com/news/releases/2005/q1/nr_050202a.pdf pp.6-7

Airbus: http://www.defense-aerospace.com "EADS Success Continues in 2004: Ambitious Financial Targets Met for Fifth Consecutive Year"

Net Profit

4

Measurement Need

Marketers need to know whether their efforts contribute to the bottom line, after total costs have been subtracted from total revenues.

Solution

This is the final profit after taxes, SGA, R&D, non-recurring and other income statement take-outs[1].

$$P_n = (V \times M_c) - E_m - E_o - I_t$$

Where

P_n = net profit (in dollars)

V = customer volume (in units sold)

M_c = margin per customer (in dollars)

E_m = marketing expenses (in dollars)

E_o = operating expenses (in dollars)

I_t = interest and taxes (in dollars)

Margin per customer is calculated by the simple formula:

$$M_c = R_c - C_v$$

Where

M_c = margin per customer

R_c = revenue per customer

C_v = variable cost per customer

Customer volume is calculated as follows:

$$V_c = MD \times MS$$

Where

V_c = customer volume

MD = market demand

MS = market share

To use a hypothetical example, Global Publishing markets business books targeted to ambitious young executives. It has the following statistics:

$V = 400,000$

$M_c = \$50$

$E_m = \$1,500,000$

$E_o = \$500,000$

$I_t = \$6,500,000$

$NP = (C_v \times M_c) - E_m - E_o - I_t$

$NP = (400,000 \times \$50) - \$1,500,000 - \$500,000 - \$6,500,000$

$ = \$11,500,000$

Therefore, Global Publishing has a net profit of \$11.5 million, which appears to be quite healthy.

Impact on Decision Making

Net profit helps managers understand how profitable their company is *after* accounting for additional, below-the-line expenses resulting from their business development efforts, including marketing. It is a good measure for determining how effective a company is with turning revenues into real profits while keeping costs under control.

This data is likely to be found in the income statement, but typically at the aggregate level. Marketers will need to check with their accounting department to review their accounts receivable to determine the number of customers the company has and to calculate the margin per customer from there. Marketing and operating expenses will be captured at the departmental level but, if a marketer works in a large company such as a Fortune 500 firm, corporate headquarters often "charges" certain cost items to each department or business unit automatically. Interest and taxes are the responsibility of the finance department as well.

A key challenge is determining the customer-volume and customer-margin figures reasonably accurately. This will require a detailed understanding of the marketer's actual customer base, the customer's purchasing specifics (to help determine average margin) and a good description of the operating expenses associated with this effort.

Another important point is to understand what net profit might be indicating. An increasing net profit is generally good news and may signal that the company and/or its products are making more profit per dollar of sales than in years past. The reasons may include greater operational efficiencies that have helped to reduce costs as a percentage of sales. Or perhaps it reflects a favorable tax situation, which is certainly good (although it may also mask inefficiencies in the operation). Increasing net profit can also indicate that customers perceive the price/value relationship for the company's products favorably and, therefore, it is able to command a price premium over the competition. Increasing net profits may also highlight management strengths, since good managers are usually more effective at leveraging the budgets and investments they oversee, and they know where to deploy resources to maximize returns.

Conversely, a declining net profit may suggest that the company is making less profit on each dollar of sales than previously, due to increased taxes, operational inefficiencies and/or costs that are rising faster than sales. In this case, lower net profit may be a warning sign that the company's control of its costs is diminishing, which could be a signal that a management change is necessary to correct this. Similarly, there may also be factors beyond the control of management, such as rising materials/suppliers costs. Or perhaps the company is no longer able to command the prices it once did for its products due to improved competitor offerings that are giving consumers greater choice.

The astute marketer will also realize that net profit is an important measure that can be a source of competitive advantage. Having a thorough understanding of one's net profit compared to that of competitors will be a key gauge in determining longer-term competitive opportunities. If the company is able to command higher net profits than its competitors, then it will have greater flexibility to invest in newer products, process or manufacturing improvements, and marketing programs to build awareness and retain loyal customers.

Endnote

1 Adapted from Best, R.J. *Market-Based Management: Strategies for Growing Customer Value and Profitability.* Upper Saddle River, NJ: Pearson Education Inc., 2005: pp.473-475.

Source

Davis, J. *Magic Numbers for Consumer Marketing*. Singapore: John Wiley & Sons (Asia) Pte Ltd., 2005: pp.60-62.

Earnings-Based Value[1]

5

Measurement Need

Marketers sometimes suffer from a lack of credibility inside companies because the effect of their marketing activities on earnings is not always easy to measure. Earnings are affected by a complex set of variables, including marketing. Marketers should know how their company is performing financially and understanding the mechanics of earnings-based value will help them recognize the connection between their marketing activities and company earnings. This is particularly important for publicly traded companies since shareholders want the value of their invested money to increase, and earnings are instrumental in determining share price.

Solution[2]

Publicly traded companies are evaluated on the performance of their stock, since it is a direct measure of value creation (or destruction) for investors. Earnings-based value is a series of calculations that helps assess the value of a company and, indirectly, may even suggest the impact of product and marketing decisions. It includes using several key financial variables: EPS (earnings per share); P/E ratio (price/earnings ratio); PEG ratio (price/earnings growth); and YPEG ratio (the year-ahead price/earnings growth). Each of the metrics is related, building from one to the next to arrive at a final earnings-based value.

To begin, it is helpful to understand a key definition: earnings. Earnings means the same thing as net profit. Earnings are evaluated by investors and business managers using earnings per share as follows:

$$EPS = \frac{P}{S_o}$$

Where

    EPS = earnings per share

    P = profits

    S_o = shares outstanding

The next piece of the earnings-based value puzzle is to determine whether EPS is good, bad or inconclusive. Earnings must be compared to the company's share price using the price/earnings ratio (P/E ratio). The P/E ratio is an indicator of a company's growth and, indirectly, its value. The P/E ratio takes the stock price and divides it by earnings from the past year (or four quarters):

$$P/E = \frac{SP}{EPS}$$

Where

    SP = share price

    EPS = earnings per share

The result is often called the "multiple", and while it is an acceptable measure of a company's value, it is incomplete and should not be relied upon as a determinant of overall company performance. Companies with a low P/E ratio may appear to be a good value and worthy of investment, but the P/E ratio is based on past performance and is not a good indicator of future potential. Since managers and investors are looking for future growth potential, a low P/E could also be interpreted as a company with a poor chance for future success.

PEG Ratio

The PEG ratio compares historical earnings growth to the P/E ratio.

$$PEG = \frac{P/E}{EPS} \ \textit{(historical growth)}$$

Where

    PEG = price/earnings growth

    P/E = price/earnings ratio

    EPS = earnings per share (historical growth)

Theoretically, as long as your P/E ratio does not exceed your growth rate, then your company is reasonably valued. A PEG of 0.5 to 1.0 is considered good or fair value, whereas a PEG of greater than 1.0 indicates that the company may be overvalued. The PEG ratio is commonly used by market analysts in their evaluation of growth companies. "Growth" companies are defined as those whose revenues and earnings are growing faster than the average company in the market.[3]

YPEG Ratio

The YPEG ratio uses the same basic assumptions as the PEG ratio, but uses projected future growth rates and not PEG's historical earnings growth rates. YPEG is more commonly used by companies with lower rates of growth, which tend to be mature firms and/or companies in slow-growth markets. Overall, the same logic applies as with the PEG ratio: 0.5 to 1.0 is good and greater than 1.0 is a potential problem. The YPEG ratio equals the current P/E ratio divided by the future earnings growth rate:

$$YPEG = \frac{P/E}{EPS \ (future \ growth)}$$

Where

$YPEG$ = year-ahead price/earnings growth

P/E = price/earnings ratio

EPS = earnings per share (future growth)

Let's look at examples of how these formulas are used.

EPS

A company called Boring Widgets (BW) has five million shares outstanding and has earned $2.5 million in the previous 12 months. BW's trailing EPS is 50 cents:

$$\frac{\$2,500,000}{5,000,000 \ \ shares} = 0.5$$

By itself, EPS is a relatively unhelpful and only becomes more important as management includes it into the rest of the earnings valuation analysis.

P/E Ratio

Now let's assume that BW has a stock price of $50 per share. Using the P/E ratio, we find:

$$P/E = \frac{\$50}{0.5}$$

$$= 100$$

The P/E is 100. If BW competes in a rapidly growing industry, such as the dot.com companies of the late 1990s, then a P/E of 100, while generally considered high, may be normal for this market. However, it would also suggest an "expensive" company and stock.

PEG Ratio

Assuming BW's historical growth rate is 25%, this gives us the following:

$$PEG = \frac{P/E}{EPS} \text{ (historical growth)}$$

$$\frac{100}{25} = 4.0$$

The PEG is 4.0. This indicates that Boring Widgets is valued four times higher than it should be, thus it appears to be overvalued.

YPEG Ratio

Completing our BW illustration, but assuming that it is now a more mature firm and that growth is expected to be closer to 10% in the coming years, produces the following result:

$$YPEG = \frac{P/E}{EPS} \text{ (future growth)}$$

$$\frac{100}{10} = 10.0$$

The YPEG is 10.0, an indication of a significantly over-valued company in this case.

Impact on Decision Making

Earnings-based value is used to help managers and investors value a company. Of course, there are many factors that contribute to the value of the company. Earnings-based value can be a useful series of calculations when comparing value over time, particularly as it relates to profitability. An increase in earnings-based value can suggest whether a company's products are accepted in the market, whether it can command premium margins and even whether it is growing share profitably. It is important to recognize that earnings-based value does not directly describe these factors. Rather, it serves as an indicator of the possible factors contributing to earnings performance.

While it is challenging to correlate a direct increase or decrease in value to specific product or marketing decisions, marketers have a responsibility to ensure their decisions result in positive growth, increased market awareness and profitable product lines. Earnings-based values are complex and make certain assumptions that must be considered in the context of the company's historical performance, that of its industry competitor set, and the future potential of the firm. It is prudent to recognize that earnings-based values reflect only a subset of the potential value a firm, brand or product represents. By itself, it is interesting and helpful, but hardly conclusive or prescriptive. Yet the danger is that many business decisions are made based on this information.

Businesses are more than an earnings stream. In fact, earnings, in their simplest form, are merely a measure of success during a particular period of time. Economics assumes a rational consumer in many of its theories, yet in reality many consumer decisions are made based on a combination of intuition, experience and logic. Similarly, earnings-based valuations assume that the ideal world is one in which the P/E ratio and the EPS growth rate are equal, or should be very close to equal. But there are numerous factors that affect the performance of companies and the perceptions of their products beyond the concept of "fair value".

Earnings-based valuation is helpful as one measure among many that facilitates understanding whether your company and its products are enjoying success in the market. As with earlier definitions, publicly traded companies have this information in their annual reports, typically in their financial statements in the sections called "Notes to Financial Statements" or "Notes to Consolidated Financial Statements".

Endnotes

1 Adapted from The Motley Fool. http://www.fool.com/School/EarningsBased Valuations. htm

2 Davis, J. *Magic Numbers for Consumer Marketing.* Singapore: John Wiley & Sons (Asia) Pte Ltd., 2005: pp.65-69.

3 Adapted from The Motley Fool. http://www.fool.com/school/Glossary/glossarya.htm

Return on Sales

6

Measurement Need

Businesses must have sales to survive and profits to thrive. To thrive, the quality of the sales must be understood by management and marketing, so an important question is the amount of profit produced relative to each dollar of sales.

Solution*

Return on sales (ROS) is a measure of a company's ability to generate profits from sales. It is effectively the profit resulting from each dollar of sales and is based on net profit after tax and total sales. It is represented as follows:

$$ROS = \frac{P_{nbt}}{S}$$

Where

ROS = return on sales

P_{nbt} = net profit before tax

S = sales

Our hypothetical company, Global Publishing (from Chapter 4, Net Profit), is quite successful. Its business generated $300 million in sales and, from our earlier net profit calculation, it generated $11.5 million in profits. Calculating the return on sales reveals the following:

$$ROS = \frac{\$11,500,000}{\$300,000,000} = 3.8\%$$

These figures may indicate that Global Publishing needs to improve its margins. On the other hand, their market characteristics may also suggest that 3.8% is a reasonable ROS. To know for certain, marketers need to understand the market in which they compete and the relative performance of their main competitors. If their competitors' ROS is in the 1-2% range, then Global Publishing is performing well.

Let's look at an actual industry example. The charts in Figure 7 below are from the consumer electronic games and toys market in the U.S[1]. The years are 2002, 2003 and 2004.

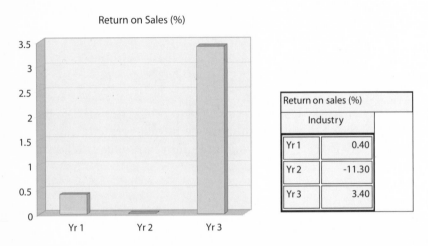

Return on Sales (%)

Return on sales (%)		
Industry		
Yr 1	0.40	
Yr 2	-11.30	
Yr 3	3.40	

Figure 7: Three-Year Return on Sales for the U.S. Electronic Games and Toys Market, 2002—2004

It is noteworthy that in 2003, the industry's collective return on sales declined 11.3%. This may suggest several influencing factors reflecting shifts in industry dynamics:

- Perhaps fewer new products in this category were introduced; therefore, consumer interest dropped in this category

- Conversely, perhaps several new products were introduced that were not well received by consumers, compelling companies to drop prices to clear inventory and, temporarily, making their actual profits per dollar of sales generated less efficient

- Prices for new products may have been too high, causing consumer resistance

- There may have been a dramatic shift in consumer interest in this category of products in general, perhaps away from packaged games and toward online games

Further investigation would undoubtedly provide clues as to the factors that led to the ROS results shown here.

Impact on Decision Making

ROS is a practical indicator of the profitability of your marketing efforts. It is most effectively used when reviewed over time, rather than for a single period, since departures from historical and industry trends can be detected.

In the example, as Global Publishing grows, it may want to focus more on increasing margin to take advantage of the investment and effort made to produce its current line of products. The income statement is the best place to find this information since its main components, total sales and net profits before tax, are captured here.

Return on sales measures the financial efficiency of a company's recent sales efforts, particularly in comparison with other companies in the same industry. ROS does vary significantly by industry and, at times, within industries. It can be a useful indicator of a given company's ability to respond to changes in its own operating performance, general market conditions or pricing. For example, an increase in ROS may signal improved operational efficiency (i.e. lower expenses). On the other hand, it may reflect a change in a company's pricing strategy. Therefore, marketers should investigate further before drawing conclusions based on initial ROS results. Higher prices may have led to the increased return on sales, but are the increased prices sustainable over the long-term? Is the company adding sufficient value to justify the increased price? Whatever the reasons, ROS results should provoke additional curiosity and inquiry if marketers wish to understand the reasons behind the figures, as illustrated by the electronic games and toys data above.

Endnote

1 BizMiner report on Consumer Electronic Games and Toys Market, The Brandow Company, 2005. http://www.bizminer.com/search/details/industries/Electronic-games-and-toys-Manufacturing.asp?profile=SMI&showALL=1

Sources

Davis, J. *Magic Numbers for Consumer Marketing*. Singapore: John Wiley & Sons (Asia) Pte Ltd., 2005: pp.69-70.

http://www.investopedia.com/terms/r/ros.asp

http://prosearch.businessweek.com/businessweek/GENERAL_FREE_SEARCH.html?Button=Description&CRITERIA=038

*Note: ROS can also be calculated based on P_{nat} (net profit after tax). Whether before-tax or after-tax profits are used, the convention should be applied consistently across all return ratios (ROA, ROE). The formula is as follows:

$$ROS = \frac{P_{nat}}{S}$$

See Best, R.J. *Market-Based Management: Strategies for Growing Customer Value and Profitability.* Upper Saddle River: Pearson Education Inc., 2005: p.478 for more information.

Return on Assets

7

Measurement Need

Operational efficiency and resource allocation are ongoing business imperatives. Inefficient operations reduce profits and stress company resources, including people and equipment. Many consumer products companies, in particular, manufacture their products, as well as market and distribute them. Management must measure the usefulness and productivity of these assets (such as machinery) since significant financial investment was made to develop them. Marketers must pay attention as well, since the product plans they develop must be feasible from an operational and manufacturing standpoint.

Solution*

Return on assets (ROA) is a measure of efficiency based on a company's ability to generate profits from its existing assets.

$$ROA = \frac{P_{nbt}}{A}$$

Where
$\quad ROA$ = return on assets
$\quad P_{nbt}$ = net profit before tax
$\quad A$ = assets (assets are invested capital, comprised of debt and equity)

Continuing with our previous Global Publishing example from Chapters 4 and 5, our hypothetical management team wants to understand its effectiveness in getting as much productivity and profitability out of their assets as possible. The company's assets are quite valuable, as is true for many firms in the "content" business, and Global Publishing is sitting on a rich treasure trove of book titles and educational programs. Let's assume its total assets are valued at $425 million.

$$ROA = \frac{\$11,500,000}{\$425,000,000} = 2.7\%$$

ROA describes how effective a company is at converting its assets into net profit. The 2.7% figure for Global Publishing must be viewed in the context of the company's own past performance and also the performance of a close competitor before determining if the result is good or bad.

Using the electronics games and toys industry example introduced in Chapter 6, Return on Sales, Figure 8 shows results for 2002, 2003 and 2004[1].

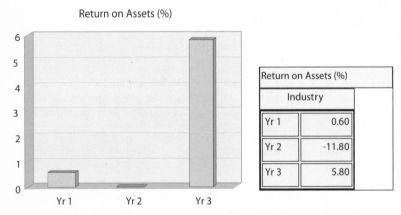

Return on Assets (%)	
Industry	
Yr 1	0.60
Yr 2	-11.80
Yr 3	5.80

Figure 8: Three-Year Return on Assets for U.S. Consumer Electronic Games and Toys Market, 2002–2004

These ROA figures provide another piece of evidence that 2003 was a challenging year for the electronic games and toys market.

Impact on Decision Making

ROA will show significant variation when different industries are compared. Heavy manufacturing and capital-intensive industries (such as commercial aircraft manufacturing, utility plants and earth moving equipment) will have a lower return on assets, simply because a significant investment in expensive assets (factories, machinery, equipment) is necessary for them to do business and compete successfully. Furthermore, these capital-intensive assets require significant additional investment in maintenance and replacement, which decreases the return on assets further. Less capital-intensive businesses, like management consulting, software firms, and accountancies will have a much higher ROA since these investments (people, ideas) do not require building factories, purchasing expensive maintenance contracts or replacement costs resulting from equipment failure, breakdown or obsolescence. The income statement will have information on the net profit before tax. The balance sheet will have information on assets.

In considering this 2% ROA figure from our Global Publishing example, a marketer may wonder whether this is good or bad. Generally speaking, the higher the number, the better. As described above, some industries may see any number greater than 1% as a good ROA figure. Alternatively, a technology company may see 8% or more as a reasonable indicator of effectiveness for that sector. Just be aware that ROA by itself is a helpful indicator, but it is better to appraise it in the context of the company's industry and competitor set. Management may feel good about its own 8% ROA, but if the competitors are at 11% or 12%, then they may have to take a closer look at their business to understand why their performance is below that of the industry.

To illustrate, let's look at two PC manufacturers: Dell and Gateway. Both compete in the direct-to-customer market (versus PC makers who sell to retailers that then sell to customers). Dell's ROA in 2004 was 13.6%. Gateway's was 0.91% for the same period (their fiscal years are slightly different). For Gateway, this may suggest that it needs to take a closer look at its use of key assets (computer assembly, inventory and even people), review how those are deployed and evaluate where the most likely changes can occur to improve performance. In fairness, Gateway has undergone significant restructuring and change since 2000 and is undoubtedly dealing with this transition, whereas Dell has been operating relatively consistently for many years, allowing it to refine its business model rather than dealing with the challenges of restructuring.

Nevertheless, ROA can be an insightful tool for management and marketers.

Endnote

1 BizMiner report on Consumer Electronic Games and Toys Market, The Brandow Company, 2005. http://www.bizminer.com/search/details/industries/Electronic-games-and-toys-Manufacturing.asp?profile=SMI&showALL=1

Sources

Davis, J. *Magic Numbers for Consumer Marketing*. Singapore: John Wiley & Sons (Asia) Pte Ltd., 2005: pp.71-73.

http://www.investopedia.com/terms/r/returnonassets.asp

*Note: ROA can also be calculated based on P_{nat} (net profit *after* tax). Whether before-tax or after-tax profits are used, the convention should be applied consistently across all return ratios (ROS, ROE). The formula is as follows:

$$ROA = \frac{P_{nat}}{A}$$

See Best, R.J. *Market-Based Management: Strategies for Growing Customer Value and Profitability.* Upper Saddle River, Pearson Education Inc., 2005: p.478 for more information.

Return on Equity 8

Measurement Need

Companies are funded by shareholders, whether publicly held (whereby ownership of the company is widely dispersed among members of the public in the form of shares of stock, and the company financial performance is subject to specific transparent reporting requirements), or privately held (whereby ownership is usually kept to a much smaller group of investors and company financial performance is not publicly reported). Owners are interested in knowing how much profit is generated from their investment. Management is responsible for the effective use of the investor's capital. And marketers must ensure that the resources allocated are properly deployed to grow revenues profitably.

Solution*

Return on equity (ROE) is a measure of efficiency based on a company's ability to generate profits from its stockholders' equity.

$$ROE = \frac{P_{nbt}}{E}$$

Where

ROE = return on equity

P_{nbt} = net profit before tax

E = book value of shareholder (owner's) equity

Global Publishing, our continuing example from Chapter 7, Return on Assets, still seeks more information to measure management's effectiveness. The hypothetical board of directors is under pressure from investors and financial analysts because, as it turns out, its 2.7% ROA is well below the industry average. They run another calculation, this time based on owner's equity. Global Publishing has $92 million in owner's equity. This is plugged into the equation to calculate the ROE:

$$ROE = \frac{\$11,500,000}{\$92,000,000} = 12.5\%$$

The same question as in previous measures should arise: is this a good or bad figure? The answer is, yet again, "it depends", which will be discussed in the Impact on Decision Making section below.

The example with which we ended Chapter 7 compared Dell and Gateway. A review of the ROE in 2004 shows that Dell's ROE was 59.18% and Gateway's was -11.87%, which suggests that Dell is more effective at creating a return on its assets (equity, in this case). Management must look deeper, to fully understand the implications of these numbers.

Impact on Decision Making

In the case of our Global Publishing example, if an ROE of 12.5% is above average for the industry, then the stockholders and board of directors will probably be satisfied temporarily. However, the low ROA and ROS ratios should be of concern, and suggest that management must focus on improving effectiveness and profitability in those areas if it wants to avoid significant changes in the future. The balance sheet liabilities will describe the equity values, while the income statement will describe the net income before tax.

ROE has limitations as a measure of effectiveness, however. It looks at the amount of invested capital as assets minus liabilities (this is the traditional definition of owner's equity). This means it does not fully account for all invested capital accurately. There is debt in the form of both short-term and long-term financial capital. So a more complete analysis would measure the return on invested capital to give investors and the board of directors a clearer picture of the effectiveness of invested capital in generating profits.

ROE, ROS and ROA each use net profit before tax (P_{nbt}) in the numerator as the dependent variable. However, in practical terms, P_{nbt} is an imprecise figure at best, since it is the result of each company's internal tracking and measurement systems. While these systems do following generally accepted accounting and financial guidelines, there is room for interpretation in each of the cost/expense areas as well as in the approach a company uses to recognize revenue.

ROE can overstate (or understate) economic value due to several factors:

1. Capitalization policies: companies use different accounting methods to determine when and at what rate to capitalize an investment, whether short-term or long-term. If the total amount of investment capitalized is larger, then ROE is likely to be lower or understated. The converse is true as well.

2. Depreciation policies: there are rules that govern the life of an asset or investment, but these are subject to some interpretation as well. Faster depreciation rates compared to straight-line methods will yield a higher ROE, possibly distorting the actual value.

3. Leverage: companies will borrow money under the assumption that they can earn higher rates of return from investing it than the cost of the borrowing, which can distort the ROE calculation since it may tempt management to finance growth with greater leverage.

4. Project lifespan: if an invested project has a long lifespan, then the ROE is likely to be overstated since the equity resources are assumed to be productively used for a longer period of time.

5. Growth rates: if a company is growing rapidly, its ROE will be lower.

6. Lag: there is usually a lag between the investment made and when the resulting cash flow turns positive. The longer the time lag, the larger the overstatement of ROE.

As marketers review their product and marketing decisions, it is their responsibility to understand the implications their investment decisions may have on each of these ratios and, more importantly, what the resulting figure could be indicating about their programs and asset deployment. While it is challenging to precisely link a market or product investment to a return on equity (or assets or sales) ratio, there is little question that marketing has a direct impact on attracting customers. If planned and executed well, then marketers will be able to confidently correlate their efforts to improved financial performance and the metrics used to measure it.

Sources

Davis, J. *Magic Numbers for Consumer Marketing.* Singapore: John Wiley & Sons (Asia) Pte Ltd., 2005: pp.73-75.

http://www.investopedia.com/terms/r/returnonequity.asp

*Note: ROE can also be calculated based on P_{nbt} (net profit before tax). Whether before-tax or after-tax profits are used, the convention should be applied consistently across all return ratios (ROA, ROS). The formula is as follows:

$$ROE = \frac{P_{nbt}}{E}$$

See Best, R.J. *Market-Based Management: Strategies for Growing Customer Value and Profitability.* Upper Saddle River, Pearson Education Inc., 2005: p.478 for more information.

Marketing Cost Per Unit

9

Measurement Need

Marketers do not have unlimited budgets, therefore they must use the money allocated to their efforts as effectively as possible. Since many marketers are responsible for managing products and product lines, the number of units sold indicates the relative success of the products compared to the competition's offerings. Each unit sold has a marketing cost associated with it, enabling marketers to measure how much it cost to market each unit.

Solution[1]

The marketing cost per unit calculation is simple:

$$MCPU = \frac{E_{mt}}{U_t}$$

Where

$MCPU$ = marketing cost per unit

E_{mt} = total marketing expense in time period t

U_t = total unit sold in time period t

In 2005 the MP3 player market was dominated by Apple's iPod. Total unit sales were 22.5 million. Depending on the source, market share estimates for Apple ranged from 73% to over 80%.[2] Let's use 73%. Total MP3 player sales were therefore 30.82 million units.

Creative Technologies, based in Singapore, is one of the competitors in this market. Industry reports show that Creative's market share was 2.4%

in 2005, which translates to around 740,000 units sold. Creative also said it spent $100 million on marketing in 2005. Using these figures, we can calculate Creative's marketing cost per unit as follows:

$$\frac{\$100,000,000}{740,000}$$

$$= \$135.14$$

Creative spent a great deal to market its various MP3 players!

Impact on Decision Making

The marketing cost per unit should decline as a product matures. As more consumers buy a company's product, distribution expands, word of mouth builds up the reputation, and the product becomes more familiar as a consequence. Marketing efforts must not stop as the business grows. Instead, the dollars allocated shift to different marketing vehicles, reflecting the changing nature of the growing customer base. Once a product catches on favorably with the public, the number of units sold quickly outpaces the dollars spent to market it, which is desirable. However, if the marketing cost per unit increases, then that may be a warning signal that consumers are losing interest and competitors are offering more attractive products at better prices. Marketers need to investigate the increasing costs per unit to determine the appropriate response.

Endnotes

1 LaPointe, P. http://www.marketingprofs.com/6/lapointe2.asp

2 http://money.cnn.com/2006/03/29/technology/apple_anniversary/index.htm

Source

http://playlistmag.com/news/2005/12/08/creative/index.php?lsrc=mwrss

Program/Non-Program Ratio

10

Measurement Need

There is little question that marketing's purpose is to provide strategic and tactical guidance in understanding customers, positioning products, building a strong brand and creating communications that capture the interest of the public. This is an important role, and a vital source of growth for companies. Given this mandate, companies must ask how efficient their marketing is given the amount of money invested in this area.

Solution[1]

The program/non-program ratio (PNPR) compares the amount of money spent on marketing activities designed to create value with the amount spent on the overhead and administrative inputs needed to support those activities. The result is a measure of efficiency, with higher ratios indicating a more efficient operation.

$$PNPR = \frac{P_t}{TP_t}$$

Where

$PNPR$ = program/non-program ratio

P_t = marketing program \$ spending in time period t

TP_t = total support \$ spending in time period t

Note: Total support \$ spending is comprised of program and non-program expenses.

Rhodesian Ridgeback Rescue, Inc. (RRRI)[2], a not-for-profit organization in North America dedicated to finding homes and basic medical care for orphaned Rhodesian ridgeback dogs, reported that its 2004 program expenses were $93,537 and its non-program expenses were $18,616, for a total expense of $112,153. Its PNPR is 83%.

$$PNPR = \frac{\$93,537}{\$112,153}$$

$$= 83\%$$

RRRI's non-program activities are related to the administrative costs associated with fundraising and other administrative expenses, including telephone, legal and postage.

Impact on Decision Making

PNPR is a general guideline for measuring marketing efficiency and is one of several steps marketers would undertake to evaluate their marketing program efforts. Since a higher ratio is desirable, marketers would use the result to set goals for the next budget period, proposing programs for improving the ratio by increasing the percentage. The challenge is determining the actual variables that comprise program and non-program activities, so marketers will need to recommend a clear set of definitions that are agreed upon with senior management. This will ensure the metric measures the same variables each time. For example, a marketer may define program activities as any marketing communications designed to sell a specific product. This would include promotions, specific advertising, price lists and discount programs. Correspondingly, non-program activities might include legal and accounting costs plus an allocation of payroll for administrative tasks unrelated to the programs.

Endnotes

1 LaPointe, P. *Marketing by the Dashboard Light*. Patrick LaPointe, 2005: p.99.

2 http://www.ridgebackrescue.org/articles/2005_may_year_2004_in_review.pdf

Program/Payroll Ratio 11

Measurement Need

Chapter 10 described the PNPR, which compares costs devoted to value-producing marketing activities with support inputs such as overhead, administration and legal. Marketing management can gain further insight by focusing specifically on the ratio of program expenses to payroll, removing other overhead and administrative costs.

Solution

The program/payroll ratio (PPR) compares the amount of money spent on marketing activities designed to create value with the amount spent on payroll in support of those activities.

$$PPR = \frac{P_t}{MP_t}$$

Where

PPR = program/payroll ratio

P_t = marketing program $ spending in time period t

MP_t = marketing payroll $ spending in time period t

Note: Marketing payroll $ spending is salary, benefits and related payroll costs.

If a company had $1 million in total marketing expense, of which $400,000 was program spending and $600,000 was payroll, then the PPR is 67%:

$$PPR = \frac{\$400,000}{\$600,000}$$

$$= 67\%$$

As marketing program expenditures are increased (assuming payroll remains constant), the percentage increases, and as program expenditures are decreased, the percentage decreases as well. The ratio is useful primarily as a period to period comparison (such as year over year) for the same company, since competitor and industry comparisons offer little meaningful guidance due to differences in budget priorities.

Impact on Decision Making

Each company has different guidelines for payroll and non-payroll activities. A worst-case scenario would have little or no program expenses, meaning most expenses are for payroll activities. Organizations with this imbalance are not likely to last long, since salaries are being paid to managers providing little or no customer-related development activities. Ratios are subject to interpretation or even abuse by those seeking to disguise or reallocate expenses to create a more favorable PPR result. To legitimately improve the efficiency, a marketer would need to persuasively argue for an increase in the amount of program-related spending (advertising, promotions) while holding payroll expenses constant (or not increasing them as much as program expenditures). Since the goal is marketing efficiency, marketers have a fiduciary and ethical responsibility to portray their budget requests accurately. Patrick LaPointe, Managing Partner of MarketingNPV, points out that industrial and B2B firms often have high payroll costs relative to their advertising expenditures, which suggests that the organizations are spending a great deal of money on non-customer facing activities. B2B organizations usually have higher sales and business development costs as well, since a significant portion of their customer activities are related to one-to-one selling and relationship development. The key is for each firm to understand its own goals and establish agreed-upon definitions of program and non-program activities.

Endnote

1 LaPointe, P. *Marketing by the Dashboard Light.* Patrick LaPointe, 2005: p.99.

Net Sales Contribution

12

Measurement Need

Segmentation is an important tool to help marketers identify groups of customers with similar characteristics, for which they then develop marketing programs that appeal to each segment while also maintaining consistency with their company's goals. Segments are broadly organized around four common themes, and marketers want to understand more clearly how much each segment contributes to overall sales. The need, therefore, is to measure the specific sales contribution of each segmentation category:

- demographics (age, ethnicity, sex, income…)
- psychographics (behaviors, likes, needs, wants…)
- geography (location)
- product use (how the product or service is actually used by the customer)

Solution

Net sales contribution calculates the financial sales contribution of a specific segment to total sales for all segments, expressed as a percentage. The formula for net sales contribution is:

$$S_{ni} = \frac{S_i}{\sum S_t}$$

Where

S_{ni} = net sales contribution for segment i

S_i = sales from segment i

$\sum S_t$ = total sales from all segments

Net sales contribution measures each segment's contribution to total sales, and can serve as an indicator for planning future sales and marketing strategies. For example, the 2004 annual report for Agrium Inc., a Canadian-based company specializing in the manufacture of agricultural nutrients and industrial products, gives detailed analysis of its various activities' contribution to net sales. This also gives shareholders a good idea of where the company's focus lies and where it is concentrating its efforts.

Table 4: Segmented Financial Results[1]
By Geography (millions of U.S. dollars)

	Retail	WHOLESALE			Total
		North America	South America	Other	
Net Sales	$1,114	$1,703	$143	($122)	$2,838
Net Sales Cont. %	39%	60%	5%	4%	100%

Table 5: Segmented Financial Results[1]
By Product (millions of U.S. dollars)

	Ammonia	Urea	Nitrate, Sulfate	Phosphate	Potash	Total
Net Sales	$397	$499	$284	$309	$214	$1,703
Net Sales Cont. %	23%	29%	17%	18%	13%	100%

Impact on Decision Making

Measuring net sales contribution helps marketers understand each segment's portion of total sales. It is a more general, less-detailed indicator of performance, serving as a useful starting point for further analysis when marketers wish to clarify the underlying factors of each segment's contribution, particularly as measured against the marketing plan for the time period under review. Using Agrium's figures in Tables 4 and 5, a North American marketer would want to review his or her region's performance versus plan. Assuming the region performed better than expected, the marketer might then review the sales contributions of each product versus the original plan to determine any variances. If, hypothetically, urea product sales were significantly higher versus plan, then the marketer would want to research the underlying causes. A market by market, or even account by account (within North America) review of each product's sales would probably reveal where urea is gaining the most business, resulting in sales beyond expectations. The marketer might then modify the marketing plan to take advantage of this growing market opportunity, perhaps by developing new pricing programs, focusing sales resources toward winning more accounts of a particular type within the best growing regions, or encouraging the development of new products or product extensions based around the urea product category.

Knowing the performance of each segment helps marketers and their companies be more effective in their future marketing and product efforts, and net sales contribution is a valuable metric in this process.

Endnote

1 http://calgwebe.agrium.com/ir2004AnnualReport/index.html

Time-Driven Activity-Based Costing

13

Measurement Need

To paraphrase Peter Drucker, the purpose of a business is to create a customer, and marketing and innovation are the only two areas that produce results[1]. Part of marketing's role is to identify segments based on customer needs and characteristics, target the segments that are likely to yield maximum profits, and develop a unique position for the product or service that is relevant to the target audience. Ensuring that customers are profitable is often perceived as a pricing tactic. But focusing solely on pricing is one-dimensional because it minimizes or even ignores add-on features such as product enhancements, additional service and training.

The measurement need for marketers is how to more effectively measure customer profitability, accounting for the work inputs that support customer-related activities. Robert S. Kaplan, a professor at Harvard Business School, has pioneered much of the research about activity-based costing (ABC), as well as the balanced scorecard. ABC is designed to help company management measure the indirect costs involved in supporting their customers. Kaplan suggests that some companies have struggled to successfully measure costs using ABC due to implementation challenges (including development costs) and the complexity of their own operations, which were not always adequately captured by ABC. His solution is time-driven activity-based costing (TDABC).

Solution[2]

TDABC measures two factors: the cost per hour of each department working on customer, product or service-related activities; and the specific time devoted to the activities themselves.

Let's take database companies as an example to illustrate TDABC. Database companies sell business software. The software is usually part of a packaged solution that includes services, such as engineering support, designed to help customers answer questions, particularly in the early stages of implementation. If the engineering support costs $120 per hour and the length of time needed to service a customer is 45 minutes, then the cost is $90:

$$TC = C_h \times T_u$$

Where

TC = total cost

C_h = cost per hour

T_u = time in units

$$TC = \$120 \times \tfrac{3}{4} \text{ hour}$$
$$= \$90$$

Impact on Decision Making

Marketers are responsible for understanding customers, analyzing their needs and measuring their profitability. Marketers utilize several tools to capture customers and, ultimately, grow the business. Pricing strategies are designed partly to help position products (and recover costs, at a minimum). Differentiation strategies enable customers to understand why a company's products are distinctive. TDABC allows marketers to understand the indirect costs that go toward supporting and communicating the pricing and differentiation strategies they have employed.

While the enterprise software example is simplistic, the lesson is powerful and useful in helping marketers understand the true profits resulting from each customer. Kaplan's approach can help companies reveal previously unknown drivers of poor customer profitability. For example, while a customer's purchase of your products may be growing, that does not necessarily mean that profits are increasing. The cost to service that customer may have increased as well, perhaps due to the temptation to add product features or services to keep the customer from defecting to a competitor. Yet the additional cost to support those services and features is not captured by a corresponding increase in prices, resulting in reduced profitability.

To understand customer profitability, it is important to know all costs, not just those that are fixed. TDABC is a useful approach for identifying the specific indirect costs of each activity related to creating that customer in the first place.

Endnotes

1 Drucker, P. *The Concept of the Corporation.* New Jersey: Transaction Publishers, reprint edition, January 1, 1993.

2 Kaplan, R.S. "A Balanced Scorecard Approach To Measure Customer Profitability". *Harvard Business School Working Knowledge*, August 8, 2005.

Causal Forecast 14

Measurement Need

Causal forecasts help managers measure the relationship between two types of variables: dependent and independent. Managers may seek to understand how much product (the dependent variable, or the "output") should be ordered under given demand conditions (the independent variable, or the "input"). As demand conditions change, so too should the amount of product ordered. In other words, the value (size, quantity, amount) of the dependent variable is directly influenced by the independent variable. Thus, a change in a product or marketing program can affect buyer behaviors (a price reduction might lead to increased purchases). Or an emerging trend may signal greater opportunity for existing or new products, changing the performance of the business as a result. Causal forecasting enables managers to measure the possible impact to their business (and/or customers or other value chain participants) from these changes.

For example, companies such as Nike or Adidas, both of which make athletic footwear, would be interested in forecasting how many basketball shoes they may sell to teen basketball players in the U.S. over the next three years. By reviewing census data of the teen population and surveys of growth trends in teen basketball, they can project the potential demand for their respective products. Assuming the teen population in the U.S. is forecast to grow (the independent variable), as is the interest in basketball, then it is plausible to project an increase in sales (the dependent variable).

Other examples (not exhaustive):

- Demand increases for air-conditioners during summer months
- Increases/decreases of ice-cream sales due to temperature changes
- More workers needed at restaurants on busy nights

Solution

A commonly used technique in causal forecasting is linear regression. In the linear regression method, when the dependent variable (usually the vertical axis on a graph) changes as a result of the change in another variable (plotted as the horizontal axis), it reflects a causal relationship and is represented by a straight line drawn through closely-related data points on a graph with an x and y axis. Simply put, linear regression is used to determine if there is a trend to the data, and is represented by a line formula:

$$y = a + bx$$

Where

y = the dependent variable

a = the intercept

b = the slope of the line

x = the independent variable

As one can surmise, to determine the line formula both the slope of the line, designated as "b" above, and the intercept, designed as "a", must be calculated. The reason is that the slope describes the effect of the independent variable, x, on the dependent variable, y (i.e. the changes in y if x changes by one unit). If there is no relationship between the dependent and independent variables, then the slope of the line would equal zero. The intercept describes where the linear regression line intersects with the y axis. The formulas are:

$$Intercept = a = Y - bX$$

$$Slope = b = \frac{\sum xy - nXY}{\sum x^2 - nX^2}$$

Where

a = intercept

b = slope of the line

$X = \sum x$ = mean of x

$Y = \sum y$ = mean of y

n = number of periods

From here, the strength of the relationship between the dependent and independent variable must be measured. This is known as correlation and is represented by:

$$r = \frac{n\sum xy - \sum x \sum y}{\sqrt{[n\sum x^2 - (\sum x)^2][n\sum y^2 - (\sum y)^2]}}$$

Where

r = correlation coefficient

n = number of periods

x = the independent variable

y = the dependent variable

Finally, forecasters need to calculate the percentage of variation in the dependent (y) variable that is attributed to the independent (x) variable. The coefficient of determination is used (which measures the relationship between the dependent and independent variables). If the independent variable is changed, then what affect does that have on the dependent variable? Do the two variables "go together"? The closer the relationship, the larger the coefficient of determination, up to 1.0 (or -1.0 for negative relationships). It is calculated by:

$$r = r^2$$

Let's use an example to illustrate how these various formulas work together.

- Restaurant Steak House
- Forecasting food sales
  - How many meals will be sold each week
- Forecasting inventory
  - Perishable food
  - Non-perishable food

Table 6 shows the linear regression

Table 6: Linear Regression

Week	# of meals served	Quantity of beef ordered (lbs)			
	x	y	xy	x^2	y^2
1	100	125	12,500	10,000	15,625
2	150	186	27,900	22,500	34,596
3	90	125	11,250	8,100	15,625

4	125	142	17,750	15,625	20,164
5	130	150	19,500	16,900	22,500
6	120	135	16,200	14,400	18,225
7	115	140	16,100	13,225	19,600
8	75	96	7,200	5,625	9,216
9	100	130	13,000	10,000	16,900
10	105	133	13,965	11,025	17,689
Total	1,110	1,362	155,365	127,400	190,140

A linear regression is then calculated as follows:

$$X = 1,110/10 = 111$$

$$Y = 1,362/10 = 136.20$$

$$b = \frac{\sum xy - nXY}{\sum x^2 - nX^2} = \frac{(155,365) - (10)(111)(136.20)}{(127,400) - (10)(111)^2}$$

$$b = 0.9983$$

$$a = Y - bX = 136.20 - 0.9983(111)$$

$$a = 25.3887$$

These results are plugged into the original line formula:

$$y = a + bx$$

$$y = 25.3887 + 0.9983(x)$$

For x, the forecaster should select the number of meals to be served (using this example) to calculate y. Let's select 130 as that is the approximate average number of meals served per day:

$$y = 25.3887 + 0.9983(130)$$

$$y = 155.17$$

Therefore, 155 pounds of beef should be ordered.

Next, the correlation coefficient is calculated to determine the strength of the relationship (also known as "interdependence") between x and y.

$$r = \frac{n\sum xy - \sum x \sum y}{\sqrt{[n\sum x^2 - (\sum x)^2][n\sum y^2 - (\sum y)^2]}}$$

$$r = \frac{10(155,365) - (1,110)(1,362)}{\sqrt{[10(127,400) - (1,110)^2][10(190,140) - (1,363)^2]}}$$

$$r = 0.9783$$

$$r^2 = 0.9571$$

The results suggest there is a strong relationship between the number of meals served and the quantity (in lbs.) of beef ordered. This restaurant can therefore feel confident that its forecast will be accurate.

Impact on Decision Making

For marketers, this result also suggests that the costs of their product can be fairly accurately predicted. By extension, the final price offered to the customer can even be determined as well. Marketers in this example will want to set prices based on their strategic objectives for the positioning of their restaurant, its image (premium, mass market, value), cost factors and the projected amount of business in the future.

For salespeople, causal forecasts are useful, particularly with controllable activities such as short-term promotions, where the outcome can be reasonably anticipated.

Causal forecasting is not useful in every situation. It works best when the correlation between the dependent and independent variables is strong.

Sources

Lapide, L. "New Developments in Business Forecasting". *Journal of Business Forecasting Methods & Systems*, Vol. 18, Issue 2 (Summer 1999).

http://morris.wharton.upenn.edu/forecast, *Principles of Forecasting, A Handbook for Researchers and Practitioners*. Edited by J. Scott Armstrong, University of Pennsylvania.

www.uoguelph.ca/~dsparlin/forecast.htm

Cachon, G. and Terwiesch, C. *Matching Supply with Demand: An Introduction to Operations Management*, International edition. New York: McGraw-Hill, 2006.

Time Series Analysis

15

Measurement Need

Marketers must regularly make decisions about future marketing activities. Strategic alignment with overall corporate objectives, marketing program investments and budgets, pricing, and customer development are among the many activities included in the typical marketing manager's responsibilities. These activities are part of the overall marketing planning effort, and many of the marketing planning decisions are based on forecasting future sales. Understanding past sales performance is helpful in this regard as historical results often reveal trends that, depending on anticipated business conditions, influence the marketing plan recommendations.

Solution

Time series analysis is a useful method for using past quantitative data to predict future performance. Three popular methods are:

- Naive forecast
- Averaging forecasts
- Exponential smoothing

Naive forecast

The naive forecast, as shown in Table 7, assumes the next period's demand will match the previous period's. It is important that the selected forecast quantity is consistent in both the actual and forecast columns (i.e. use dollars in both, or units).

Table 7: Naive Forecast Chart

Period	Actual Sales (dollars)	Forecast Sales (dollars)
January	75	
February	75	75
March	90	75
April	110	90
May	120	110
June	120	120
July	150	120
August	110	150
September	100	110
October	90	100
November	100	90
December	130	100

Averaging forecasts

Averaging forecasts have several approaches. Moving and weighted moving averages are two of the most common approaches.

Moving average

Forecasters would select a representative number of periods and calculate the average of those periods. The result becomes the forecasted amount for the next period. Let's assume a four-month forecast period using the previous chart. In this case, the forecast would represent the total sales in the January-April timeframe divided by the number of periods (four), to arrive at May's moving average. As Table 8 illustrates, May's forecast sales are 88. The same process is repeated to determine June's forecast sales (99), July's (110), and so on.

Table 8: Moving Average Forecast

Period	Actual Sales (000s dollars)	Forecast Sales (000s dollars)
January	75	
February	75	
March	90	
April	110	
May	120	88
June	120	99

July	150	110
August	110	125
September	100	125
October	90	120
November	100	113
December	130	103

The moving average forecast helps correct the simplistic assumptions of the naive forecast since it is likely that the previous period's sales are not perfectly repeatable in the next period. Moving average helps smooth over variations attributable to seasonal patterns. The moving average of sales performance based on the preceding three months (in this example) reduces the chance that any one month's exceptional performance (good or bad) will unduly influence the next month's forecast. However, more recent sales data is usually considered more reliable than older data since it may be indicative of current market conditions. Moving average forecasts do not account for this since the impact of recent data is reduced due to the inclusion of older data in the average. The weighted moving average can help overcome this bias.

Weighted Moving Average

The weighted moving average (or "simple" weighted average) assigns weights to data in different periods with, generally speaking, more recent periods receiving a higher weighting because they are considered more influential. The sum total of all the weights equals one, therefore, each weight is a fraction of one. Let's continue with the same example, assigning the lowest weight to the earliest month and the highest weight to the most recent as follows: 0.1, 0.2, 0.3, 0.4:

May = January (75x0.1) = February (75x0.2) + March (90x0.3) = April (110x0.4) = 93.5

June = February (75x0.1) + March (90x0.2) + April (110x0.3) + May (120x0.4) = 106.5

July = March (90x0.1) + April (110x0.2) + May (120x0.3) + June (120x0.4) = 115

August = April (110x0.1) + May (120x0.2) + June (120x0.3) + July (150x0.4) = 131

September = May (120x0.1) + June (120x0.2) + July (150x0.3) + August (110x0.4) = 125

October = June (120x0.1) + July (150x0.2) + August (110x0.3) + September (100x0.4) = 115

November = July (150x0.1) + August (110x0.2) + September (110x0.3) + October (90x0.4) = 106

December = August (110x0.1) + September (100x0.2) + October (90x0.3) + November (100x0.4) = 98

Table 9 shows the weighted moving average forecast.

Table 9: Weighted Moving Average Forecast

Period	Actual Sales (000's dollars)	Forecast Sales (000's dollars)
January	75	
February	75	
March	90	
April	110	
May	120	93.5
June	120	106.5
July	150	115
August	110	131
September	100	125
October	90	115
November	100	106
December	130	98

Exponential Smoothing[1]

Exponential smoothing is a more sophisticated approach to weighted moving average. It, too, is a popular forecasting technique used in computerized forecasting programs and wholesale and retail inventory ordering programs. Like the weighted moving average, exponential smoothing favors more recent data over older data. A key difference, however, is the use of a "smoothing constant" called alpha, represented by á. Alpha describes the level of smoothing deemed reasonable and the speed of a company's reaction to differences between forecasts and actual occurrences. As per weighted moving average, smoothing is a technique for reducing the impact of seasonality or more extreme variances from typical demand performance. It is always less than one and is based on the marketing forecaster's intuition of what comprises a good response rate combined with the nature of the product itself.

$$F_t = F_{t-1} + á(A_t - F_{t-1})$$

Where
F_t = new forecast
A_t = actual demand that occurred in the forecast period
F_{t-1} = previous/most recent forecast

Forecasters begin the analysis with a previous period, building sequentially to arrive at the forecast for the period needed. This requires the forecaster to have past data and/or the initial forecast from which to develop the analysis. Adapting the earlier table, let's develop a forecast for April. To determine this, the forecasts for February and March must be calculated. For February, we need to know F_{t-1}, the previous/most recent forecast (January, in this case). Let's assume it was 70 and that alpha is 0.6. The following result occurs for February:

$$F_t = 70 + 0.6(75 - 70) = 73$$

An identical approach is used to determine the figures for March:

$$F_t = 73 + 0.6(75 - 73) = 74.2$$

Finally, April is then calculated:

$$F_t = 74.20 + 0.6(90 - 74.20) = 83.68$$

Table 10 shows the exponential smoothing.

Table 10: Exponential Smoothing

Period	Actual Sales (000's dollars)	Forecast Sales (000's dollars)
January	75	70
February	75	73
March	90	74.20
April		83.68
May		
June		
July		
August		
September		
October		
November		
December		

Once the actual data for April is known, May can then be forecast, and the process continues as each month's actual sales are included.

Impact on Decision Making

Marketing managers have the responsibility to develop forecasts that help their companies determine demand for products and services. A thoughtful time series forecast utilizes historical data (otherwise they are unreliable guesses). It serves as a starting point guide of your company's possible future(s), from which your marketing recommendations logically flow. It helps marketers observe and understand seasonal variation patterns in data as well as any growth rate changes. However, marketers must be alert to the pros and cons of time series forecasts:

- They are never 100% reliable
- Time series forecasts tend to be more accurate with shorter time frames (i.e. it is easier to predict tomorrow than it is next month, or next year)
- Time series analysis tends to assume that the future will be like the past
- They tend to be more credible when based on longer data histories (i.e. using several months or years of data is better than several days)
- Newer data tends to be more reliable than older data and receives a higher weighting as a result

Marketers must ask themselves a key question when considering forecasting needs: is the sales trend increasing, decreasing, flat? Time series analysis can be helpful in answering basic trend questions as it may suggest emerging opportunities or, conversely, warning signs. But time series analysis is less useful for understanding and determining the causes that underlie trends. How do anomalous events such as external market disturbances (natural or man-made disasters), aggressive new marketing campaigns or competitive behavior affect demand? What are the reasons for the seasonal variation? Time series analysis is a good first step toward developing a better forecast, but marketers must consider these other influences when developing their marketing plans.

Endnote

1 Cachon, G. and Terwiesch, C. *Matching Supply with Demand: An Introduction to Operations Management*, International edition. New York: McGraw-Hill, 2006.

Sources

Cachon, G. and Terwiesch, C. *Matching Supply with Demand: An Introduction to Operations Management*, International edition. New York: McGraw-Hill, 2006.

Doyle, C. *Collins Internet-Linked Dictionary of Marketing*. Harper Collins, 2003, 2006: p.296.

Imber, J. and Toffler, B.A. *Dictionary of Marketing Terms*, Barron's Educational Series, 2000: p.545.

http://www.bized.ac.uk/timeweb/crunching/crunch_analysis_illus.htm

http://home.ubalt.edu/ntsbarsh/stat-data/Forecast.htm#rgintroduction

http://www.referenceforbusiness.com/management/Ex-Gov/Forecasting.html

http://gbr.pepperdine.edu/001/forecast.html

http://www.tutor2u.net/business/marketing/sales_forecasting.asp

Market Growth 16

Measurement Need

One of marketing's most important tasks is identifying growth opportunities along two dimensions: market share and financial performance. Growth has direct implications for a firm's competitive position. Company growth signals market acceptance of the firm's products (since customers are unlikely to adopt a new product if it does not satisfy their needs) and a potential competitive advantage (particularly if the growth is faster than the competition's). Marketing management is keenly interested in whether company growth is faster, equal to, or less than market growth since the answer will affect future marketing plans about customer segments, product choices, channels and even marketing communications programs.

Solution

Market growth is determined by measuring the total sales in your market and then comparing this figure to the sales changes in preceding time periods (typically years). It is represented by the following formula:

$$G_m = \frac{R_I}{R_L}$$

Where

G_m = % market growth

R_I = dollars/units increase this year

R_L = dollars/units last year

To illustrate using dollars, if the total revenues in your market are projected to be $500 million this year and were $400 million last year, then the market growth rate is 25%. This was calculated by dividing the revenue increase, $100 million, by total revenues last year, $400 million:

$$\frac{\$100 \ \text{million}}{\$400 \ \text{million}} = 0.25 \ \text{or} \ 25\%$$

Using units, Sony sold 850,000 units of its Walkman digital music player in 2004. It forecast sales of 4.5 million units in 2005, for a projected growth rate of 529%. The market for portable digital music players was 37 million units in 2004 and was expected to be 57 million units in 2005, for a growth rate of 54%[1]. Knowing the market growth rate assists companies in determining whether their own performance is stronger, consistent or weaker than the rest of the market.

Projected Sony Digital Music Player Growth

$$\frac{4,500,000 \ \text{units}}{850,000 \ \text{units}} = 5.29 \ \text{or} \ 529\%$$

Projected Digital Music Player Market Growth

$$\frac{20,000,000 \ \text{units}}{37,000,000 \ \text{units}} = 0.54 \ \text{or} \ 54\%$$

Impact on Decision Making

Knowing the market growth rate can provide marketers with insight into the future potential for their businesses (although there is no guarantee that historical growth rates will continue into the future). Market data can be easily obtained from industry trade publications, independent market-research firms, product analysts, reputable business magazines, government reports and trade associations.

Marketers must measure their own company's growth first, for two reasons: first, to see what the growth trend has been over the past few years and determine whether their current pace is above or below the recent historical average; and second, to compare their business's growth to that of the competition.

Market growth can serve as a good indicator of dynamics in the marketplace. It provides guidance on the market's potential (the total number of customers in the target market segment), the level of customer penetration (how many customers have entered the market) and the rate of customer entry (how quickly new customers enter the market)[2]. As the Sony example hints, the market growth rate can also suggest important trends, which can be further understood by comparing growth rates for the past four or five years and/or projected growth for the next few years. In Sony's case, their projected pace of growth far exceeds the overall market, which means Sony expects to gain market share, most likely at the expense of its rivals. Further analysis reveals that part of Sony's projection is influenced by the launch of new digital music player models in 2005, probably with the hope that these new devices will capture the hearts and minds of consumers and eat into the market leading position of its rival, Apple. Marketers will want to understand the forces driving this market growth and, in this instance, the reasons their growth far exceeds the pace of the market. Demographic changes, purchase behavior patterns, product or market innovations and lower interest rates are examples of factors that may drive or influence the growth rate. Once marketers understand the driving forces, they can use this information to develop new products, communications campaigns and price changes to create a competitive advantage for their products.

Market growth provides strategic guidance regarding the potential attractiveness of a given market in the years to come and assists marketing managers in understanding the associated opportunities and challenges. It is also a useful tool for senior management when evaluating its marketing investments, since it provides a snapshot of likely growth opportunities. Venture capitalists, as well, find market growth an important factor in evaluating the viability of start-up companies, since it can suggest whether a venture has a long-term future or not.

Developing a clear understanding of market growth is not complex, but it does require more effort than merely scanning the daily paper. Publicly-traded companies produce annual reports for shareholders, containing detailed financial information and often providing insight into senior management's view of future opportunities. Marketers can and should avail themselves of this information as it will provide some general insight into their competition, albeit that annual reports rarely reveal detailed strategic choices. But because public companies have an obligation to report their performance to shareholders, a diligent marketer may succeed in gaining a clearer sense of the competitor's management style and will certainly be able to compare specific business performance to that of their own comparable products. Marketers working in privately held companies will benefit from their public company competitor's annual reports as well. But to learn about other private companies and their respective strengths and weaknesses, marketers will need to conduct their own market research, hire a market research firm, or review industry trade publications for their sector.

The thoughtful reader will quickly note that the Sony example provides a frame of reference. In other words, Sony's projected 529% growth rate appears quite strong compared with the market overall. However, be aware that to measure growth, a marketer must be quite clear about what is being measured and why. Is it growth of total market revenues? Or growth of total market dollars available for purchasing? Or is it the rate at which new customers are being acquired? Or the rate at which the three-to-five most significant competitors are growing? The answer depends on the industry. Furthermore, even within industries there are segments that may perform far differently from others.

Endnotes

1 Hall, K. "Can Sony's New Walkman Run?". *BusinessWeek Online*, September 9, 2005.

2 Best, R.J. *Market-Based Management: Strategies for Growing Customer Value and Profitability.* Pearson Education, 2005: pp.72, 73.

Source

Davis, J. *Magic Numbers for Consumer Marketing.* Singapore: John Wiley & Sons (Asia) Pte Ltd., 2005: pp.18-22.

Market Share 17

Measurement Need

Marketers use the Four Ps of the marketing mix (product, price, place, promotion) to attract customers and develop a competitive advantage for their company's products. To measure success, marketing managers need to assess their performance compared to the competitors.

Solution

Market share describes a company's sales as a percentage of total sales volume in a specific industry, market or product area. It can be expressed with the following formula:

$$M_{it} = \frac{S_{it}}{\sum S_t}$$

Where:

M_{it} = company i's market share in time t expressed in percentage terms

S_{it} = sales of company i in time t (in units or dollars)

$\sum S_t$ = sum of all sales in time t (in units or dollars)

To illustrate, Nike had $12.3 billion in total sales in 2004 out of total sales of the global athletic market of $33 billion[1]. Nike's market share was over 37%, calculated as follows:

$$\frac{\$12,300,000}{\$33,000,000} = 37.3\%$$

Impact on Decision Making

Market share helps management understand the success of its efforts to penetrate the market relative to its competitors. A rising market share is generally a good sign, although it is subject to several qualifications. The company's market share (in units) may have risen because the company lowered its price substantially and may now be losing money. Or its share may have risen because the product category is aging and smarter firms are quickly abandoning the category, leaving the crumbs to this firm. The data used to measure market share will likely come from several sources. The marketer's finance or accounting departments should have up-to-date information on the company's sales provided from the company's sales management or distribution operations. Total sales in the market will come from several outside sources, including industry trade reports, consulting firms, market research specialists and even business magazines. Marketing managers should compare data from multiple sources because of differences in data collection time periods, precision of measurement criteria, reporting time periods and the collection methodology.

Building on the athletic market example, Adidas announced in 2005 its intention to acquire Reebok. With this acquisition, Adidas would move closer to Nike's number one market share position. The Adidas-Reebok deal would have created a company with $11.1 billion in revenue in 2004, or nearly a 31% market share. Pre-acquisition, Adidas' global market share was closer to 21-22%. Adidas' market share increase is due to acquisition, not necessarily a rising overall market, although that may be a possible contributor in the future.

Market share is typically used in several planning areas. As a business planning metric, senior management may set a market share target for a forthcoming time period (typically 1-2 years) for the company. Marketers would typically include the market share figures when discussing strategies and objectives in the marketing plan and in their internal efforts to build support from other departments. If marketing managers are responsible for a specific product, product line or product category, then individual market share goals may also be set for each specific product, in addition to overall company objectives.

Marketing managers need to analyze their market share in depth to better understand the sources of their market share performance. If market share gains were made over a specified period of time, were they ahead of schedule or behind schedule? Is this increased share sustainable? If market share declined, what were the factors that may have caused this? Competitor innovation? Competitor pricing? Customer dissatisfaction? Changing customer preferences?

The key takeaway is that market share is a useful metric for both review and planning purposes.

Endnote

1 Adapted from two business reports: Hirsch, S and A. Tucker. "In a bid to step on Nike's toes, Adidas plans to buy Reebok". *The Baltimore Sun*, August 4, 2005; and Kang, S and M. Karnitschnig. "For Adidas, Reebok Deal Caps Push to Broaden Urban Appeal". *The Wall Street Journal*, August 4, 2005.

Source

Davis, J. *Magic Numbers for Consumer Marketing*. Singapore: John Wiley & Sons (Asia) Pte Ltd, 2005: pp.30-34.

Market Demand 18

Measurement Need

Chapters 16 and 17 describe market growth and market share, which are both key measures in a marketer's performance assessment "toolbox". Marketers need to measure total demand since it helps describe additional growth opportunities, if any.

Solution

Market demand describes the total demand for a particular product and/or service. It is the sum of existing/repeat customers plus new customers and it can be used to measure company-level or market-level demand. It is represented by the formula:

$$M_{dt} = P_{rt} + P_{nt}$$

Where

M_{dt} = market demand during time period t

P_{rt} = repeat or replacement purchases in time period t (in dollars)

P_{nt} = new purchases in time period t (in dollars)

Let's assume that a Southeast Asian dried foods manufacturing business sells its products direct to retailers. Last year, purchases from their existing/repeat retail customers totaled $5 million while purchases from new customers amounted to $2 million. Market demand for their product is $7 million.

$$\$5,000,000 + \$2,000,000 = \$7,000,000$$

Impact on Decision Making

Market demand helps marketers understand the sources of customer demand for their products and/or services. It provides basic insight into their target customer base and can be an early indicator of the effectiveness of marketing and sales programs. An increasing demand from new customers is generally considered a positive signal that the market is growing and wants more of your product. A decline in existing customers may be cause for concern, suggesting that competitors are offering better products, lower prices or a combination of both. However, it would be wise to investigate the market more deeply before reaching conclusions from market demand data alone. At the market level, data for demand, repeat purchases and new purchases can be found in industry trade journals, industry research reports, general business magazines with special issues devoted to specific industry sectors and the marketer's own research into market trends. At the firm-level, marketers will have to rely on a combination of their own internal reports for information on current and new customers as well as market research to gauge market demand.

Market demand is particularly useful for marketers when discussing their target customers in planning meetings with senior management and in the written marketing plan itself. To be measured properly, a marketer must have a clear and empirically based explanation of the new and existing customer figures used. Otherwise, the market demand figure will be purely an exercise in guessing, which will harm the marketer's ability to convincingly defend the rest of their marketing plan.

Market demand is an important planning metric, particularly in combination with market growth (Chapter 16), since an increase in both measures may indicate that a company is taking thoughtful advantage of a rising market in both retaining existing customers and capturing new ones. Furthermore, market demand can be a useful starting point for establishing sales objectives at both the strategic and tactical levels. Strategic sales objectives include revenue targets at the market and segment levels. Tactical sales objectives would focus on more detailed expectations at the individual customer account level. A clear understanding of market demand will therefore help sales management establish appropriate sales quotas for their field sales personnel. This will be discussed at greater length in the sections on both customers and sales force quotas.

Sources

Best, R.J. *Market-Based Management: Strategies for Growing Customer Value and Profitability.* Pearson Education, 2005: p.77.

Doyle, C. *Collins Internet-Linked Dictionary of Marketing.* Harper Collins, 2003, 2006: p.177.

Davis, J. *Magic Numbers for Consumer Marketing.* Singapore: John Wiley & Sons (Asia) Pte Ltd, 2005: pp.46-47.

Market Penetration

19

Measurement Need

Marketers are responsible for attracting, retaining and growing customer business, and market penetration is one of four strategies companies can employ to improve their success with customers and increase market share as a result.

Solution[1]

Market penetration is a comparison of current versus potential market demand of a company's products.

$$M_p = \frac{D_c}{D_p} \times 100$$

Where

M_p = Market penetration
D_c = Current market demand
D_p = Potential market demand

Current market demand describes the total number of products that could be purchased by a pre-defined target customer group in a specific market area under specific business conditions and marketing programs for all firms in the market.

Potential market demand describes the *added* opportunities available to the same companies for the same products under the same conditions. Potential market demand is influenced by type of product, pricing, new marketing appeals and competitor actions. Some products lend themselves to added potential, such as many consumer non-durables (food, beverage and grocery products, for example), while other products have less added potential, such as a sports or entertainment events. This is due partly to the types of products (when popular grocery items are discounted, for instance, it often drives temporary demand and increases the total dollars in the market than would otherwise have "naturally" been spent. Sports and entertainment events have a narrower appeal (everyone needs food, not everyone needs to see a professional soccer match) and limited live seating. Additional marketing spent on it will generate increased costs per remaining seat.

Market penetration is effectively a method for measuring potential opportunities for the market overall. A corollary measure in this evaluation is known as the market share index, a particularly useful measure for individual companies. Market share index helps marketing management determine which areas of their operation need adjustment to improve market penetration. It is closely related to market share, providing more specific information about the factors that influence customer purchase decisions and, ultimately, market share.

The market share index formula is[2]:

$$M_{si} = P_a \times P_p \times B_i \times A \times P_{pur}$$

Where
   M_{si} = market share index
   P_a = product awareness (the number of people aware of your product in your target market compared to the overall population in the target market)
   P_p = product preference (is the product and/or its features attractive?)
   B_i = intention to buy (is the product's price attractive?)
   A = availability of product (can the product be found in the marketplace?)
   P_{pur} = product purchase (is buying the product a positive experience?)

Using the first formula for market penetration, let's assume we are analyzing the market for pizza in a selected city. The market is highly fragmented, meaning multiple competitors are vying for market share, but no single pizza operation overwhelmingly dominates. Current demand indicates a market totaling $8 million in sales annually. However, past industry marketing efforts indicate that price promotions boost business by 25%. Therefore, the market potential is $10,000,000 ($8,000,000 × .25 = $2,000,000. This result is added to the $8,000,000 current demand to determine potential demand). Therefore,

$$M_p = \frac{\$8,000,000}{\$10,000,000} \times 100$$

$$= 80\%$$

The result shows a market penetration of 80%. For most markets, this result would be quite high, suggesting that acquiring the remaining potential customers would be increasingly expensive on a per-customer basis. However, let's assume that, based on current market dynamics, a price promotion at this time will lead to business increases of 75%. Therefore, the market potential is $14,000,000 ($8,000,000 × 0.75 = $6,000,000. This result is added to the $8,000,000 current demand to determine potential demand), as follows:

$$M_p = \frac{\$8,000,000}{\$14,000,000} \times 100$$

$$= 57\%$$

Market penetration is now 57%, which suggests that there is more room for all pizza companies in the market to improve their growth. The market penetration calculations describe the market overall.

Now let's look at growth opportunities for individual companies in this highly fragmented market. Using the second formula for market share index, let's assume that a pizza company's data gathering reveals the following statistics for their business:

- P_a = Product awareness = 52% (48% are unaware)
- P_p = Product preference = 76% (24% find it unattractive)
- B_i = Intention to buy = 55% (45% do not intend to buy)
- A = Availability of product = 40% (60% product not available)
- P_{pur} = Product purchase = 38% (62% had a disappointing purchase experience)

Plugging these figures into the formula reveals that our small pizza firm has a market share index of 3.3%

$$M_{si} = P_a \times P_p \times B_i \times A \times P_{pur}$$

$$M_{si} = 0.52 \times 0.76 \times 0.55 \times 0.40 \times 0.38$$

$$= 0.033$$

$$= 3.3\%$$

Marketing management of this pizza firm now has data indicating that the overall pizza market is only 57% penetrated by all competitors and that their own share is 3.3%. Therefore, with the right mix of promotions, their market share can improve, perhaps dramatically. Had the market penetration rate been closer to 100%, the task of improving share grows significantly harder since all companies are vying for a limited set of remaining customers.

A helpful framework when conducting market penetration analysis is the Ansoff Matrix, conceived by Igor Ansoff in his 1957 *Harvard Business Review* article "Strategies for Diversification"[3]. Ansoff describes growth opportunities in a simple two by two matrix, with products across the horizontal axis and markets along the vertical access, as shown in Figure 9.

PRODUCTS

		Present	New
MARKETS	**Present**	Market Penetration	Product Development
	New	Market Development	Diversification

Figure 9: Strategic Growth Choices

The Ansoff Matrix is a useful supplement in determining market penetration because it provides clear guidance on the marketing growth choices: growth opportunities are limited to existing products in existing markets. This prescribes a set of activities available to marketing managers in order to successfully penetrate existing markets. The activities are:

1. Increase market share in the existing market—marketers are attracting customers within the segment who are either buying competitor products or who fit the target profile but have not yet committed. Marketers can influence this through more advertising, new pricing, short-term promotions or, most expensively (but it can also be the most productive over the long term), increased customer relationship development and personal selling. This is the competitive situation commonly associated with many branded consumer products, with similar or identical ingredients, but frequently updated marketing messages. The challenge is the expense of regularly creating fresh and new marketing campaigns that are relevant to consumers and resonate with them as well.

2. First mover advantage—also known as securing dominant share. Usually, the marketer is representing an innovative product that attracts the market's attention before the competition has a chance to enter, allowing the firm to capture a dominant market share. However, securing a long-term majority share is very difficult without substantial investment in continuous

marketing and R&D (the latter also begins to shifts the company from a market penetration to a product development growth strategy). Technology markets, including software and consumer electronics, often have this approach. The challenge is sustaining the advantage beyond the short term.

3. Deep price penetration—this is an aggressive, low-price-point strategy designed to steal share aggressively from competitors by undercutting them on price. A classic example is from the 1980s in the U.S., when Japanese chip manufacturers flooded the market with below-cost chips to gain market share. The challenges are determining the break-even point and raising prices later on, as customers adopt your offerings and the company seeks to improve profitability.

4. Increase product usage by current customers—this can be done by developing new uses for the product or creating customer loyalty plans. Examples include the airline and hotel industries. The challenges are the cost of staying updated on customers information (often through expensive software systems and databases), the cost of accumulated points programs or frequent flyer miles redeemed within a short-period of time, and the cost of finding new personalized marketing approaches that continue to reinforce the importance your company places on the relationship.

Impact on Decision Making

Market penetration helps companies assess remaining growth potential. The market share index analysis indicates where firms may have problems in their "go to market" efforts, highlighting those areas that can help improve penetration. For example, in the above analysis, 76% of the people who are aware of the pizza company's product prefer it, which is a reasonably strong level of preference for the product. Interestingly, only 52% of the market is aware of the product. Therefore, the company can focus its marketing efforts on communications to increase awareness. If, through these efforts, this individual pizza company succeeds in increasing awareness to 75%, then their market share index increases from 3.3% to 4.7%.

$$M_{si} = 0.75 \times 0.76 \times 0.55 \times 0.40 \times 0.38$$
$$= 0.047$$
$$= 4.7\%$$

In this example, another area of improvement is in the buying experience. Only 38% of the buyers had a good buying experience. Therefore, the company could undertake a point-of-sale training program that teaches sales and customer service employees how to improve service with a view to enhancing customers' purchasing experience. Let's assume the company is able to flip these numbers through just such a training program, so that 62% of the buyers report a positive buying experience. Keeping the aforementioned increase in awareness level and now factoring in the improved buying experience level yields a market penetration of 7.8%.

$$M_{si} = 0.75 \times 0.76 \times 0.55 \times 0.40 \times 0.62$$

$$= 0.078$$

$$= 7.8\%$$

Be aware that understanding each variable in the market share index has its own challenges. Product awareness describes the percentage of customers in the target market that are aware of a company's products (the percentage of people overall in the market that are aware of your product could be measured, but it would be less meaningful because this would presume that all people in the market may have an interest in the product if they were only aware of it). If awareness is low, then this result indicates that the company has the potential to increase awareness. The corollary is that it will cost money to increase awareness since marketing will have to invest in advertising, sales promotions and other marketing communications efforts. Improving the buyer's satisfaction at the time of purchase will also cost money. But if the company's goal is to improve penetration and beat the competition, then these are worthy of serious consideration.

As the Ansoff Matrix indicates, decision making for market penetration is clear cut since marketing management is concerned only with known products and known markets. While the investment can be heavy in marketing plans (pricing and advertising, in particular) and sales programs (promotions and volume selling), it is unlikely to involve much market research or R&D, since both of those would shift the company's strategy to different growth quadrants and, correspondingly, different marketing and product approaches. Firms focusing on market penetration may have a unique relationship with customers, developed over many years or even decades of tradition, thus minimizing the need to seek growth elsewhere. It is a unique and conservative business approach, but if your company is too successful, it is a matter of time before competitors enter, forcing you to consider a response from the other quadrants.

To determine potential market demand, marketers must conduct and analyze customer research, evaluate trends, establish product pricing, determine distribution, and create promotional campaigns to generate awareness. Sales management then works directly with customers, developing relationships, understanding customer profiles and determining specific solutions to address customer needs. Once a customer base is established, the challenge is how to continue growing this increasingly valuable asset.

Collecting the data for the market share index is challenging, but not impossible. It implies that marketers undertake some basic market research to determine each of the formula's components. Each of the components can be determined from surveys, with the exception of product preference and availability of product. Product preference can be calculated using a technique called *conjoint analysis.** Availability of product is determined through an analysis of your own distribution asking:

- Is the product available and easy to buy?

- What is the number of actual distribution points compared to the total number of distribution points, which provides a percentage of share or penetration?

Endnotes

1 Kotler, P., Siew, M.L., Swee, H. A. and Tan, C.T. *Marketing Management: An Asian Perspective.* Upper Saddle River, NJ: Prentice Hall, 2003. p.137

2 Best, R.J. *Market-Based Management: Strategies for Growing Customer Value and Profitability.* Pearson Education, 2005: pp.72, 86-87

3 Ansoff, H.I. "Strategies for Diversification". *Harvard Business Review*, 35(2), September-October (1957).

Sources

Davis, J, *Magic Numbers for Consumer Marketing.* Singapore: John Wiley & Sons (Asia) Pte Ltd, 2005: pp.34-36.

*For more information on conjoint analysis, readers are encouraged to review the following sources:

- http://www.quickmba.com/marketing/research/conjoint/

- http://www.surveysite.com/conjoint_tutorial.html

- http://www.questionpro.com/conjoint/

- http://www.populus.com/techpapers/conjoint.php (this site contains helpful Adobe PDF downloads of articles and papers about conjoint analysis)

- http://www-marketing.wharton.upenn.edu/forecast/intro_ pdf/05-conjointanalysis.pdf(a brief Adobe PDF download describing conjoint analysis is available)

Segment Profitability[1]

20

Measurement Need

Marketers must have a clear sense of their company's strategic opportunities within the overall market, and STP (segmentation, targeting and positioning) is the tool most frequently used. STP, specifically segmentation, breaks the market into smaller groups of customers who share common characteristics and/or have similar needs so that the marketing effort can be tailored to those specific groups. The company then targets those segments that are best addressed by the company's core competencies and capabilities. As products gain favor and the business grows, marketers need to pay close attention to the target segment's profitability, and not just the revenues it generates.

Solution

Segment profitability allows marketers to measure whether an attractive customer segment, from a revenue standpoint, will also be profitable. Three formulas are used, each of which contributes to describing the overall understanding and attractiveness of the market segment in question[1]:

1.
$$C_{nm} = \{D_s \times S_s \times (P_{pu} \times M)\} - E_m$$

Where

C_{nm} = net marketing contribution

D_s = segment demand

S_s = segment share

P_{pu} = price per unit

M = percentage margin

E_m = marketing expense

2.
$$Marketing\ ROS = \frac{C_{nm}}{S} \times 100\%$$

Where

Marketing ROS = marketing return on sales

S = sales

3.
$$ROI = \frac{C_{nm}}{E_m} \times 100\%$$

Where

ROI = return on investment

Let's look at the following hypothetical example. Euro Bikes is based in Europe and manufactures bicycles. We will further assume that demand for bicycles across the European continent is three million units per year. Euro Bikes has been in this market for 20 years and has developed a strong reputation for reliable and affordable bicycles targeted at the entry-level consumer. It has been able to garner a 25% market share in what is otherwise a fragmented industry. Euro Bikes' bicycles are built of quality parts but have few extra features, thus selling for $50. By contrast, premium bikes with composite materials, sophisticated gear technology and state-of-the-art shocks sell for as much as $3,500. Bicycle manufacturing is expensive because of the number of parts that are put together by hand. Euro Bikes' main facilities are located in Estonia, where wages are lower. Consequently, Euro Bikes' costs are slightly more manageable than most competitors' in the industry, which helps it maintain 15% margins. It focuses its marketing efforts on point-of-purchase (POP) displays and minor promotional giveaways such as seat covers and reflectors. Its total marketing expenses are 10% of sales.

These figures are plugged directly into the formulas:

$$C_{nm} = \{D_s \times S_s \times (P_{pu} \times M)\} - E_m$$

$$= \{3,000,000 \times 25\% \times (50 \times 15\%)\} - \$3,750,000$$

$$= \$1,875,000$$

This means that Euro Bikes' efforts to target the entry-level bike buyer have a net marketing contribution of $1,875,000.

Now, let's bring in the other two formulas to fully measure the attractiveness of this segment:

$$ROS = \frac{C_{nm}}{S} \times 100\%$$

$$ROS = \frac{\$1,875,000}{\$37,500,000} \times 100\%$$

$$= 5\%$$

$$ROI = \frac{C_{nm}}{E_m} \times 100\%$$

$$ROI = \frac{\$1,875,000}{\$3,750,000} \times 100\%$$

$$= 50\%$$

Euro Bikes' return on sales is 5% and its return on investment is 50%. While these results may be consistent with the bicycle industry overall, Euro Bikes would have to compare its figures with those of specific competitors in the sub-segment of entry-level bicycles to help determine if this is a good performance. Of course, the company should have its own internal performance expectations as well. Assuming its industry research suggests comparable performance and its internal performance targets are met, then Euro Bikes ought to be pleased.

Segment demand and segment share statistics are gathered through market research, both *primary* (conducted or commissioned directly by a company's marketing management to study the market), and *secondary* (trade journals that publish annual statistics, general business magazines like *BusinessWeek, The Economist, Fortune*…). The net marketing contribution, margin percentages, marketing expenses and price per unit are all found in the company's detailed account records for each customer, which are most likely summarized in the income statement. The marketing plan and programs may also list pricing information, although this is likely to be in a more hypothetical "ideal world" stage and not in the actual market data.

Impact on Decision Making

The decision to target a particular segment is influenced by whether the segment has the potential to achieve a specific or desired level of profitability. The first formula, net marketing contribution, helps marketers understand a given segment's profit potential and, therefore, its general attractiveness as a business opportunity. Marketing ROS describes the return on total sales, which is dependent on knowing the net marketing contribution. It is an important indicator of the efficiency of the business's operations. A lower marketing ROS signals either a decrease in pricing or an increase in expenses. This helps marketers understand whether or not the return is attractive from the perspective of total sales generated, and is an indicator of the effectiveness of the sales effort. Finally, marketing ROI measures the total return on the marketing investment, indicating whether the expenditures on marketing are yielding maximum results.

Segment profitability is a useful method to assess both the attractiveness and success of specific audiences a marketer is targeting. It can help companies understand how different components of their marketing investments affect profitability, which can guide marketing decisions for the future. Each segment, however, is likely to be unique and success (or failure) in one does not guarantee a similar performance in another. Marketers need to use the various marketing tools at their disposal to adjust the value proposition, ensuring that they are fine-tuning their efforts based on the characteristics of a given segment. This is one of the central challenges in marketing and it is a reason why marketing programs can often be disappointing when reviewed by CFOs and CEOs. Marketers may implement a campaign consistent across multiple segments, yet only one segment may respond favorably. Consequently, the overall marketing effort looks wrong; yet the useful lesson is the response of the segment that found the proposition attractive (and, of course, the marketer now knows tactics that do not work with the other segments). Marketers must develop their budgets and programs with an eye toward the different programs required to reach each audience *before* going to market, so that the power of marketing can be fully realized. In consumer products companies, marketers often pre-test new products and marketing campaigns in niche markets, or even with focus groups, to gain a better understanding of the potential attractiveness of the offering.

Furthermore, products face different lifecycle stages in different markets, depending on the newness of the product, the maturity of the market, or even geographic issues, thus requiring different marketing approaches to reach satisfactory performance levels.

Segment profitability is important in both the planning and review stages of the marketing planning effort. Marketers must justify their overall budgets and proposed expenditures and segment profitability is a key measure to support specific marketing programs they recommend. Additionally, segment profitability can be a useful tool in reviewing the success of total marketing activities targeted toward a specific segment since marketers can compare actual performance to expectations from the start of the planning period.

Endnote

1 Adapted from Best, R.J. *Market-Based Management: Strategies for Growing Customer Value and Profitability*. New Jersey: Pearson Education Inc., 2005: pp.145-147.

Sources

Gilligan, C. and Wilson, R.M.S. *Strategic Marketing Management: Planning Implementation and Control*. Elsevier Butterworth-Heinemann, 2005: pp.318-320.

Davis, J. *Magic Numbers for Consumer Marketing*. Singapore: John Wiley & Sons (Asia) Pte Ltd, 2005: pp.145-150.

Customer Profitability 21

Measurement Need

Marketing helps companies identify, capture and retain customers. The challenge is recognizing, increasing the number of and measuring *profitable* customers.

Solution

Customer profitability models are used by managers to make resource allocation decisions for individual customers. This approach measures total revenues and total costs for customers during the period of time being measured. While companies face differing revenue and cost structures, the simple calculation of revenues minus costs attributable to each customer is sufficient for determining profitability. Of course, one-time customers can skew this approach, since it is likely that the costs to acquire the customer are higher (versus established customers familiar with the company and its products) relative to the return (measured via increased revenues, profits or both). Therefore, it may be more useful to review loyal customers whose cost to service and purchase patterns are better known.

$$Customer\ Profitability = r_t - c_t$$

Where
r_t = revenues from the customer during time t
c_t = costs incurred to acquire and support the customer during time t

A product manufacturer is interested in knowing customer profitability, but not at the individual consumer level, even though the final end-user is the mass consumer. Acquiring such knowledge would not be an effective use of the marketing effort since the manufacturer is structured to deliver large volumes of product to numerous intermediaries and locations. The marketing effort will instead be directed toward programs that strengthen relationships with wholesalers and retailers. Wholesalers can be offered such incentives as volume pricing, preferred terms and rapid inventory replenishment. Retailers, on the other hand, are targeted with cooperative allowances such as slotting allowances, which are fees paid to retailers to ensure product placement on store shelves, and co-op advertising, which is an agreement between manufacturers and retailers to share product advertising and/or promotion costs. Customer profitability in this situation is an aggregated figure, based on the revenues resulting from sales to wholesalers and the costs associated with those transactions, including any fees paid to retailers.

Impact on Decision Making

The measurement of customer profitability is an exercise in simple calculation. However, astute marketers know that customers have different values. Don Peppers and Martha Rogers, of Peppers & Rogers Group, are among the leading experts in customer profitability. They assert that not all customers are equal, let alone equally profitable, and their One-to-One model describes approaches for enhancing the value of every customer relationship. Most businesses experience the 80/20 rule (80% of the money comes from 20% of the customers) or a similar dominance of a few customers contributing the majority of the revenues and profits. Determining specific profitability per customer is challenging, however, since costs are hard to accurately assign or allocate. Managers must take the time to understand the profile of customers contributing the most profits and develop programs that continue to develop these important relationships. To find the revenue and cost figures, marketers can begin their research as follows:

> **Revenues figures:** The accounting department in most companies should have sales data attributable to specific products and for specific periods of time. This information is summarized in the income statement, although it is unlikely to have a breakdown of each product's revenue performance. Accounting (or finance) should have a separate transactions record for each product for the specific period of time being reviewed, derived from actual payments received from each customer.

> **Costs figures:** Determining costs accurately can be challenging due to varying materials costs, labor differences, royalties paid to different suppliers, support costs and different marketing programs for each customer. The accounting department will typically aggregate all costs associated with a specific product, allocating it evenly across various customers, even though each customer may have unique purchase patterns.

Sources

Drucker, P. *The Effective Executive*. New York: Harper Collins, 1967.

Ofek, E. "Customer Profitability and Lifetime Value". *Harvard Business School Article*, 9-503-019, August 7, 2002.

www.peppersandrogers.com

Share of Customer

Measurement Need

Measuring marketing's customer success extends beyond acquiring customers and growing market share to include increasing the company's share of each acquired customer's business.

Solution

Share of customer describes a company's sales to a specific customer as a percentage of that customer's total purchases of products of that specific type. Conceptually, it similar to market share, except that market share equals sales as a percentage of total sales of all companies in a given product and/or market. A more informal description is known as "share of the customer's wallet".

The formula for share of customer is similar to market share:

$$S_i = \frac{S_{it}}{\sum M_t}$$

Where

S_i = share of customer i (in percentage terms)

S_{it} = your sales to customer i in time t (in units or dollars)

$\sum M_t$ = sum of all customer spending in time t (in units or dollars)

For example, if a customer has $1 million to spend on a given type of product, and a company's sales to that customer total $100,000, then the company has a 10% share of customer.

$$S = \frac{\$100,000}{\$1,000,000}$$

$$= 10\%$$

Conversely, of course, if that customer buys $900,000 of the product from the company, then the share of customer is 90%.

The athletic footwear industry, for example, uses share of customer as one of the measures for evaluating the many retail buyers with which they work. Buyers from large retail sporting goods and footwear chains have budgets comprised of planned purchases and units that have already been ordered. The difference between these two is called "open to buy" dollars, which is the remaining money a buyer has available to spend on footwear products. A footwear sales representative who knows his/her retail buyer well will also know the amount of open to buy dollars that are uncommitted. Successfully persuading the retail buyer to allocate most, or all, of their remaining budget toward purchases of the sales rep's footwear products will increase his/her share of customer.

Impact on Decision Making

While market share measures an individual company's share of total market sales, share of customer analyzes it at the individual customer account level, measuring the percentage share of the total dollars for a type of product that the customer has spent with a specific company. It can be a useful guide for marketers in assessing success at persuading a customer to purchase a larger share of their products over the competition's. Share of customer is also a valuable measure for assessing the performance of individual sales representatives since it is a partial indicator of how successful they are in developing their customer relationships.

Share of customer information is likely to be kept in the reports of those who work closest with customers—field sales and marketing. Managers in these functions have deep customer knowledge and direct account responsibility, which is often a combination of quantitative data and qualitative insights about the unique profiles of each customer. Top performing sales people are quite familiar with the resources and spending patterns of their customers. However, this information is rarely stored in formal accounting or financial reports since these reports are designed to review performance in aggregate and not at the individual customer level. Furthermore, the information salespeople have about their customer accounts includes subjective insights, based on their personal experiences and observations from direct interactions. Most of this information is not useful for formal accounting and financial tracking purposes, yet it is vital to a salesperson's understanding of individual customer accounts.

Share of customer results can be a driver of customer relationship programs designed to improve loyalty, yet they are also an early indicator of product problems if there is a decline in average per customer purchases over time or if the customer increases purchases of the competitor's products. However, marketers must also be aware that individual customers are subjected to business cycles that will undoubtedly influence purchase decisions. Sales and marketing should work closely together since the field sales organization works with customers on a daily basis and can therefore inform marketing of potential purchase pattern changes. Sales management is usually a separate function and it establishes its own customer goals at the national, regional and local levels. Sales plans set performance targets for each sales representative, often including share of customer. The Sales Force section later in this book delves further into key sales metrics for detailed performance analysis. Finally, share of customer is quite useful when meeting with the company's senior management as it provides insight into specific customers, their value and potential. It assists senior management in understanding how effective and successful their field-based people are in developing their customer relationships.

Sources

"Market Segmentation/Share of Wallet Understanding the characteristics of High-Potential Customers". A case study by Harte-Hanks Research & Analytics. http://www.hartehanksmi.com/content/pdf/Share%20of%20Wallet%20Case%20Study.pdf

Davis, J. *Magic Numbers for Consumer Marketing*. Singapore: John Wiley & Sons (Asia) Pte Ltd., 2005: pp.167-168.

Customer Acquisition Costs 23

Measurement Need

With growth as a key marketing objective and STP (segmentation, targeting and positioning) as an important strategic marketing tool, marketers have to determine the cost of reaching, attracting and ultimately acquiring the customers they are targeting.

Solution

Customer acquisition costs are the costs incurred to acquire new customers. In its simplest form, it can calculated by dividing total acquisition expenses by total new customers. However, this simpler approach leaves out key details about the figures that determine an acquisition expense.

Alternative methods shed additional light on these costs. One method multiplies the numbers of times or frequency a marketing vehicle is used to acquire one customer by the cost of using that vehicle.

The formula for customer acquisition costs in this case is:

$$C_{ac} = CD_m \times C$$

Where

C_{ac} = customer acquisition costs

CD_m = number of compact disc (CD) mailers needed to acquire one customer

C = cost to send each mailer

Another method calculates it by dividing the cost of each marketing vehicle by the conversion rate it generates, as shown by this formula:

$$C_{ac} = \frac{C}{C_r}$$

Where

C_r = conversion rate*

*see Chapter 46 on the response rate and Chapter 47 on the conversion rate

To illustrate, let's assume a company wants to calculate the cost of acquiring customers through one of its marketing vehicles, CD mailers (AOL-America Online did this regularly in the 1990s as it invested heavily in building up its customer base). We will examine both random and acquired-list mailings.

Random mailing

Let's assume that the cost of mailing CD mailers is $0.35 each, and the average conversion rate is 1% (marketers learn this based on past experience with mailers and/or industry statistics). Thus, one person purchases for every 100 CD mailers sent. The cost of acquiring each customer using a random mailing is:

First formula: 100 x 0.35 = $35

Second formula: $\dfrac{\$0.35}{0.01} = \$35$

Depending on the metrics for the given industry as well as the average order size per customer, $35 to acquire a customer may be perfectly reasonable, too low or too high. Marketers will need to research their market and competitors to develop their own expectations.

Acquired-list mailing

A smart marketer will want to analyze other options beyond a random mailing to see if there are more effective ways to acquire customers. This marketer may know, or determine, that renting or acquiring a list of qualified prospects will yield a probable conversion rate of 3% (three times more effective than a random mailing). This means that for every 100 CD mailers sent, three people will purchase. Thus, our marketer may decide to rent a list from a reputable list broker, knowing that the names on the list have a higher likelihood of purchasing the company's products. List brokers are in their business to make money and they expend a fair amount of effort to develop their lists through research, so they generally charge a fee. In this example, assume the broker charges $0.25 per name.

The smart marketer can now compare the random mailing to the list mailing and decide which is better. The cost of acquiring a customer using an acquired list is:

$$\frac{\$0.60}{0.03} = \$20$$

The $0.60 is the result of the cost of mailing each CD, $0.35, plus the cost of acquiring each name, $0.25, divided by the conversion rate expected. The upfront cost of sending out CD mailers is clearly more expensive when a list is rented—71% more in this example. But the overall cost of acquiring customers is reduced substantially *and* the company is reaching an audience more likely to respond favorably to the company's offer.

Impact on Decision Making

Customer acquisition costs vary across industries and media. When acquisition data is available, marketers must determine if they are comparing apples with apples. As discussed in the section above, using the formula successfully means knowing more about the characteristics of the market being researched. For example, marketing research may reveal that sending CD mailers to prospective customers in the U.S. to promote a new product will yield one new customer for every 25 mailers. When expanding to another country however, it turns out that 100 CD mailers are needed to acquire one customer. Marketers then have to ask a few simple questions:

- Is sending 100 mailers reasonable, given the four-fold increase in costs?

- What is the break-even point before I cross from loss to profit?

- Is that new market attractive over the long term?

- Is the longer-term market potential large enough to warrant the increased costs?

Knowing customer acquisition costs, even projected, helps marketers assess the best way to allocate their resources and design their marketing programs accordingly. A key question that often precedes the customer acquisition costs analysis is the overall goal of the proposed marketing efforts. If the goal is to raise awareness in the market overall before refining the marketing efforts to target a particular segment, then marketers must factor in these "awareness-building costs", since they will directly affect the receptivity to the direct-marketing program aimed at the final target audience. A market that has a high level of awareness will require less subsequent customer education and explanation in the direct-marketing programs. Conversely, if a direct-marketing program is implemented in the absence of developing market awareness, then the conversion rate is likely to be much lower. Marketers must be aware of the relationship between their various marketing efforts so that they can maximize the return on their marketing investment for each program.

Much of the data depends on the target audience profile. Marketers gather this information from their own company records, plus primary and third party research methods. Most industries have research reports written about them, usually by market research firms, financial analysts and product analysts. Furthermore, the direct marketing association in the United States (www.the-dma.com) provides a range of information tools and services that will help marketers determine statistics specific to their industry. Once a marketer determines who they are targeting, they must decide whether a random mailing or acquired lists from brokers is more suitable for their program. The list broker is usually a more cost-effective approach, as the simplified example above demonstrated.

Also, the costs for the marketing vehicle (in this example, CD mailers, but the same approach can be used with other media) depend on the numbers of CDs the marketer sends with each mailing and whether any additional literature is included (since that increases the mailing costs due to added weight and/or changes in the mailing dimensions). Response and conversion rates are usually based on industry trends and, therefore, should not be guessed. If a marketer does not know the response rates for their particular products or industry, then they must try to find a reasonably similar industry and benchmark their metrics accordingly. In the worst case, if there are no comparable metrics, then a marketer should assume conservative rates that are marginally better for rented lists than a purely random mailing (i.e. 2% conversion versus 1% conversion).

A question that inevitably arises is how to determine the number of marketing vehicles needed to acquire one customer ("CD_m"or CD mailers in this case). This information will vary from one industry to the next and from one country to another. However, the aforementioned Direct Marketing Association (DMA) website is a great place to obtain information. It contains links to other DMA sites in many countries around the world, including Singapore, Japan, Thailand, Australia and much of Europe, as well as North and South America. Contacting the relevant experts in each location and asking them how and where to find these metrics will help marketers determine a variety of metrics common to that country. It is important for marketers to conduct basic research for the country in which they are interested. Often, the general metrics cited are U.S.- or Euro-centric and may mislead one into thinking the same metric applies to every country or region. But the cultural differences around the world are vast and what is common practice in the U.S. may be quite different from what is common and acceptable in, say, Thailand.

However, once marketers have done their homework, they can then begin using this formula with the confidence of knowing that the ensuing analysis of their direct-marketing program (CD mailers, in this case) is based on supportable data. The secret to success with this measure, therefore, is in using data and metrics that are consistent with the country context in which the marketer is operating.

Once marketers have run through the analysis, they still have to make the final choice as to whether to enter the new market or not. This is not always easy, as customer-acquisition data can be scarce, and the methodology is often foggy. Furthermore, it is a wise move to compare various list brokers and ask them for their customer names. Then, contact a few of their customers to learn whether the broker is as good as he or she claims. While list brokers will generally charge similar rates, there may be variation in quantity and quality of associated information with each name (i.e. some lists may come only with name and address, while others may come with name, address, company name, title and more). Brokers may also charge marketers more for each additional line of information requested beyond the basic name and address.

Also, list rentals are just that—rentals. Marketers do not own the names in most cases. The name is "owned" once that target customer responds to the mailing. List brokers usually include several "dummy" contacts in their mailings to ensure that renters do not use their list more than once.

Not all customer acquisition efforts yield a satisfactory return, despite strong market development efforts and targeted direct-marketing campaigns with an attractive offer. Many companies from the dot.com era displayed, in retrospect, a disregard for the value of thoughtfully-developed marketing programs, making careless marketing investments. CDnow (now owned by Amazon.com) spent nearly $40 to acquire each new customer. Purchase patterns revealed that these customers bought only $25 of products on average[1]. Therefore, the costs outweighed the benefits.

The more marketers know about their customers, the greater their chances of keeping their customer acquisition costs affordable and manageable.

Endnote

1 *Optimize Magazine,* http://www.optimizemag.com/article/showArticle.jhtml?articleId=177
00715&pgno=2

Source

Davis, J. *Magic Numbers for Consumer Marketing.* Singapore: John Wiley & Sons (Asia) Pte
Ltd. 2005: pp.173-177.

Cost Per Lead   24

Measurement Need

Attracting customers is one of the responsibilities of marketers. While mass market advertising offers the possibility of an extensive reach (see Chapter 40), its primary purpose is to create awareness. Alternatively, targeted marketing (also known as "one-to-one marketing") helps marketers have more personalized communications with customers since specific messages (such as a limited-time promotion) can be tailored to the needs of specific groups of customers, hopefully resulting in a purchase. Marketers use lists comprised of their target customers, which are usually acquired from third party firms specializing in direct marketing. Each name on the list is known as a "lead". Acquiring customer lists, and each lead on them, is expensive due to the time, money and people resources utilized in acquiring information about customers in different segments. Marketers need to measure the cost of acquiring these leads because this information ultimately helps determine if their customers are profitable.

Solution[1]

Cost per lead is simply the cost the advertiser pays to acquire each lead. A lead can be anything from an e-mail address to a complete customer profile, including name, company, job title, and all corresponding contact information. The cost per lead will increase as the customer information sought grows. Determining cost per lead requires that the marketer knows the specific costs underlying the total advertising cost, represented by the following:

$$CPL = \frac{TAC}{TLG}$$

Where

CPL = cost per lead

TAC = total advertisement costs

TLG = total leads generated

TAC is composed of direct and indirect advertising costs and is easily calculated:

$$TAC = DAC + IAC$$

Where

DAC = direct advertisement costs

IAC = indirect advertisement costs

Marketers will appreciate that we do not yet have all of the required information, since both DAC and IAC are aggregates of other fees:

$$DAC = AAF + DC + AF$$

$$IAC = AO$$

Where

AAF = all advertisement fees (placement costs, based on insertion frequency, ad size, and related specs)

DC = design/development costs (fees incurred to create the campaign)

AF = agency fees (salaries and non-wage expenses associated with work on the specific campaign)

AO = administrative overheads (hourly wages x number of hours)

To illustrate, let's look at a hypothetical example of a timeshare purchase.[2] Timeshares are joint ownership of a property. Owners use the property according to an agreed-upon schedule. Timeshare properties are located all over the world and are a particularly popular form of vacation home ownership since costs are shared, plus owners can "trade" their schedules with owners of other timeshares in different locations.

In this example, a timeshare company owns two condominiums, each with a market value of $100,000. The company wants to sell each condominium to 12 different owners (each owner would have the right to occupy their unit for one month). 24 total buyers paying $8,333 each are needed. The marketing department develops two different campaigns. The first campaign is a more personalized, targeted marketing campaign aimed at a focused number of high quality leads. The second campaign is a broader program, designed to attract potential buyers to a seminar in which they hear a sales presentation that hopefully convinces them to buy. Both campaigns incur a $60 administrative cost to service each lead.

Campaign 1 acquired 200 qualified leads from a third party firm specializing in providing high quality customer lists. Cost per lead is $35. Total lead cost is $7,000 (DAC—direct advertising costs). Twelve purchases resulted from this effort, a 6% conversion rate.

- The timeshare firm's marketing department discovered it took eight hours to create, develop and track this campaign at $75 per hour. This equals $600 total administrative overhead (IAC— indirect advertising costs).

- Total ad costs (TAC) = $600 (IAC) + $7,000 (DAC) = $7,600

- Cost Per Lead = $7,600 / 200 = $38

At this point, our revised cost per lead includes the campaign costs plus total add costs. While we now have a clearer picture of the cost per lead, the analysis is more useful if we determine the ROI. Administrative costs and the cost per buying customer must be included to calculate ROI:

- Administrative cost = $12,000 (200 leads x $60 administrative cost per lead)

- Cost per buying customer = ($7,600 + $12,000) / 12 = $1,633

- ROI = ($8,333/$1,633) − 1 = 4.10 = 410%

The marketer now conducts a similar analysis to evaluate Campaign 2.

Campaign 2 contracted with an online ad agency for 2,000 clicks at $3 cost per click.

- It took 20 hours for a staff member to set up and monitor the campaign at a rough cost of $60 per hour

- The web-site and email design cost $1,500 to develop

- Campaign 2 generated 100 leads and ten purchases (10% conversion)

TAC = $1,200 set up costs (IAC) + ($1,500 web + $6,000 ad costs) (DAC) = $8,700

Cost per lead = $8,700/100 leads = $87/lead

Administrative costs = $60 x 100 = $6,000

Cost per buying customer = ($8,700 + $6,000) / 10 = $1,470

ROI = ($8,333/$1,470) − 1 = 4.67 = 467%

Impact on Decision Making

Cost per lead tells marketers the rough costs of each lead. But to add accuracy, a marketer must factor in both the direct and indirect costs. Furthermore, the ROI should be calculated to determine whether the proposed campaign yields positive results. In the hypothetical examples used, the cost per lead in Campaign 2 was more than double that of Campaign 1. Had our marketer stopped the analysis at this point, he might have assumed Campaign 1 was more financially attractive since it created 12 buyers at a lower cost per lead. Our marketer may also be interested in the absolute quality of the leads generated. Campaign 1, therefore, offered better quality leads even though there were fewer leads overall. If the goal was to generate buyers, then Campaign 1 did this better than Campaign 2 and, therefore, the marketer may choose this for future campaigns even though it yields a lower ROI.

However, the ROI analysis reveals that Campaign 2 had a higher return, even though the total number of actual buyers was lower, the cost per lead was higher, as was the total advertising cost. Campaign 2 was also $163 cheaper per buying customer and 13.9% more efficient than Campaign 1 (467% ROI versus 410% ROI: 57% difference divided by 410%). If the goal was to generate a higher ROI, then Campaign 2 would be the choice for future campaigns.

The final evaluation will be based on the goals outlined at the beginning of these campaigns.

Endnotes

1 Adapted from http://www.100best-free-web-space.com/glossary257.html

2 Adapted from http://www.elearners.com/resources/sloan/metrics.asp

Sources

http://www.goarticles.com/cgi-bin/showa.cgi?C=29058

http://www.oakwebworks.com/articles/article-6-analytics-part-1.htm

Break-Even Analysis

25

Measurement Need

Before launching a new product, management wants to know how many units it must sell at a certain price to break even and offset the costs incurred.

Solution

Three break-even analysis methods will be discussed, each addressing different but related parts of the business' needs.

1. Conventional break-even: determining the number of units to be sold where gross revenues equal total costs

2. Break-even market share: translate unit break-even into a market share equivalent

3. Customer break-even: determining break-even for regular versus infrequent customers

1. Conventional break-even (or break-even *volume*) is calculated as follows[1]:

$$BE = \frac{FC}{(P - AVC)}$$

Where

BE = break-even

FC = fixed costs

P = price per unit

AVC = average variable costs

Note that the denominator, (P-AVC) is the contribution margin of each unit sold, known as M_{pu}.

Let's assume an auto parts company has the following *pro forma* financials for a new product launch:

$$FC = \$10,000,000$$

$$M_{pu} = \$4 \ (P = \$12, \ AVC = \$8)$$

$$BE = \frac{\$10,000,000}{\$4}$$

$$BE = 2,500,000 \text{ units}$$

2. Break-even market share[2]

$$BE_{ms} = \frac{BE}{MD} \times 100$$

Where

BE_{ms} = break-even market share

MD = market demand

If market demand for this product was 50 million units total, then the break-even market share would be:

$$BE_{ms} = \frac{2,500,000}{50,000,000} \times 100$$

$$= 5\%$$

3. Customer break-even

Assuming that profitable customers are the goal, then it can also be assumed that there are customers who are frequent or regular purchasers of products, and customers who are infrequent or occasional purchasers of products. Both will be discussed here.

Customer break-even analysis is a formula based on a series of data points:

- Margin on each purchase
- Survival rate
- Cost of each marketing communication
- Expected profit per customer

Two extended examples will be used to illustrate customer break-even. The second will include margin per unit:

Example 1: An Auto Parts Company

Let's assume that our auto parts company launches new products to the market twice per year, in winter and summer. Furthermore, the company's marketing team sends six CD mailers per year in the first year to all customer types. In the second year and beyond, regular customers will continue to receive six CD mailers each year. Less-frequent buyers, though, will receive only two per year thereafter as there is no need for the company to spend the money on them until they start buying more.

Since this auto parts company launches new products twice each year, its regular customers receive CD mailers with the same content for three consecutive mailings before changes are made to the CD mailer. Less-frequent customers receive two different CD mailers with no repetition. The regular customers purchase this company's auto parts products three times each year, with an average order size of $30, while the less-frequent buyers purchase once each year, with an average order size of $60.

The retention rate (the rate at which a customer is likely to return the following year) for regular customers is 90%, while the retention rate for less-frequent customers is 45%. Knowing the retention rates helps marketers determine the long-term survival rate of each group of customers (i.e. whether or not they will be around for a given number of years). In the case of the regular customer with a 90% retention rate, his survival factor in year five is 65.6% ($0.90^4 = 0.656$) [3]. The less-frequent customer's loyalty or survival rate in year five is 4.1% ($0.40^4 = 0.041$) [4].

The marketer must know the gross margin on each purchase because it helps determine how many purchases a customer type must make over a given period of time before they become profitable. The marketer can then forecast the length of time he will be "investing" in CD mailers before converting a customer to profitability, and the auto parts company's senior management wants to know when its customers will be profitable using CD mailer marketing to acquire them. The gross margin for these products is 25% of total sales. With these figures, we can construct comparisons between the regular and less-frequent customers with random and purchased list mailings to review the break-even levels.

Random mailing

Regular customer

- Receives six CD mailers per year
- Makes three purchases per year at $30 per purchase
- There is a 90% retention rate of regular customers who make purchases in the next time period
- Mailing cost = $0.35 per CD mailer
- 1% response rate
- Gross margin = 25%

Table 11 shows the analysis.

Table 11: Random Mailing—Regular Customer Analysis

Regular Customers	Year One	Year Two
Margin per purchase	$7.50	$7.50
Retention Rate	100%	90%
CD Mailing Cost	$0.35 x 6 = $2.10	$0.35 x 6 = $2.10
Profit per Customer	3 x 7.50 – 2.10 = $20.40	0.9 x (22.50 – 2.10) = $18.36
Total Profits per Customer (factoring in acquisition costs)	$(14.60)	$3.76

Acquired-list mailing

Regular customer

- Receives six CD mailers per year
- Makes three purchases per year at $30 per purchase
- 90% retention rate of regular customers who make purchases in the next time period
- Mailing cost = $0.60 per CD mailer
- 3% response rate
- Gross margin = 25%

Table 12 shows the analysis.

Table 12: Acquired-List Mailing—Regular Customer Analysis

Regular Customers	Year One	Year Two
Margin per purchase	$7.50	$7.50
Retention Rate	100%	90%
CD Mailing Cost	$0.60 x 6 = $3.60	$0.60 x 6 = $3.60
Profit per Customer	3 x 7.50 – 3.60 = $18.90	0.9 x (22.50 – 3.60) = $17.01
Total Profits per Customer (factoring in acquisition costs)	$(1.10)	$15.91

In this first set of examples with regular customers it is apparent that acquiring a mailing list enhances profitability over the random mailing. While the cost per mailing is higher by 71%, the customer acquisition cost is lower with the acquired list, making the profit margin higher. In this example, upfront investment in smart marketing (i.e. a mailing list) leads to larger profits. Costs, therefore, are not the only factor that should be considered when choosing a marketing program.

Now we will look at the same framework, but using less-frequent customers.

Random mailing

Less-frequent customer

- Receives six CD mailers per year in year one, and two per year thereafter

- Makes one purchase per year, at $60 per purchase

- 45% retention rate of regular customers who make purchases in the next time period

- Mailing cost = $0.35 per CD mailer

- 1% response rate

- Gross margin = 25%

Table 13 shows the analysis.

Table 13: Random Mailing—Less Frequent Customer Analysis

Less-Frequent Customers	Year One	Year Two	Year Three
Margin	$15	$15	$15
Retention Rate	100%	45%	20.25%
CD Mailing Cost	$0.35 x 6 = $2.10	$0.35 x 2 = $0.70	$0.35 x 2 = $0.70
Profit per Customer	$15-$2.10 = $12.90	0.45 x (15-0.70) = $6.44	0.2025 x (15-0.70) = $2.90
Total Profits per Customer (factoring in acquisition costs)	$(22.10)	($15.66)	($12.76)

It will take several years using this approach before a less-frequent customer becomes profitable. The final example incorporates the cost of an acquired mailing list.

Acquired-List Mailing

Less-frequent customer

- Receives six CD mailers per year in year one, and two per year thereafter
- Makes one purchase per year, at $60 per purchase
- There is a 45% retention rate of regular customers who make purchases in the next time period
- Mailing cost = $.60 per CD mailer
- 3% response rate
- Gross margin = 25%

Table 14 shows the analysis.

Table 14: Acquired-List Mailing—Less Frequent Customer Analysis

Less-Frequent Customers	Year One	Year Two	Year Three
Margin	$15	$15	$15
Retention Rate	100%	45%	20.25%
CD Mailing Cost	$0.60 x 6 = $3.60	$0.60 x 2 = $1.20	$0.60 x 2 = $1.20
Profit per Customer	$15 – $3.60 = $11.40	0.45 x (15 – 1.20) = $6.21	0.2025 x (15 –1.20) = $2.79
Total Profits per Customer (factoring in acquisition costs)	$(8.60)	($2.39)	$0.40

Impact on Decision Making

Customer break-even analysis is straightforward mathematically, but there are several less visible factors that marketers should consider when calculating it. In these examples, break-even is dependent on list quality, customer retention rates, gross margin, mailing costs, purchase price and purchase frequency. The analysis ignored other variables such as when a company decides to stop sending its mailers to customers who are no longer active. Determining when to get rid of a customer should be an important part of marketing planning, acknowledging that there will be exceptions. Since most business and budget planning is done annually, it is reasonable to use one year as the planning horizon. Therefore, the decision to eliminate customers would occur after the normal sequence of CD mailers has been sent since it will not be known until the end of a full year that a customer is no longer active. When this occurs, marketers should modify their profit-per-customer calculations by multiplying the previous year's retention rate by the CD mailer's mailing cost. The reason is that the previous year is when the customer was last "active", and an influence on the company's profitability.

Marketers may also have other costs not reflected in this analysis, such as additional marketing promotions and communications connected to the CD mailer. These should be included in the next mailing analysis. As marketers learn how many products are returned, cancelled or discounted, adjustments in the mailing program content and number of mailers will be inevitable.

Customer break-even analysis is a useful tool in assessing the potential of almost any marketing campaign, with some exceptions: this analysis is less reliable if the marketer is attempting to correlate a general-awareness advertising campaign with increases in customers and sales. Unless the advertising campaign has a specific offer that asks for customers to respond, it is problematic linking an advertising campaign to any specific increase in business.

Example 2: A Wallet Company

The definitions and formulas are effectively the same, but a different approach to calculating break even will be described.

In this example, margin per unit (M_{pu}) is included as a variable.

Margin per unit is defined as the amount of money that remains to cover fixed costs after all variable costs are deducted.

Wallets made by this company sell for $10. The retail margin is 30%. The wholesalers who purchase the wallet maker's products take an 8% margin. To determine M_{pu}, price, fixed and variable costs are needed. The variable costs are $3 per wallet. The total fixed costs (aggregated costs, not per unit) are $1,800,000 (for salaries, equipment, etc.).

Despite early success, the wallets are facing reduced demand as a result of competition. Furthermore, customers believe the wallets are overpriced. The marketing manager is considering reducing the price by $2. To assist with a strategic response, the marketing manager is considering hiring a consumer products consulting firm to provide recommendations and to ensure a high quality marketing effort. The consulting firm has proposed a contract for $250,000 to help the marketing manager for a month.

The marketing manager is going to make a presentation to the board of directors about her solution for improving the wallet's sales. The plan includes several preliminary formulas needed to determine a defensible break-even level.

The marketing manager knows the following about her products:

- Retail price is $10

- Retail margins are 30%

- Wholesale margins are 8%

- Wallet market is 35 million customers

- Market share is 20%

- Variable costs are $3 per wallet

- Total fixed costs are $1,800,000

- Considering price reduction of $2 per wallet

- Considering hiring McKinsey, a consulting company, for $250,000

She begins by determining the manufacturing sales price (MSP), using the following formula:

$$MSP = P_r - M_r - M_w$$

Where

P_r = retail price

M_r = retail margin percentage

M_w = wholesale margin or mark-up

She calculates MSP as follows:

$$MSP = \$10 - \$3 - \$0.8 = \$6.20$$

Next, she calculates the margin per unit (M_{pu}):

$$M_{pu} = MSP - VC$$

Where

VC = variable cost

This works out to:

$$M_{pu} = \$6.20 - \$3 = \$3.20$$

The marketing manager begins the break-even sequence, beginning with break-even volume, using the formula:

$$BE = \frac{FC}{(P - AVC)}$$

Recall that (P-AVC) is the same as margin per unit (M_{pu}), so the equation simplifies to this:

$$BE = \frac{FC}{M_{pu}}$$

$$BE = \frac{\$1,800,000}{\$3.20}$$

$$BE = 562,500 \text{ wallets}$$

The marketing manager wants to calculate the break-even volume with the $2 price reduction included. She uses the following formula:

$$BE_{\Delta} = \frac{(Original\ M_{pu})}{New\ M_{pu}} \times Original\ BE$$

Where

BE_{Δ} = breakeven volume after price change

$Original\ M_{pu}$ = \$3.20

$New\ M_{pu}$ = \$1.20

$Original\ BE$ = 562,500 wallets

Solving with the new figures:

$$BE_{\Delta} = \frac{(\$3.20)}{\$1.20} \times 562,500$$

$$= 1,500,000 \text{ wallets}$$

Lowering the price by $2 has a significant impact on the break-even figures.

The marketing manager then focuses on determining break-even market share under the regular price, using the formula:

$$BE_{ms} = \frac{BE}{MD} \times 100$$

Where

BE_{ms} = break-even market share

BE = 562,500

MD = 35,000,000

This is calculated as follows:

$$BE_{ms} = \frac{562,500}{35,000,000}$$

$$= 2\%$$

The break-even market share for the price reduction is now calculated:

$$BE_{ms} = \frac{1,500,000}{35,000,000}$$

$$= 4\%$$

Finally, the marketing manager wants to know break-even when it includes the cost of hiring the consulting firm.

$$BE = \frac{FC}{M_{pu}}$$

$$= \frac{\$250,000}{\$3.20}$$

$$= 78,125 \text{ units}$$

Therefore, the marketing manager would need to sell another 78,125 wallets to cover the added cost of the consulting firm.

This alternative analysis shows the different ways to look at determining break-even. Both approaches in customer break-even highlight the importance of understanding the costs involved in acquiring customers. A good way to use both is to determine the various break-even levels as demonstrated in the second approach, then factor in the marketing costs, customer retention and customer response rates to provide an in-depth analysis that provides credible analytical guidance on the measures needed to achieve success.

The different approaches to break-even analysis are important because of the interdependency between measures. For example, break-even analysis influences lifetime customer-value analysis and it is influenced by customer acquisition costs.

Knowing the cost of acquiring customers is helpful in determining when a customer will bring profits to the company. There are different types of customers as we have discussed before. Developing long-term customer loyalty is usually the ideal, but only when loyalty leads to ongoing profitability. Companies have to face the decision of keeping or eliminating unprofitable customers. The decision rests on marketing's view of that customer's long-term potential and how long management is willing to wait for the customer to turn profitable.

Even with this analysis, actual results will not be 100% consistent with the planning assumptions. But the analysis does provide an added sense of the conditions needed to achieve break-even. It is then the marketing team's responsibility to make it happen. No amount of analysis will make the customer transactions occur.

Historical data will provide most of the information required to perform the break-even calculations. Smart companies know their customers' purchase patterns, whether they sell direct (such as Dell) or they sell through retailers (such as Nike). Start-ups can acquire industry data from benchmark companies in their industry and apply it to their target audience to get a sense of how long it will be before their customers, and ultimately their growing business, are profitable.

Endnotes

1 Doyle, C. *Collins Internet-Linked Dictionary of Marketing*. Harper Collins, 2003, 2006: p.47.

2 Best, R.J. *Market-Based Management: Strategies for Growing Customer Value and Profitability*. New Jersey: Pearson Education, 2005: pp.255-256.

3 Loyalty/Survival Factors:

Year 1 = 0.90^0 = 1

Year 2 = 0.90^1 = 0.9

Year 3 = 0.90^2 = 0.81

Year 4 = 0.90^3 = 0.729

Year 5 = 0.90^4 = 0.656

4   Year 1 = 0.450 = 1

Year 2 = 0.45^1 = 0.45

Year 3 = 0.45^2 = 0.2

Year 4 = 0.45^3 = 0.091

Year 5 = 0.45^4 = 0.041

Sources

Ofek, E. "Customer Profitability and Lifetime Value". *Harvard Business School Article*, #9-503-019, August 7, 2002.

Davis, J. *Magic Numbers for Consumer Marketing*. Singapore: John Wiley & Sons (Asia) Pte Ltd., 2005: pp.178-190.

Customer Equity and Customer Lifetime Value

26

Measurement Need

Conventional wisdom in business tells us that it is more expensive to recruit new customers than focusing on retaining existing ones; therefore more management effort should be directed toward developing and growing customer loyalty. Customer-related measures have therefore become a key determinant of marketing effectiveness.

But an important challenge for managers is calculating how much their customers are worth. One solution is to measure customer equity, which is the sum of the present values of the company's future customer cash flows.

Solution

Two methods are described here, measuring different (but related) factors in customer lifetime value (CLTV). There are more sophisticated treatments for those readers who are interested in exploring this topic further. The endnotes provide information on these.

1. Marketing managers developing customer loyalty need to be concerned with maximizing retention and minimizing defection. Retention efforts should involve more than merely maintaining the existing relationship and purchase patterns with existing customers, although that is a good starting point. Given that loyal customers have already "voted" in favor of their company by purchasing its products, the opportunity lies in increasing cross-selling (selling similarly priced complements) and up-selling (selling a more expensive product or complement).[1]

This formula assumes a constant customer defection rate, a constant net margin and a discount rate.

$$CLTV = m/(k+d)$$

Where

m = constant net margin (profits – retention costs)

k = discount rate

d = constant defection rate

This simplified approach calculates the basic financial value of the customer. Each customer represents potential cross-selling and up-selling value, which is captured by factoring in a constant growth rate g.

$$CLTV = m/(k+d-g)$$

The growth rate is subtracted because it is unlikely that a customer's long-term growth rate will remain constant. The rate of increasing cross or up-selling purchases will diminish over time as customer's added satisfaction and enjoyment from each additional purchase is reduced.

2. A related approach to CLTV estimates the dollar value (typically, the flow of profits) of a customer's long-term relationship with a company. While it, too, measures how much a customer is worth while remaining a loyal purchaser of a company's products, it also factors a value for new customers referred by existing customers, adding further value to the relationship developed with the referring customer. As with the first approach, retention is a primary objective. However, this approach does not factor in cross or up-selling opportunities, focusing instead on new customer referrals. The second example illustrates this method[2].

The marketing manager needs to be acquainted with the key data associated with their loyal customers, derived from:

M = average amount of money spent per purchase

C = average costs to service each purchase

P = number of purchases per year

Y = number of years managers expect to keep this customer

A = new-customer acquisition cost

N = number of new customers referred by original customer

F = customer adjustment factor for the period of time being evaluated.

Allen Weiss, founder and publisher of Marketingprofs.com, describes F, the customer adjustment factor, as follows:

> "…(F) captures changes in a customer's behavior over time. If you estimate that the customer will increase the money spent per visit over time (because you estimate you will increase their loyalty), then put in a higher number—say, 1.4. If you estimate the customer will decrease their spending over time, put in a lower number—say, 0.9. This is obviously a subjective estimate."

Therefore, one is considered steady state, so no correction is needed. The subjective nature of the correction factor reveals the importance of including both qualitative and quantitative measures in the customer analysis. Next, the terms are grouped into individual equations.

$M - C$ = the average gross profit generated by the customer per visit

$P \times Y$ = total number of visits over the customer's lifetime

$A \times N$ = the amount of money saved by the customer's referral

The lifetime value of the customers can now be determined using the formula:

$$CLTV = [(M - C) \times (P \times Y) - A + (A \times N)] \times F$$

To illustrate, let's assume the management of a hotel chain wishes to determine the lifetime value of their average customer. Management reviews the guest statistics for its hotels:

M = average amount of money spent per purchase (guest)   = \$220

C = average costs to service each purchase (guest)   = \$70

P = number of purchases/visits per year   = 3

Y = number of years managers expect to keep this customer   = 20

A = new customer acquisition cost   = \$25

N = number of new customers referred by original customer   = 5

F = customer adjustment factor   = 1.3

CLTV of the average guest equals $11,830, as shown below:

$$\{(\$220 - \$70) \times (3 \times 20) - \$25 + (25 \times 5)\} \times 1.3 = \$11,830$$

In this illustration, hotel management has determined that its loyal customers are likely to spend more in the future with each visit, hence the higher customer adjustment factor.

Impact on Decision Making

CLTV in these approaches can be influenced by what data is used and how it is interpreted. For example, determining the average spending per customer is dependent on whether managers are using transactions or customers in their calculation. If a manager adds together total purchases and divides by the number of transactions, then the value of some customers may be under-represented since their separate multiple purchases would be viewed purely as if they were separate customers. On the other hand, accurately determining actual customer purchases requires a more sophisticated tool which not all retailers may have, such as loyalty cards that can be scanned with each purchase. Furthermore, loyalty cards may not be used consistently by customers, which can skew the analysis.

Cost figures are quite challenging to determine at the individual purchase level. Are managers measuring the cost of the entire operation at the time the customer made his or her purchase? Or are they assessing the costs specific to that transaction? If managers are measuring the costs specific to the transaction, they will find those are very hard to determine with any degree of precision. Therefore, it is most useful if managers determine a set of costs that are normal for each operation and that are applicable to customer-specific transactions, then consistently apply these every time costs are measured.

There is no single formula that is perfect and the same is true with CLTV. Even with more sophisticated modeling, managers must be comfortable knowing that their customers simply will not behave according to predictions. This is similar to the economic theory that assumes a rational customer. It is convenient from a modeling and analytical point of view, but it does not reflect the nuances of day-to-day consumer behavior.

The important takeaway for marketing managers is the sizable long-term value represented by a loyal customer, which should provide the incentive to develop marketing programs designed to reinforce retention. The process reinforces why businesses should try to develop long-term relationships rather than short-term or, worse, one-time purchase gains.

The data is found in several areas. For retailers, the average customer-spending information can be found in scanner data simply by adding together total purchases and dividing by the number of customers, or transactions, depending on how sophisticated their point-of-purchase system is. Average costs can be found in the income statement or daily bookkeeping records. The forecast numbers are estimates, based either on historical experience, industry benchmarks or perhaps even new services, products or technologies that managers believe influence customers' buying patterns. The customer-acquisition costs have already been discussed in the previous sections. Accurately finding out the number of new customers a customer refers to the company requires a fair amount of individual customer knowledge and/or a CRM system, or even a basic database designed to track these kinds of activities. The correction factor is a subjective assessment, affected by several factors, including: the manager's experience in the business, competitor performance and market factors. Given this, managers should be able to estimate a reasonable correction factor.

Endnotes

1 Reibstein, D. and Srivastava, R. "Metrics for Linking Marketing to Financial Performance". Working paper submitted to Marketing Science Institute, October 19, 2004: pp.8-9.

2 Adapted from http://www.marketingprofs.com/5/weiss7.asp

Sources

Additional resources about CLTV for the enthusiastic and curious:

http://www-stat.stanford.edu/~saharon/papers/ltv.pdf

http://hbswk.hbs.edu/item.jhtml?id=1436&t=marketing

http://executiveeducation.wharton.upenn.edu/globals/documents/metrics.pdf

http://www.interactionmetrics.com/customer_equity.htm

http://www.businessknowhow.com/manage/client-value.htm

Lemon, K.N., Rust, R.T. and Zeithaml. V.A. "Customer-Centered Brand Management". *Harvard Business Review*, September 2004.

Consumer Franchise 27

Measurement Need

Since marketing is responsible for creating and developing the customer base, marketers need to evaluate which customers have the highest value. This will allow them to determine how best to deploy marketing resources.

Solution[1]

As implied, consumer franchise identifies those customers who are regular, core buyers. They have the highest likelihood of continuing to purchase the company's products. Additionally, a company's sales include purchases from less committed buyers. The following formula represents a company's total sales derived from a combination of committed and uncommitted buyers:

$$Sales = (P_1 \times N_1) + (P_2 \times N_2)$$

Where

P_1 = customer probability of buying if committed

N_1 = number of committed buyers

P_2 = customer probability of buying if uncommitted

N_2 = number of uncommitted buyers

For example, let's assume that the hypothetical firm, Grinner Teeth Dentistry (GTD), has 1,000 committed customers (dental patients) who believe in GTD's services. 60% of these patients buy services each year. GTD also has another 1,000 uncommitted customers who have used their services infrequently or even just once. They also use the services of other dentists. Since these uncommitted customers purchase non-GTD services as well, their probability of purchasing just GTD is 20%.

$$Sales = (60\% \times 1,000) + (20\% \times 1,000)$$

$$Sales = 600 + 200$$

$$Sales = 800$$

A marketer might be tempted to increase the sales from the committed and uncommitted buyers, spending money and marketing time trying to convert the uncommitted buyers into higher probability committed ones. Let's assume the marketer pursues this and converts 50 buyers:

$$Sales = (60\% \times 1,050) + (20\% \times 950)$$

$$Sales = 630 + 190$$

$$Sales = 820$$

This represents an improvement. However, if the marketer chooses to try to convert uncommitted buyers, it is reasonable to assume that a disproportionate share of the marketing budget would be spent on educating these uncommitted buyers. The certainty of conversion is unknown, but one can surmise that only some of the uncommitted buyer would convert and, of those, not all would become high-probability committed buyers.

Common sense suggests the marketer should focus his efforts on the consumer franchise, since committed buyers have a higher probability of buying in the first place and have demonstrated their loyalty and commitment already. Let's now assume that the marketer is able to increase the probability of purchase from the committed buyers to 65%, with the uncommitted buyer efforts remaining the same:

$$Sales = (65\% \times 1,000) + (20\% \times 1,000)$$

$$Sales = 650 + 200$$

$$Sales = 850$$

Another option is to increase the number of committed buyers. The marketer's research may have revealed that there is a segment of customers whose characteristics are similar to those of his committed buyers, so he allocates a portion of the marketing budget specifically to these new customers and attracts 50 more as a result:

$$Sales = (60\% \times 1,050) + (20\% \times 1,000)$$

$$Sales = 630 + 200$$

$$Sales = 830$$

The marketer has attracted 50 new committed buyers, with the overall sales result still better than the first option above of allocating marketing resources toward converting uncommitted buyers.

Impact on Decision Making

Assuming the marketer has concluded that uncommitted buyers are not the focus of their marketing efforts, there are three ways to improve sales: increase the probability of buying from committed buyers; increase the number of committed buyers; or a combination of both.

To increase the probability of buying from committed buyers, promotions may be most effective. The marketer knows that this buyer will purchase at least 60% of the time, so the marketing challenge is to increase this by increasing usage. Promotions are an effective method for doing so. However, the disadvantage is that the promotion may only "spike" usage for the duration of the promotion and not permanently increase the probability of purchase. To sustain the desired higher probability of purchase levels, marketers will have to engage in more sophisticated marketing communications and customer relationship building that offers higher value without resorting to discount-driven promotions. Otherwise, the committed buyers will become trained to expect discounts and may wait to purchase when the next discount is offered. This unfortunate result has the effect of increasing the probability of purchase but, over the longer term, actually reducing profitability.

To increase the number of committed buyers, the marketer may focus more on advertising, product and service enhancements, and similar value-added activities. This approach has the distinct advantage of attracting more committed buyers and eliminates the influence of discounts, arguably a more responsible long-term approach since it yields more committed buyers who, when purchasing, pay full price.

The final option, improving the probability of purchase and increasing the number of committed buyers, may sound appealing (after all, who wouldn't want a larger pool of committed buyers who have a high probability of purchase as well?), but marketers must be aware of the challenges. First, the marketing expense is likely to be higher since the marketer is allocating dollars both to increase the purchase probability through developing promotions and increase committed buyers through increased advertising activities. Second, the same risk exists when the marketer tries to increase the probability of purchase through promotions: long-term margins may suffer. In effect, the marketer may actually end up with larger pool of committed buyers, all of whom now expect discounts, making the cost of servicing each customer higher than before.

The bottom-line lesson is that the consumer franchise is a valuable measure to help marketers understand how to use the marketing levers at their disposal to increase sales profitability and effectiveness for the business.

Endnote

1 Gilligan, C. and Wilson, R.M.S. *Strategic Marketing Management: Planning, Implementation & Control*. Richard M.S. Wilson and Colin Gilligan, 2005: p.527.

Retention Rate 28

Measurement Need

To maintain a consistent financial performance requires customers. Marketing must not only attract customers so that initial sales are created, but retain customers over time since doing so is usually less expensive financially than new customer prospecting. Furthermore, retained customers are generally less expensive to maintain since marketing has to invest less in marketing communications that educate the customer. However, it can be argued that the marketing effort does shift to a different type of communication, typically one-to-one, relationship-driven marketing. Nevertheless, marketers have a very real need to measure the customers they have retained.

Solution

The retention rate measures the percentage of a company's customers that it is able to retain over a specified time period. The formula for retention rate is:

$$Retention\ rate = \frac{C_a}{C_{at}}$$

Where

C_a = the number of active customers at end of time period t

C_{at} = the number of active customers at start of time period t

One recent study conducted by *Road and Travel* Magazine[1] concluded that Chevrolet, a General Motors brand, has the highest customer retention rate in the passenger vehicle market. This was based on the J.D. Power and Associates[2] 2003 Customer Retention Study[SM]. According to the study,

Chevrolet retained 60.8% of its customers, far ahead of its competitors. The reason given for this high retention rate was the inability of another brand to offer features present in the customers' current Chevrolet model.

Impact on Decision Making

Customer retention (loyalty) has been a long-cherished objective of businesses for the simple reason that losing a customer costs companies money in terms of lost revenues, plus the costs incurred to attract the customer in the first place. Additionally, loyalty is often perceived as verification that a company's products have been regularly accepted by customers over those of their nearest competitors. Furthermore, loyalty is seen as an avenue to develop a deeper relationship with customers and, hopefully, convince them to buy even more of the company's offerings. Finally, loyal customers usually require less investment from the business to maintain the relationship than the costs incurred to develop the relationship at the outset. Once customers are educated about a company and its products, the company does not need to expend as much effort to explain itself as it did at the "courtship" stage of the relationship. Therefore, marketers, for the most part correctly, see high customer retention rates as a desirable and worthy objective.

A central responsibility of marketing is to attract and retain customers. However, merely retaining customers is insufficient. While customer loyalty is an important and usually desirable objective, it must be in the context of profitable retention. This is a critical point for marketers and business leaders to understand since loyalty, by itself, may not be financially attractive without a clear use of the marketing mix (product, price, place, promotion) to create a profitable set of customers.

In their July 2002 *Harvard Business Review* article entitled, "The Mismanagement of Customer Loyalty", Professors Werner Reinartz and V. Kumar argue persuasively that customer loyalty and profitability must be managed concurrently to ensure maximum positive results. Even then, profitability, should it result, may vary dramatically among customers. Furthermore, customers that were both profitable and loyal in the past may not be so in the future.

The takeaway is clear: while a high retention rate is an important goal, it is not cause for celebration unless it also results in a profitable relationship. Marketers must be aware of the balance between loyalty and profitability so that they can design marketing programs that yield the best possible customer results.

The retention rate data can be derived from retention surveys, which track customer defection. Such surveys are conducted on both current and former customers. Alternatively, marketers may be able to find this information in their customer account summaries, which are usually found in the accounting or financial reports that summarize business activities for a given period of time. Sales management may, and very likely does, have detailed and accurate customer account information in its reports, since sales representatives are in direct contact with their respective customers, often on a daily basis.

NOTE: an alternative approach to measuring retention rate is described by Roger J. Best, Emeritus Professor of Marketing from the University of Oregon. He uses a simple formula[4]:

$$CR = \left(1 - \frac{1}{N}\right) 100$$

Where

CR = customer retention

N = period of time (usually # of years)

For example, if the average lifespan of a customer is 10 years, then the expected retention rate is 90%:

$$CR = \left(1 - \frac{1}{10}\right) \times 100$$

$$= (1 - 0.10) \times 100$$

$$= 0.90 \times 100$$

$$= 90\%$$

Of course, the average customer lifespan is subject to innumerable influences. Assuming the customer has demonstrated past loyalty, there is still no guarantee that the customer will continue a similar relationship into the future. For marketing planning, customer retention estimates are just that: estimates. Marketers must not fall in love with the metrics, even if historical trends suggest future retention looks promising. As with any business, clever competitors will always try to lure away customers, so a concerted effort with ongoing programs and activities, regularly reviewed for progress against plan, is required to achieve the retention expectations.

Endnotes

1 http://www.roadtravel.com/newsworthy/newsandreviews04/jdpowercustomerretention.htm

2 http://www.jdpower.com/corporate/news/release/pressrelease.asp?ID=2003175

3 Best, R.J. *Market-Based Management: Strategies for Growing Customer Value and Profitability* Upper Saddle River, NJ: Pearson Education, Inc. 2005 pp 16-17

Churn Rate 29

Measurement Need

When a company attracts a customer, the next step is to acquire and retain that customer. Not all customers are loyal, or profitable or desirable. Some cost more to service than others, for example. Nevertheless, a vital component to a successful customer strategy is converting first time buyers into long-term, profitable relationships. Of the customers initially attracted, some inevitably choose to move on to another company and its products. Part of a marketer's challenge is knowing how many customers a company loses versus how many are retained.

Solution

Churn is a measure of customer attrition. It refers to the percentage of customers a business loses over a specific period of time. It is calculated as follows:

$$Churn = \frac{C_t}{C_{at}}$$

Where

C_t = the number of customers a business loses over time period t

C_{at} = the number of active customers at the start of time period t

Churn is a common phenomenon in the telecommunications industry, particularly in the U.S. (where consumers regularly receive marketing communications in the form of discounts, low or no penalty provider switching plans, and a wide variety of pricing schemes within), but increasingly around the world as telecommunications is deregulated. It is a highly competitive, commodity-driven market in which provider offerings are often indistinguishable from one another. Consequently, consumers frequently switch service providers to pay the lowest possible price. The industry average churn varies within the telecommunications industry. In the wireless sector, annual churn rates have ranged from 23.4% to 46%[1]. The Internet sector experiences similarly high churn rates, ranging from 21% to 63%[2].

Impact on Decision Making

It is important that marketers learn why customers left so they can reduce churn in the future through revised marketing communications programs, improved product offerings, better pricing and more effective customer targeting. Most businesses regularly face customer churn challenges, trying to develop strategies and programs that will minimize it. It is necessary to address churn since losing a customer is often expensive in both time (amount of time invested to attract and retain a customer), resources (manpower deployed to service customers) and money (the actual outlay of cash spent on customer development programs). Churn rates also affect customer lifetime value analysis (see Chapter 26) since a higher churn rate indicates customers are not staying long with the company. This leads to higher costs since more money has to be invested to educate and attract new customers.

Churn is somewhat similar to retention (Chapter 28), but there are subtle differences. Churn is calculated with former/lost customers only while retention can be determined with former or existing customers[3]. Churn research focuses on why they left, whereas retention focuses on how to maintain and increase loyalty. Furthermore, churn is subject to interpretation, blurring the differences even more with retention. Returning to the telecommunications example, different providers may use slightly different methodologies in calculating churn. When a customer moves from one geography to another, and consequently changes telephone numbers, yet remains with the same provider, the provider might count this move as churn. This phenomenon occurs regularly in the U.S. Alternatively, when a customer's service contract expires and that same customer selects a different plan with the same provider, this may also be counted as churn. In these two instances, the customer has remained with the provider, but individual circumstances have created the need to change their previous plan.

Marketers must be clear on their definition of churn, since it affects the kinds of marketing programs designed to attract and retain customers in the future. A conservative definition of churn suggests that it pertains only to customers the company has lost to a competitor as opposed to another division or product within the same firm. This definition would lead the curious marketer to explore why the customer switched to a competitor, whether it is isolated or an indication of a larger, unsettling trend and, consequently, how to improve the situation for remaining and new customers. However, large companies (such as telecommunications) often "lose" customers to another division. Corporate marketers, with broad strategic responsibilities for marketing across the entire company, may view this as retention, since the customer remains with the company overall. But divisional and/or product line marketers may count this as churn and, therefore, concern themselves with how to reduce it in the future.

It stands to reason that whether a customer is lost to a direct competitor or to another division within the same firm, marketers can use this as an opportunity to improve their offerings and their running of the business.

Churn numbers typically come from one of two sources: reactive, or post-customer departure, reports; and proactive, or pre-customer departure, reports. Reactive reports are generated by any of several key areas in a company, depending on its size, complexity and customer account practices. Sales, customer support, customer service, telemarketing and even customer account managers in accounting may track this information. As it implies, reactive reports capture customer departures after a customer has contacted the company and indicated they are leaving. It is a more straightforward metric, although it can also be frustrating since it is usually much harder to convince an already lost customer to return. Proactive efforts attempt to predict which customers are likely to leave, allowing marketers the opportunity to target them with new programs and incentives designed to retain them and, thereby, reduce churn[4].

Endnotes

1 Gupta, S., Kamakura, W., Lu, Mason, J.X.C., and Neslin, S.A., "Defection Detection: Improving Predictive Accuracy of Customer Churn Models". March 2004 (working paper).

2 Ibid.

3 Ibid., pp.4-7

4 http://www.polarismr.com/customer_ret.htm

Source

http://www.investopedia.com/terms/c/churnrate.asp

New Customer Gains   30

Measurement Need

Chapter 19 on market penetration introduced the Ansoff Matrix, which describes the growth choices available to management. It is shown again as Figure 10, but with market development and diversification highlighted, since both of these options require the acquisition of new customers, through geographic expansion and/or the addition of new customer segments. With respect to diversification, growth also comes from new products.

Marketers need to measure the success of their new customer efforts.

PRODUCTS

		Present	New
MARKETS	**Present**	Market Penetration	Product Development
	New	Market Development	Diversification

Figure 10: Strategic Growth Choices

Solution

New customer gain measures the number of new, unique customers for a given company over a specific period of time. The measure is:

$$New\ Customer\ Gain = C_{et} - C_{bt}$$

Where

C_{et} = the number of customers at end of time period t

C_{bt} = the number of customers at beginning of time period t

New customer gain provides marketers with a basic gauge of a new product's acceptance in the market. Customer gain can also be used to judge whether new strategies are needed to increase market share for an existing line of products.

Professional sports provide an interesting example on new customer gain. Most of the professional leagues around the world have programs designed to attract new fans. The National Football League (NFL) is the governing body for professional football in the U.S. The NFL has 32 teams, and each team develops its team and market appeal based on the needs of the city in which it is located. Most teams have a variety of mechanisms to attract new fans, including different pricing programs. The different pricing programs include:

- single-game tickets (purchased for specific games, often on the game-day itself)

- season tickets (tickets paid-in-full for every home game prior to the commencement of the season)

- personal seat licenses (PSLs—a one-time purchase of a specific seat and its associated rights). PSLs theoretically allow a fan to own a specific seat forever. Clubs still charge a fan for the annual season tickets as well, but the PSL guarantees that the fan will have the same seat every year) and luxury boxes/suites (larger rooms that accommodate several people and also include many amenities like televisions, personalized food service, more spacious and comfortable seats…)

The objective of an NFL sports franchise (like any business, for that matter) is to maximize revenues and attract as many new customers as possible. The pricing programs discussed above illustrate the different approaches NFL sports franchises atempt to attract fans.

Impact on Decision Making

New customer gain provides marketers with a basic indication as to whether they are making positive progress in developing their company's and product's customer base. As with most marketing measures, the answer this calculation provides requires marketers to investigate the sources of the gain to better understand how to capture additional gains in the future. Marketers must identify the factors that contributed to the gain in new customers. Did the gains result from new marketing programs? If so, which programs yielded the greatest return? It is important for marketers to compare the actual costs to acquire each new customer to the additional revenues and profits generated. While start-up companies and new product launches regularly incur higher costs than revenues until they have developed their customer base and resulting revenue stream, it would be disadvantageous to spend more on new customer acquisition than the business gains in new revenues for a sustained period of time.

Often, organizations may encounter difficulty in determining new customer gains as a number of other factors are involved. For example, customers may switch from one line of product to another, but within the same company. While some companies may consider this as customer gain for one product, others may ignore such customer movements. However, marketers must be clear in explaining what they are measuring. For example, Steve Jobs of Apple Computer announced at the January 2006 MacWorld Conference that in the first quarter of fiscal 2006, it sold 14 million iPods compared to 4.5 million iPods in the same quarter of 2005[1]. By most standards, this represents a significant increase in units sold. Does the year-over-year increase mean that Apple acquired 9.5 million new customers as well? That is unlikely. Undoubtedly, some customers bought more than one iPod. It is reasonable to assume, however, that some of the 9.5 million increase included several million more customers. It is tempting to misread or misjudge what this metric is describing, so marketers must be clear about the results of this calculation.

Endnote

1 CNN.com January 11, 2006 http://edition.cnn.com/2006/TECH/ptech/01/10/apple. macworld.reut/index.html

Source

Ansoff, H. I. "Strategies for Diversification". *Harvard Business Review*, 35(2), September-October, 1957.

Customer Losses 31

Measurement Need

Losing customers is expensive since money and resources have been invested to educate and attract them. Once customers have "voted" in favor of your products (by purchasing them), a marketer's next step is to leverage the initial purchase into a long-term, profitable relationship. For planning and budgeting purposes, marketers need to see how many customers have been lost, versus retained, so that future marketing plans can be adjusted to reduce losses.

Solution

Customer loss refers to the number of customers that stop purchasing a company's products or services over a given period of time. The simplified formula below uses the same variables as that in Chapter 30, New Customer Gains, but the measure now focuses on customer attrition versus gain over the same period of time.

$$Customer\ Loss = C_{bt} - C_{et}$$

Where

C_{bt} = the number of active customers at beginning of time period t

C_{et} = the number of active customers at end of time period t

Impact on Decision Making

Customer loss is an effective tool for assessing the continued value of an existing product to customers as it matures over time. If an existing product is losing customers or revenues, marketers are faced with three choices:

invest in new strategies and tactics to improve customer acceptance of the product and increase the product's profitability as well; stop doing business with unprofitable or low margin customers; or, remove the product from the portfolio.

The logic of the formula assumes that C_{bt} is larger than C_{et}, resulting in a number equal or greater than zero. The reason is simple: if C_{et} were larger than C_{bt}, then it would suggest a gain in total customers over the same period of time. Assuming customer losses are larger than customer gains during the time period being measured, marketers can begin analyzing the defections to determine if there are any patterns and their potential causes. If the customer losses occur in only one period and not over several periods, then it may be an anomalous event requiring only minor analysis to ensure the causes are limited. However, if customer losses persist, it may well signal significant problems, including:

- a decline in the level of trust customers have in a company's products

- products that are no longer relevant to the customer's needs

- a decrease in quality

- the price-value relationship is no longer attractive

- new competitor offerings are better/cheaper/more trustworthy/more innovative

- a shift or changing trend in the overall consumer market

While marketers do not like to lose customers, it is important to measure the losses and understand the causes to eliminate or at least minimize them in the future. A persistent pattern of customer losses will inevitably negatively impact cash flow unless those customers that remain are extraordinarily profitable (which would suggest the customers lost are acceptable since they were generating losses). Determining the actual causes of customer loss is, of course, easier said than done since the influencing factors can be numerous and quite complex. The potential complexity should not deter marketers from undertaking the analysis, however, since the resulting benefits will include a clearer understanding of the variables that impacted customer loss.

Marketers should create a plan for retaining high-profit customers and enhancing their value to the firm further. However, this can be a difficult analysis to get right since high value customers often have complicated relationships with companies across multiple business areas, from products and services to support and finance. Customers may switch from one line of product to another, but within the same company. Some managers may consider this as customer loss for one product, while others may see this as a gain for the company, just in a different area.

The U.S. auto industry used customer satisfaction scores for years, assuming incorrectly that it was a predictor of happiness with the product and, indirectly, an indicator of product and even financial success. Yet through the mid-1990s, while the customer satisfaction scores remained high, the repurchase rate stayed between 30% and 40%, suggesting a customer loss of 60% to 70%[1]. Interestingly, one can easily imagine the bottom line impact if the auto industry could reduce customer losses to "only" 50% or 55%.[1]

Endnote

1 Reichheld, F.F. "Learning from Customer Defections". *Harvard Business Review*, March-April, 1996: pp.4-5.

Return on Customer^{sm}   32

Measurement Need

Just as managers seek to understand how much profit will result from each investment within a specified period of time, marketers must understand the added value derived from their customer investments.

Marketers are familiar with the targeting and segmentation techniques designed to help them understand their customers, including:

- Geographic
- Demographic
- Psychographic
- Product uses
- Segmentation options ranging from a single segment emphasis to full market coverage.

A sizable investment in time, money and resources is usually necessary to gather enough useful details about customers to ensure that the ensuing marketing programs (advertising, pricing, promotions) are properly designed and directed to the most appropriate audience.

To complete the analysis, marketers must evaluate the potential return on these customer investments. Calculating Return on Customer^{sm} enables marketers to more confidently demonstrate that their customer investments are paying off.

Solution[1]

According to Don Peppers and Martha Rogers of Peppers and Rogers Group, a leading consultancy focused on improving business performance through a customer-centric focus, Return on Customer^{sm} (ROC^{sm}) is another way of measuring shareholder value. The ROC^{sm} formula is:

$$ROC^{sm} = \frac{p_i + DCE_i}{CE_{i-1}}$$

Where

ROC^{sm} = return on customer

π_i = cash flow from customers during period i

ΔCE_i = change in customer equity during period i

CE_{i-1} = customer equity at beginning of period i

Peppers and Rogers illustrate Return on Customer^{sm} with two useful charts. The first one illustrates a steady customer response rate over time to a marketing program.

	Year 1	Year 2	Year 3	Year 4
Total prospects	1,000,000	1,000,000	1,000,000	1,000,000
Response rate	1%	1%	1%	1%
Cost per campaign	$1,000,000	$1,000,000	$1,000,000	$1,000,000
Cash flow per campaign	$1,250,000	$1,250,000	$1,250,000	$1,250,000
Profit per campaign	$250,000	$250,000	$250,000	$250,000
Profit per year (6 campaigns)	$1,500,000	$1,500,000	$1,500,000	$1,500,000
Year-end customer equity	$6,000,000	$6,000,000	$6,000,000	$6,000,000
Change in customer equity	-	-	-	-
Total value created	$1,500,000	$1,500,000	$1,500,000	$1,500,000
Return on Customer^{sm}	-	25%	25%	25%

The second example assumes a declining response rate over time. A number of factors can contribute to a decreasing response rate including consumer weariness from repeated messages or uninspiring offers. As Peppers and Rogers argue, companies risk destroying customer equity, even as they appear to be making a profit.

	Year 1	Year 2	Year 3	Year 4
Total prospects	1,000,000	1,000,000	1,000,000	1,000,000
Response rate	1%	0.95%	0.90%	0.85%
Cost per campaign	$1,000,000	$1,000,000	$1,000,000	$1,000,000
Cash flow per campaign	$1,250,000	$1,187,500	$1,125,000	$1,062,500
Profit per campaign	$250,000	$187,500	$125,000	$62,500
Profit per year (6 campaigns)	$1,500,000	$1,125,000	$750,000	$375,000
Year-end customer equity	$6,000,000	$4,500,000	$3,000,000	$1,500,000
Change in customer equity	-	$(1,500,000)	$(1,500,000)	$(1,500,000)
Total value created	$1,500,000	$(375,000)	$(750,000)	$(1,125,000)
Return on Customer[sm]	-	(6.3%)	(16.7%)	(37.5%)

Impact on Decision Making

The objectives of marketing programs and campaigns must be clearly enumerated from multiple perspectives. Depending on the business need, a marketer may be tempted to boost short term revenues using promotional offers. This may improve sales (and perhaps profits), but the cost may be the loss of loyal customers, the destruction of customer equity, or both. Therefore, marketing managers have to assess the implications of their communications plans before launching them. Marketers are responsible for measuring communications program and campaign effectiveness. The implications of declining customer equity must be recognized by marketers when they are designing marketing communications programs. A promotional campaign with an attractive price offer may increase sales, but it may also dilute any brand premium.

Endnote

1 Peppers, D. and Rogers, M. *Return on Customer: Creating Maximum Value From Your Scarcest Resource* 2005 Don Peppers and Martha Rogers. Published by Doubleday, a division of Random House, Inc. Chapter 1 "An Open Letter to Wall Street" pp.16-18.

NOTE: Return on Customer and ROC are registered service marks of Peppers and Rogers Group, a division of Carlson Marketing Group, Inc. Readers who are interested in a more comprehensive treatment of ROC[sm] are encouraged to review Peppers and Rogers' book as footnoted above. Furthermore, their website, www.peppersandrogers.com, provides additional insight into their consulting and research work.

II

THE OFFERING

"The offering" describes what the company is offering to customers via products, their prices and the value conveyed by the brand.

The measures covered in this section are:

Products and New Products

- New product purchase rate
- Profit impact

Prices

- Price
- Mark-up pricing
- Target-return price

Advertising

- Share of voice
- Advertising to sales ratio
- Reach
- Frequency
- Gross rating points
- Cost per gross rating point

Sales promotion

- Premiums
- Promotion profit

Direct marketing

- Response rate
- Conversion rate

- Direct mail revenue goals
- Direct mail profit goals
- Direct mail gross profit
- Direct mail net profit
- Direct mail ROI

Internet marketing

- Click-through rates
- Gross page impressions/gross page requests
- Cost per click
- Cost per action
- Cost per sales dollar
- Hits
- Pay per lead

Brands

- Brand equity
- Brand premium
- Recall
- Recognition
- Usage

Retail

- Transactions per customer
- Returns to net sales
- Transactions per hour
- Hourly customer traffic
- Inventory turnover
- Percent inventory carrying costs

- Gross margin return on inventory investment
- Sales per square foot
- Sales/profits per employee
- Average transactions size
- Average items per transaction
- Retail close ratio
- Retailer's margin percentage
- Markdown goods percentage
- Percent utilization of discounts
- Shrinkage to net sales

The marketer has shifted emphasis from the strategic work discussed in Marketing Planning and Customers, into the more tactical work represented by the marketing mix Four Ps: product, price, place and promotion. Developed over 40 years ago, the Four Ps is the classic marketing framework, and is still largely relevant today for marketers as they shape their basic offering.

Figure 11 shows the marketing mix Four Ps.

Product	Price
Place	Promotion

Figure 11: Marketing Mix Four Ps

Product

Products are more than a physical item or tightly defined service. Consumers see products as a promise of quality and a provider of value. The purchase of a product does not end the relationship for the company—it begins the relationship for the consumer. Customers expect the products they purchase to work, and if not, then redress is sought. The product must include warranties, replacement and return policies, customer service, technical support and an image of assumed quality.

Marketers have an obligation to develop and promote products that are reliable, foster goodwill with customers and advance the company's reputation and perceived value. Before launching a product, a marketer should evaluate its potential for success. For products that are global, a marketer must factor in overseas support for the product, develop distribution relationships, identify the most attractive markets and understand the competitive conditions.

The relevance of products to the overall marketing effort has taken on new significance in recent years with the burgeoning economies of Southeast Asia. For years, Japan was considered the only Asian country producing products and services that succeeded in western markets. Toyota, Honda, Nissan, Nintendo, Sony, Mitsubishi, Fujitsu and Panasonic were the world's most talked about companies. Additionally, Japanese banks were well represented among the world's top 50 financial institutions. Korea began emerging in the 1990s, with the growth of Samsung and Hyundai in particular. Now Thailand, Singapore, Vietnam, China and India are taking center stage. New products from companies in these markets are found in the U.S. and Europe. Marketers in these countries have observed the success of western multi-nationals around the world and are copying as well as developing their own approaches to the product effort. This is creating a formidable and stimulating challenge for marketers in Europe and the U.S., who have long dominated the multi-national business environment.

Marketers throughout the world know that they can market their products almost anywhere and, equally, their competition can come from anywhere as well. Developing smart products and product strategies to compete successfully begins with measuring a product's potential before launching into new markets.

Price

A product's image is influenced by price. High prices convey high quality and the corollary is true for low prices and low quality. At a minimum, price is a mechanism for marketers and their companies to recapture their costs. Beyond recovering costs and hopefully making a profit, pricing strategies are quite varied. Each company's financial needs are different, even for companies in the same region, industry and product market. These unique conditions dictate different pricing strategies.

For marketers, beyond recapturing costs, the most important consideration is how price fits with the company's strategic positioning objectives and influences perceptions in the market. Pricing strategy will vary by market as well. But marketers must know the needs of their own company first. Is the company's strategy based on rapid sales growth? Then a low price, economy or penetration, strategy will be chosen. Is the objective profit maximization? Then either a skimming or sustained premium price approach will be used. Is the company struggling to survive? Then crisis pricing may be used to secure as many customers as possible with the hope of converting them to higher price customers later.

Pricing strategies go beyond a single price for a single product. Payment terms are a method for controlling price by reducing the upfront cost to the customer by extending the length of time over which the price is paid. Volume pricing is used to reward customers that purchase significant quantities of product. Coupons, rebates and allowances are promotional pricing vehicles. Finally, once pricing choices have been made, market conditions will dictate whether, and how much, fine tuning is required to sustain marketplace interest and support for the products.

Place

Place describes channels, retail merchandise assortments and inventory, and distribution location. It is the marketer's tool for determining how and where customers will purchase the products.

Place strategies are not as simple as having a good location—as important as that is. Customers' demands have grown more sophisticated concurrently with the growth in product choices, competing brands and access to information (and products) via the Internet. Place decisions are also expensive because of real estate costs, store design expenses, inventory fulfillment and warehousing requirements, supplier location and relationships, IT infrastructure needs, and competitors developing and improving their own retail operations as well.

Place issues are further complicated by the fragmentation of markets and segments. Whereas it was once common place to have discount, middle market and upscale retail locations, sophisticated retailers like Crate and Barrel, IKEA, Pottery Barn, Sharper Image, Brookstone (OSIM), WalMart, and Costco, for example, have discovered that customers at all levels shop in their stores, depending on their needs. IKEA offers affordable furnishings to budget customers, yet IKEA appeals to upscale customers as well, due in part to the innovative designs, unique store layouts and vast selection.

Whether the place strategy focuses on a discount store or an exclusive, upscale environment, customers expect the merchandise to be high quality (even in discount stores), the service to be helpful, the merchandise thoughtfully displayed and the shopping environment to be friendly. The reason for this multi-part strategy is due to the increasing importance of creating experiences for customers that go beyond the purchase of a product and include the development of an emotional attachment.

The retail measures described in this book help store management assess performance results of their operations.

Promotion

The term "promotion" is misleadingly narrow. A better term is integrated marketing communications (IMC), which more accurately describes the important inter-dependence between each promotion category. Figure 12 illustrates the range of IMC tools available to marketers. The role of IMC is to provide clear marketing communications across varied media.

Figure 12: Promotion Choices

Media choices are made based on their ability to deliver an audience that the marketer seeks and hopes to convert to paying customers. No single medium works best, so sophisticated marketers are developing multi-layered campaigns that capture customers with similar (not identical) messages in different media. Volkswagen (VW), for example, ran a marketing campaign referred to as the "Da Da Da" campaign. The ad featured two young men driving around in a new VW car called the Golf, spotting an old chair on the sidewalk, and putting it in the car. The campaign was supported by VW's website, the commercial was downloaded and shared on the Internet around the world and it became the subject of free press and blogs everywhere. The campaign worked well across several of the IMC media.

Marketers are tapping into mobile communications as well, sending text messages to subscribers of services around the world. The Internet has evolved from a form of electronic brochure in the early to mid-1990s to a platform for advertising, videos, music, PR, customer blogs and new product launches.

Not all of these vehicles are successful, so marketers must determine which media reach their target audience most effectively and then craft a campaign that appeals directly to them. More problematically, the rapid advancement of the Internet, blogs and mobile communications have accelerated the pace at which products are known around the world. Many of the IMC components are driven by word of mouth, not impressions, gross rating points (GRPs) or reach. The challenge for marketers is how to manage these viral effects, because they are otherwise not controllable. Careful planning of products, pricing, market selection, media vehicles and communications strategies is more important than ever, and the need to measure these has grown as well.

The advertising, sales promotion, direct marketing and Internet marketing measures in the pages that follow will help marketers more effectively measure key communications vehicles.

The Impact of Globalization on Marketing

While the Four Ps help shape the business offering, actually implementing a go-to-market plan is an entirely different challenge. Globalization has complicated the Four Ps by compelling marketers and their companies to develop their offerings based on the needs of each international market. Planning conventions that are familiar to marketers in the western markets of Europe and North America either do not exist or are not applicable to the developing economies of Southeast Asia, China and South America. Customers in western markets have grown up surrounded by marketing communications practices that seem second nature. Yet in emerging markets, the practices may never have existed, so a common knowledge base does not exist, nor the infrastructures upon which marketers rely to gain market information.

Product variation has increased during globalization, not decreased, despite the belief that a key requirement of product and brand success is having the same look and feel everywhere. Consistency may mean a product is of the same quality everywhere, but the message conveyed is tailored to the needs of the local market. Or it may mean that the product has to be redesigned to fit local needs and country-specific regulatory requirements. Uniformity implies that an identical product and message is developed in all markets, irrespective of local tastes and preferences. But uniformity is not desired or recommended for most markets today. Part of the marketer's role is to understand the unique characteristics of each market he enters.

Language and cultural differences may prevent marketing messages from successfully translating across markets.

A memorable example is the infamous Pepsi campaign years ago with the slogan[1],

"Come Alive with the Pepsi Generation!"

It certainly sounds positive, reflecting the uplifting, youthful image Pepsi has cultivated over the years. But when it was translated into Chinese, it had a very different meaning,

"Pepsi brings your ancestors back from the grave!"

The slogan clearly lost something in the translation. For marketers, the lesson is self-evident: local adaptation is important for successful international growth.

In the B2B environment, entering new markets, specifically new countries, can be a formidable challenge as well. In the early 2000s, Tradecard, a U.S.-based software company specializing in providing a web-enabled financial transactions platform for companies in international trade, decided to enter China[2]. The company had been founded in the late 1990s and had earned success in the U.S. by streamlining the documentary and financial requirements of trade transactions, a process that was previously labor-intensive, slow and bureaucratic due to regulatory and legal requirements. In effect, Tradecard's solution took the hassle out of trade transactions since buyers and sellers could interact online. Tradecard's system worked well in the U.S., where banking, capital markets, regulatory and legal standards are well developed. There was also a sizable and growing market of companies doing business online on the equally well-developed U.S. IT infrastructure. Furthermore, U.S. businesses had been operating in this type of environment for years.

Tradecard's move to China was risky, however, since the economy and business market was not nearly as well developed as the U.S.'s. Only a few hundred companies in China were even on the Internet in 2001 and fewer still were transacting business online. Most companies conducted transactions through paper-based or even simple handshake agreements. Furthermore, the legal system was not developed enough to provide recourse for companies whose transactions were mishandled. Finally, the marketing channels familiar in the U.S. did not exist in China, so it was not clear how to reach the market. But, the company entered anyway and the business has grown steadily since. The primary reason they entered? The enormous potential China represented. Tradecard's management team believed that China's economy was rapidly changing, and would quickly develop much of the infrastructure needed for long-term success. As carefully planned as most large companies are today, new markets develop very differently and rarely according to corporate or industry specifications. Marketers, therefore, must know how to employ the key marketing frameworks for planning, then adapt as the situation warrants.

Despite these shortcomings, the fundamental simplicity of the Four Ps translates well across markets and cultures and offers marketers a useful tool for planning their general approach to the market. The measures discussed in this section help marketers answer the harder questions that the Four Ps cannot address.

Brand

Brands can be products, services, companies or experiences. Companies in almost every industry are taking their branding efforts more seriously than ever before, because of the additional value conveyed by a brand. Even if the offering is identical to a lesser-known competitor's, a well-known brand can command a higher price. With the growing complexity of markets and the expansion of product choices, brands play an increasingly important role. Brands are a form of trust between customers and companies. Today's marketing strategies involve developing brand experiences that go far beyond a product or price. A brand experience describes the multi-faceted effort by companies to connect to customers with entertainment, lifestyle, communications and relationship development. Each of these components is seen as part of the customer's overall use of, and attachment to, products and services.

Nike's NikeTown stores, first launched in the early 1990s, are richly designed, upscale retail environments in which different athletic themes are integrated into distinct product pavilions. Customers can test a basketball shoe, for example, on the store's basketball court before purchasing. Products move from a behind-the-scenes warehouse to the retail counter through clear tubes, via conveyor belts and in mini-elevators. Music changes as customers move from one pavilion to the next. The sum total leaves customers with the distinct impression that the products they purchased are extraordinarily special.

Virgin Atlantic offers its airline customers a series of pre- and post-flight experiences, including limousine service, special airport lounges with full spas and multi-screen movie theatres among its atypical traveler choices.

Apple provides customers with stylishly designed, high-quality computer and media products that work together to control most of the entertainment needs in today's home, or the more sophisticated needs of music and video artists. Their retail stores are brightly lit, energetic and stimulating, featuring Apple products for visitors to use, games for kids to play, a genius bar (where customers can get their questions answered) and store concierge.

Each of these examples of brand experience shapes the consumer's perception and strengthens their relationship with the brand. For marketers, branding has evolved from a simple effort of developing a logo and slogan into a three-dimensional experience designed to inspire customer loyalty. Brands have become strategic assets, and marketers have an opportunity to turn ordinary products into extraordinary experiences that add emotional value for consumers and financial value for companies.

Brand measures, particularly brand equity, help marketers understand the complexity in measuring brands. Non-marketers need to appreciate that brands are not easily measured, nor is there a universal standard for brand valuation. Brands are complex strategic assets composed of tangible and intangible inputs.

Endnotes

1 http://www.fuqua.duke.edu/alumni/connect/pnews/120605-imf.htm

2 Adapted from Farhoomand, A. "Tradecard: Expanding into China". Center for Asian Business Cases, University of Hong Kong, HKU273.

Source

Adapted from: Farhoomand, A. "Tradecard: Expanding into China". Center for Asian Business Cases, University of Hong Kong, HKU273.

New Product Purchase Rate[1]

Measurement Need

Most companies invest time, money and resources into new product development. Marketing plans are developed to guide companies in profitably growing the business within target customer segments, taking advantage of the company's core capabilities. Of course, this general view overlooks the details and challenges companies face in the product launch process. Marketers need to estimate whether a proposed product is likely to achieve success in the market.

Solution

The new product purchase rate formula is in a category of marketing models called "diffusion" (or, sometimes, "penetration") models, which provide guidance about the likely acceptance of a new product in a given market. It helps marketers and their companies determine the penetration rate for new consumer products. In effect, it provides guidance on the rate of acceptance of a new product over time, which can help determine the effectiveness of a company's marketing programs in building share and generating sales.

The new product purchase rate is determined by the following formula:

$$q_t = r \times q \, (1 - r)^{t-1}$$

Where

q_t = the % of total households expected to try the product in period t

r = rate of penetration of untapped potential

q = the % of total households expected to eventually try the new product

t = period of time

To illustrate, we can look at an example using San Fransisco, California, where there were approximately 330,000 households in 2003. We will assume the following variables:

r = 40%. Meaning 40% of the remaining potential new buyers are penetrated

q = 20%. Meaning 20% of San Francisco households will actually buy the product

t = period of time.

Let's input these figures into the formula over successive time periods (five years in this example) to demonstrate the changes in penetration rates.

$$q_t = rq \ (1-r)^{1-1} = (0.4)(0.2)(0.6^0) = 0.080$$

$$q_t = rq \ (1-r)^{2-1} = (0.4)(0.2)(0.6^1) = 0.048$$

$$q_t = rq \ (1-r)^{3-1} = (0.4)(0.2)(0.6^2) = 0.029$$

$$q_t = rq \ (1-r)^{4-1} = (0.4)(0.2)(0.6^3) = 0.017$$

$$q_t = rq \ (1-r)^{5-1} = (0.4)(0.2)(0.6^4) = 0.010$$

This set of equations indicates that the rate of new product penetration for the 20% who will buy the product decreases over a five year period.

From here, sales are determined by simply taking the resulting penetration rate for each period and multiplying it by the total number of San Francisco households, then multiplying by the expected price for the first purchase (each period is essentially "first purchase" expenditures since the purchases reflect first time buyers in each period) per household. Furthermore, we will assume the first-time purchase price for this product is $50.

$$q_t = rq \ (1-r)^{1-1} = 0.080 \rightarrow .08 \times 330,000 \times \$50 = \$1,320,000$$

$$q_t = rq \ (1-r)^{2-1} = 0.048 \rightarrow .048 \times 330,000 \times \$50 = \$792,000$$

$$q_t = rq \ (1-r)^{3-1} = 0.028 \rightarrow .029 \times 330,000 \times \$50 = \$478,500$$

$$q_t = rq \ (1-r)^{4-1} = 0.017 \rightarrow .017 \times 330,000 \times \$50 = \$280,500$$

$$q_t = rq \ (1-r)^{5-1} = 0.010 \rightarrow .010 \times 330,000 \times \$50 = \$165,000$$

The data on households is government census data, which is collected at different times in different countries. A quick search on the Internet provides numerous references to household data from Canada, the U.S., Australia, the U.K., Japan, and Europe (including those parts of Eastern Europe formerly under the influence of the now-defunct Soviet Union). China's data is less reliable due to differences in collection techniques, uncertainty over census dates, inconsistent transparency requirements and comprehensiveness.

Impact on Decision Making

The conscientious reader will note that questions do remain. For example, how does one determine r, the rate of penetration of untapped potential? How do marketers determine the percentage of households that are likely to try the product in a certain time period? The answers depend on several factors:

- The market in which the company competes
- The ease of determining, reaching and converting customers in the target markets
- Surveys that assess customer purchase intent
- An estimate of the remaining potential customers to be converted

Determining the number of potential customers in the target market requires marketers to learn about their actual target market, which means they will have to do more research. Predicting product adoption rates is a combination of science and art. The science comprises the data-collection techniques and subsequent analysis. The art is in deciding how much of the result should be believed, given the vagaries of consumer behavior. In other words, just because consumers say they are likely to buy your product does not mean they will behave in that way at the actual time of purchase. Intent does not necessarily lead to action or purchase. The real test will be how consumers actually respond when you introduce your products to the market.

For a marketer launching a new product, this is an interesting way to gauge its potential economic lifespan, assuming, of course, that there are no changes in target-customer penetration, audience size, product features or pricing. These latter caveats are the challenges. Furthermore, determining the potential market for your product out of the total household population and the rate of penetration is somewhat arbitrary. Marketers can mitigate some of this guesswork by gathering industry and competitor statistics for similar products and inferring the potential on their own. Therefore, a marketer's analysis will be a mixture of observable data and qualitative judgments.

Endnote

1 The formula has its origin in an article by Louis A. Fourt and Joseph N. Woodlock, entitled "Early Prediction of Market Success for New Grocery Products", in the *Journal of Marketing*, October 1960, pp.31–38. More recent, in-depth research has been conducted by Peter S. Faber, Bruce G.S. Hardie and Chun Yao Huang in their article "A Dynamic Changepoint Model for New Product Sales Forecasting", *Marketing Science*, Vol. 23, No. 1, Winter 2004, pp.50–65.

Sources

Davis, J. *Magic Numbers for Consumer Marketing*. Singapore: John Wiley & Sons (Asia) Pte Ltd., 2005: pp.162-166.

http://www.census.gov/acs/www/Products/Profiles/Single/2003/ACS/Narrative/155/NP15500US0667000075.htm

http://en.wikipedia.org/wiki/San_Francisco

Profit Impact 34

Measurement Need

When launching products, marketers want to calculate the potential profit when the costs of manufacturing, product and pricing activities are included.

Solution

Profit impact describes the effect on profits resulting from a company's product-related expenditures. Two preliminary steps must be taken before calculating profit impact: determining the manufacturing sales price (MSP) and the contribution per unit (C_{pu}).

$$MSP = P_r - M_r - M_w$$

Where

P_r = retail price

M_r = retail margin

M_w = wholesale margin or mark-up

Contribution per unit is based on the formula:

$$C_{pu} = MSP - C_v$$

Where

C_v = total variable cost

Profit impact can now be calculated with the following formula:

$$Profit\ impact = (C_{pu} \times U_s) - C_{fc}$$

Where

C_{pu} = contribution per unit

U_s = units sold

C_{fc} = total fixed costs

To illustrate with a hypothetical example, Generic Remote is a small manufacturer of generic remote controls for use with home audio-visual equipment. The remotes have the following profile:

- Retail price of $10
- Retail margins are 30%
- Wholesale margins are 8%
- Remote market is 35 million customers
- Market share is 20%
- Units sold are 7,000,000
- Variable costs are $3 per remote
- Total fixed costs are $1,800,000

Step 1: Calculate *MSP*

$$MSP = P_r - M_r - M_w$$
$$MSP = \$10 - \$3 - \$0.80$$
$$MSP = \$6.20$$

Step 2: Calculate C_{pu}

$$C_{pu} = MSP - C_v$$
$$C_{pu} = \$6.20 - \$3$$
$$C_{pu} = \$3.20$$

Step 3: Calculate profit impact

$$Profit\ Impact = (C_{pu} \times U_s) - C_{fc}$$
$$Profit\ Impact = (\$3.20 \times 7,000,000) - 1,800,000$$
$$Profit\ Impact = \$20,600,000$$

Impact on Decision Making

The profit impact figure measures the effect marketing expenditures have on the profitability of a company, product line or individual products. It does not fully account for marketing's contribution, other than from a predominantly product cost standpoint. Much of the research on profit impact is dated, conducted in the 1970s and 1980s during an era dominated by manufacturing, under-representing the impact from non-manufacturing activities. A more updated approach would include marketing's expenditures to promote products (through advertising, sales programs, promotions, PR and pricing strategies) in the period of time measured. Although not always felt by consumers in the market at the same time, the exclusion of these marketing activities distorts the marketing contribution; yet these are necessary components for a successful product launch. There is a longer-term, residual benefit from marketing activities undertaken today, just as there is from products produced today that are enjoyed over months and years.

The C_{pu} information will be found in the company's retail and wholesale pricing and margin data, within marketing and finance. The same is true with the information pertaining to units sold. Marketers may struggle to acquire timely data, but a visit to the sales department will usually provide the most recent figures since those may not have been forwarded to the finance and accounting groups yet. The fixed costs would also be in the financial figures, but could be derived department-by-department.

Sources

Gilligan, C. and Wilson, R.M.S., *Strategic Marketing Management: Planning, Implementation & Control*. Richard M. S. Wilson and Colin Gilligan, 2005: pp.112-115.

Best, R.J., *Market-Based Management: Strategies for Growing Customer Value and Profitability*. Upper Saddle River, NJ: Pearson Education, 2005: pp.14-18, 290-292.

The Profit Impact of Marketing Strategy Project. Edited by Paul W. Farris, University of Virginia and Michael J. Moore, University of Virginia, 2004.

Davis, J. *Magic Numbers for Consumer Marketing*. Singapore: John Wiley & Sons (Asia) Pte Ltd., 2005: pp.63-65.

Price 35

Measurement Need

Price is one of the four Ps of the classic marketing mix (product, price, place, promotion). It has a significant influence on a company's success since revenues result from a specific number of units sold times a price charged. Price influences customer perceptions as well. Low price usually conveys a perception of a cheaper, lower quality product, whereas higher prices connote better quality and, at the highest prices, premium and/or exclusive products. This is the amount of money you charge for a product or service.

Solutions

The matrix[1] in Figure 13 outlines four general price strategies (not exhaustive):

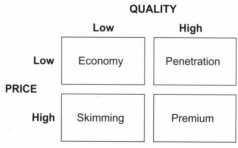

Figure 13: Price Strategies

Economy pricing means charging a small mark-up above cost.

Penetration pricing describes the price companies charge when trying to gain market share. Companies charge the lowest possible price to gain share while still making a profit or, at a minimum, breaking even. Cost or production efficiencies allow this kind of pricing to work, but the challenge is sustaining the cost efficiencies and advantages over time. **Note**: In the the 1980s, Japanese and Korean microchip makers[2] were selling their products below cost to gain market share in a pricing practice known as "dumping". This led to anti-dumping complaints with the U.S. Department of Commerce against the Japanese and Korean firms as well as an anti-dumping lawsuit filed by the U.S. Government. Dumping and penetration pricing are not the same.

Skimming is when the marketer charges the highest possible price that the market will bear relative to competitor offerings, if any. It is often used in the early stages of market development for a new product, when the quality of offerings in the overall market is low due to the market's immaturity. As the market matures, if the company maintains a quality edge as competitors enter, then their pricing strategy would shift to premium.

Premium pricing describes the highest possible price charged over time, due to the company's dominant market share position, unusually high-quality products and corresponding image, and a unique offering in the market relative to competitors.

Once marketers have planned their pricing strategy, they can then run a simple calculation to determine if a retail price yields a satisfactory net price once discounts and taxes are included:

$$P = P_L - D - A - T$$

Where

P = price (the final price realized)

P_L = list price (your target full retail price)

D = discounts (percentage reduction from list price, usually based on volume)

A = allowances (price reductions issued for trade-ins and/or promotional dollars from cooperative marketing activities between the manufacturer and retailer)

T = taxes and tariffs

Let's assume the marketer has set a retail price target of $10. Taxes and tariffs imposed by the tax authorities amount to 5%. The marketer decides a promotion program is needed to induce more sales, with the following offer:

- Discounts that average 5%

- Allowances that average 2%

$$P = \$10 - \$0.50 - \$0.20 - \$0.50 = \$8.80$$

Therefore, the list price of $10 nets out to $8.80 per product sold.

The marketer may want to test this pricing level with a selection of consumers and chooses an online survey to maximize the potential responses. Let's assume three price variations are included in the test, as in Table 17.

Table 17: Financial Impact of Price Variation

Price (before discounts and taxes)	$5	$10	$20
Orders	1,000	1,500	900
Revenue	$5,000	$15,000	$18,000

In this case, the middle price of $10 produces the highest number of orders while the $20 price produces the highest revenues. The marketer must decide which is more important: the number of customers or the revenue generated from a smaller group of premium buyers. The answer will depend on the marketing strategy and overall business objectives, as well as the company's (or product's) image and position in the market.

Impact on Decision Making

All of the price components described could have been altered to encourage demand: lower list price; higher discounts to inspire the retailer to buy larger quantities; higher allowances to encourage more promotion and support from the retailer, and so on. Marketers have no control over taxes and tariffs, but they do need to factor them into their final pricing analysis and recommendations. If the marketer's goal was to maximize profit and position the product as a premium product, then the $20 suggested price is the most appropriate.

A pricing strategy will include considering the company's volume objectives, profit objectives or some other set of considerations such as competitive parity. If volume is the primary goal, then the marketer will pursue unit and/or market share growth. Penetration pricing is the best approach in this case. This means setting prices low enough to capture market share rapidly. It is most often used when competitors have identical, similar or better products. If the objective is profitability, then a skimming pricing strategy is most often used in the early market development stages, transitioning over time to a premium pricing approach. This means that a company believes its product offering is unique and innovative and, consequently, has a probable lead over the competition. Companies price at a premium level both to capture higher profits and to establish and reinforce a market-leading position. Over time, marketers may reduce the price as competition enters (which it will inevitably do, since competitors will notice a company's success and want to get their share of it as well), but this may risk dilution of the company's premium reputation. Alternatively, the marketer can opt for value-added changes in the product that keep its price at a premium level

Marketers are not limited to these approaches. It is quite possible that a blended approach may be the most sensible, whereby a firm chooses to price mid-market. Once again, this decision must be considered in the context of a firm's overall positioning objectives. Often, a middle approach can become no-man's land in which the products are not perceived as either premium or mass market. Consequently, the consumer does not know what the product stands for. If a reasonable benefits argument for this middle approach cannot be made, then consumers are likely to buy on the basis of either lowest cost or most unique features.

Pricing data should come from the company's business and sales plans for each product. Often, sales representatives control final price (usually within pre-set guidelines) because they are dealing directly with the customer at the point of sale and know first-hand what the customer is seeking. As each order comes in from the market, this information is fed directly into the company's financial reports, where the details of each transaction are fully described. Sales people should be recording the final agreed price and quantity figures accurately so that the accountants know how to categorize the price specifics. Depending on each company's accounting practices, allowances and discounts may be counted against the marketing program's budget, or they may be counted against the sales team directly, especially if each salesperson's compensation is tied to measures of financial performance such as profitability. It could also be a combination of these methods.

Endnotes

1 Doyle, C. *Collins Internet-Linked Dictionary of Marketing.* Harper Collins, 2003, 2006: p.177.

2 Adapted from: *Knowledge@Wharton Newsletter* "How Companies Use (and Abuse) Law for Competitive Gains". http://knowledge.wharton.upenn.edu/article/978.cfm, which is based on: Shell, G. R. "Make the Rules or Your Rivels Will"; Crown Business, 2004.

Sources

Davis, J. *Magic Numbers for Consumer Marketing.* Singapore: John Wiley & Sons (Asia) Pte Ltd., 2005: pp.203-206.

Dolan, R. J. "How Do You Know When the Price is Right?". *Harvard Business Review*, Sept-Oct 1995.

Usborne, N. "How to Determine the Best Price for Your Product or Service". February 14, 2006. http://www.marketingprofs.com/6/usborne6.asp

Mark-Up Price[1]

Measurement Need

Product pricing is one of the most important elements of the Four Ps of the marketing mix since price helps to recover costs, position products and generate profits. When marketers know their costs and need to achieve a specific margin, then mark-up pricing can be used to set price.

Solution

This pricing method adds a slight increase, or "mark-up", to the product's (or service's) cost. It is often used in professional-services businesses. Companies using it would calculate their base costs for a project or product, then add a percentage mark-up to reflect the premium they believe their product or service represents. This is represented by the following formula:

$$MUP = \frac{UC}{(1 - ROSe)}$$

Where

MUP = mark-up price

UC = unit cost

$ROSe$ = expected return on sales

Unit cost must be determined to calculate the mark-up pricing formula. To calculate unit cost, use this formula:

$$UC = \frac{VC + FC}{US}$$

Where

UC = unit cost

VC = variable cost

FC = fixed cost

US = unit sales (in units, not dollars)

Professional-services firms often use mark-up pricing by estimating the total project cost, then adding in their profit, or mark-up.

Manufacturing operations have a similar approach that requires understanding certain key costs and sales estimates to calculate a cost per unit, from which the mark-up price can ultimately be determined.

In the following case, Company X makes flidgets. The following are its expected costs and sales:

- Variable costs $15

- Fixed costs $200,000

- Expected unit sales   40,000

Company X positions its flidgets at the premium end of the market because it uses premium materials, so while its costs are slightly higher than those of its competitors, it is able to command high prices due to the added value its products offer. Therefore, Company X expects a mark-up of 20%. Its pricing can now be calculated.

First, we determine unit cost:

$$Unit\ cost\ =\ variable\ cost\ +\ \frac{fixed\ costs}{unit\ sales}$$

$$Unit\ cost\ =\ \$15\ +\ \frac{\$200,000}{40,000}\ =\ \$20$$

Next, we add this figure into the mark-up price equation:

$$Mark\text{-}up\ price\ =\ \frac{unit\ cost}{(1-expected\ return\ on\ sales^*)}$$

$$Mark\text{-}up\ price\ =\ \frac{\$20}{(1-0.2)}\ =\ \$25$$

Company X's mark-up price to its retail accounts is $25. Their profit is $5 on each flidget it sells.

Impact on Decision Making

While mark-up pricing is generally simple, it is not the most effective approach to pricing. It is simple because you only need to estimate the mark-up you wish to earn above cost, and price accordingly. It is not always effective because you may not be maximizing your profit or sales potential. Perhaps the customer sees Company X's flidgets as being of only mediocre value, despite the premium materials. If so, Company X is unlikely to hit its sales target. On the other hand, customers may perceive them as being of extraordinary value at $50. Company X's marketers then have to consider whether they would sell just as many if the price was $5 or $10 higher, thereby improving their margins.

While mark-up pricing is simple, since it is really based on covering costs plus adding a little margin, it may leave out any unique positioning opportunities that could help marketers build a more reputable, exclusive brand. Even if it was not marketing's goal to be a high-end brand, money may still be left on the table if mark-up pricing is the primary pricing guide.

Mark-up pricing is based on estimates of the total costs for a project or product and, therefore, the data can be found in the company's marketing plans and accounting budgets for each department. Identifying the costs is the tricky part, so a company's systems must be sophisticated enough to measure cost inputs, both fixed and variable, to the unit level. Once the costs are known, or estimated, then the marketing manager's job is to identify a reasonable mark-up price. This is most likely driven by the company's strategic margin goals for each product line, as well as the positioning goals for each product in each product line. The reason for noting the positioning goals is that pricing has a direct impact on consumers' perceptions of a product's position vis-à-vis the competition.

Finance and/or accounting will have information on specific fixed costs allocated to the marketing department. As with all numbers that describe or affect your marketing decisions, you should double-check accounting's figures against your own budget figures to see what differences there are, if any. Usually, the accountants have specific rules that govern how to count certain costs and these tend to be more detailed than the basic budgets marketing departments (or most other departments, for that matter) would submit. It is quite likely that your figures will not match the figures from accounting or finance, but that is probably as a consequence of these rules.

Endnote

1 Adapted from: Kotler, P., Siew, M.L., Swee H.A. and Tan, C.T. *Marketing Management: An Asian Perspective*. New Jersey: Prentice Hall, 2003.

Sources

Davis, J. *Magic Numbers for Consumer Marketing*. Singapore: John Wiley & Sons (Asia) Pte Ltd., 2005: pp.216-219.

http://users.wbs.warwick.ac.uk/dibb_simkin/student/glossary/ch19.html

Note: from Chapter 6, Return on Sales, we learned that the formula for return on sales is:

$$ROS = \frac{P_{nbt}}{S}$$

Target Return Price[1]   37

Measurement Need

When the company's investment decisions are dictated by target rates of return, marketers use this information to determine the best price for a given product.

Solution

Target return price is designed to cover all costs and yield a specified or target return. Like mark-up pricing (Chapter 36), it is another cost-based approach.

$$TRP = Cpu \pm \frac{R \times I}{US}$$

Where

TRP = target return price

Cpu = cost per unit

R = expected return

I = capital invested

US = unit sales (in units)

Let's assume that a new athletic apparel company, called Corner Kick, competing only in soccer shoes, decides to launch a new product to compete against Adidas and Nike. Sales are expected to be 100,000 units in the first year, but the company believes a new fabric machine is necessary to successfully create the quality of product needed. Corner Kick's marketing manager wants to know what his target-return price would be by investing $3 million in the new fabric machine used to mechanically blend two or more specialty fabrics together. Corner Kick's apparel has always been positioned as premium products sold at premium prices. The cost per unit is $35. Senior management has premium expectations on the target returns for the $3 million investment, seeking an ROI of 25%, which means the final price should return $750,000.

Here's how the analysis looks:

$$Target \ \ return \ \ price \ = \ 35 \ + \ \frac{0.25 \times \$3,000,000}{100,000} \ = \ \$42.50$$

Therefore, to achieve a 25% ROI, the target return price must be at least $42.50.

Impact on Decision Making

Target return pricing depends on the assumptions and expectations that went into it. For example, if your expected ROI is not in line with industry standards on similar projects, then it is quite possible that your target return price will not adequately meet your needs. It is also conceivable that your unit sales assumptions are off, perhaps significantly. In this event, you would want to determine break-even at different sales volumes to see where a more accurate target-return price should be set. Keep in mind as well that target return pricing ignores competitor pricing, customer response and market trends, all of which can affect the final analysis. Preparing multiple scenarios is often the key to selecting an approach with which you are most comfortable.

The data is found in the company finance and accounting departments. One of the formula's variables, capital invested, is located in the balance sheet under liabilities, either as shareholders' equity or long-term debt.

Unit sales are found, in their final form, in the income statement. However, since those are typically completed at the end of business cycles (quarterly or annually), preliminary figures can be found in sales or in the preliminary finance reports.

Endnote

1 Adapted from: Kotler, P., Siew, M.L., Swee, H.A. and Tan, C.T. *Marketing Management: An Asian Perspective*. New Jersey: Prentice Hall, 2003: p.496.

Source

Davis, J. *Magic Numbers for Consumer Marketing*. Singapore: John Wiley & Sons (Asia) Pte Ltd., 2005: pp.220-221.

Share of Voice

38

Measurement Need

Since a substantial portion of the marketing communications budget is still spent on advertising, and advertising continues to be one of the most effective ways to reach the target audience, marketers want to measure their share of the total communications expenditures in the market. Firms can increase their share of total marketing communications by spending more on advertising.

Solution

Share of voice measures the percentage of media spending by a company compared to total media expenditure for the product, service or category in the market. Share of voice is represented by:

$$V_s = \frac{A}{\Sigma A_t}$$

Where

V_s = your share of voice expressed in percentage terms

A = your advertising spend for a given product

ΣA_t = total of all market advertising spend for the same type of product

Suppose $100 million is spent on ads for portable music players overall, and a specific company spends $5 million to promote its own player. The company's share of voice would be 5%:

$$V_s = \frac{\$5,000,000}{\$100,000,000}$$

$$= 5\%$$

Impact on Decision Making

Marketers hope to grow the business by investing in programs, including marketing communications, that inspire consumers to buy. Advertising is a specific activity within marketing communications that can have a significant influence on perception. In this regard, a high share of voice can lead to increased awareness, which, ultimately, can lead to increased sales and market share. Also, marketers will need to plan their marketing communications campaigns based on the type of audience they are trying to reach, the time of day ads are run, and the type of publication in which ads are run. Knowing the profile of their radio and television audiences ensures there is a match with the marketing plan and business goals. The time of day is important because radio and television stations charge different rates during peak versus non-peak times. The audience profile also changes depending on the time of day. Finally, the type of publication, mass market versus vertical, attracts different audiences as well. In the U.S., an example of a mass market publication is *Time* magazine whereas a vertical publication example would be *VAR Business*, a technology magazine. Each of these marketing communications choices are affected by the amount of money a marketer has budgeted to spend.

A key point to remember is the relationship between the amount spent and the number of ads a marketer is able to run as a result. While a high share of voice may indicate a larger amount of money devoted to advertising versus competitors, marketers need to carefully consider the relevance of the message to the actual consumers targeted. In other words, it is not terribly useful to have the highest share of voice if the company's message does not appeal to the target consumer.

Advertising totals for a particular product will most likely be captured in the marketing plan and marketing budget. Typical company finance and accounting reports measure advertising costs as a component of total marketing expenditures. Some companies even report advertising related to specific product launches. But, it is more likely that these individual product advertising figures are "rolled up" into an overall marketing expense line item. Market totals for category or product advertising may be found by reviewing industry trade publications, third-party research reports, business magazines with special industry sections and local business journals. Relevant statistics may also be gleaned from press releases or sales literature from businesses that have already bought industry reports and are using the information in their publicity.

Additional awareness does not mean it is necessarily positive. Assuming the marketing team and advertising agency (if the company has one) are competent, then improvements in awareness, perception, sales and market share should occur over time. Furthermore, share of voice has a direct impact on how consumers actually feel about and perceive a company, which ultimately can influence its market share.

Sources

Kotler, P., Siew, M.L., Swee H.A. and Tan, C.T. *Marketing Management: An Asian Perspective*. Upper Saddle River, NJ: Prentice Hall, 2003: p.650.

Davis, J. *Magic Numbers for Consumer Marketing*. Singapore: John Wiley & Sons (Asia) Pte Ltd., 2005: pp.228-230.

Doyle, C. *Collins Internet-Linked Dictionary of Marketing*. HarperCollins Publishers, 2003, 2005: p.287.

Advertising to Sales Ratio

39

Measurement Need

Advertising is used to build a company or product image, attract customers and, ultimately, generate, or certainly influence, an increase in sales. The amount spent on advertising will vary depending on the type of product, who the target audience is, the type of media used (online, print, broadcast) and the design and content of the message. Marketing is often asked what the return is on the various programs it implements. Measuring how effective the advertising campaigns are at creating sales is a vital piece of information that marketers supply to support their marketing efforts.

Solution[1]

The advertising to sales ratio describes the effect of advertising on a company's total sales. The formula is:

$$ASR = \frac{E_a}{S_t}$$

Where

ASR = advertising to sales ratio

E_a = total advertising expenditures

S_t = total sales during time t

Below are a number of examples of advertising to sales ratios for various well-known companies.

Nike

Nike spent $304 million on advertising in 2003, when total sales were $10.7 billion. Its advertising to sales ratio was:

$$\frac{\$304,000,000}{\$10,697,000,000}$$

$$= \quad 2.8\%$$

Reebok

Reebok spent approximately $106 million on advertising in 2003, when total sales were $3.485 billion. Its advertising to sales ratio was:

$$\frac{\$106,000,000}{\$3,485,316,000}$$

$$= \quad 3\%$$

Sony

Sony spent $1.684 billion on advertising in 2003, when total sales were just over $62 billion. Its advertising to sales ratio was:

$$\frac{\$1,684,000,000}{\$62,031,000,000}$$

$$= 2.7\%$$

Samsung

Samsung spent $489 million on advertising in 2003, when total sales were just over $45 billion. Its advertising to sales ratio was:

$$\frac{\$489,000,000}{\$45,928,109,341}$$

$$= 1.1\%$$

DaimlerChrysler

DaimlerChrysler spent $2.230 billion on advertising in 2003, when total sales were nearly $172 billion. Its advertising to sales ratio was:

$$\frac{\$2,230,000,000}{\$171,870,000,000}$$

$$= 1.3\%$$

Toyota

Toyota spent $2.669 billion on advertising in 2003, when total sales were nearly $128.9 billion. Its advertising to sales ratio was:

$$\frac{\$2,669,000,000}{\$128,965,000,000}$$

$$= 2.1\%$$

Dell

Dell spent $597 million on advertising in 2003, when total sales were $35.4 billion. Its advertising to sales ratio was:

$$\frac{\$597,000,000}{\$35,404,000,000}$$

$$= 1.7\%$$

Hewlett Packard

Hewlett Packard spent $812 million on advertising in 2003, when total sales were $73 billion. Its advertising to sales ratio was:

$$\frac{\$812,000,000}{\$73,061,000,000}$$

$$= 1.1\%$$

Table 18 provides advertising to sales ratios for numerous industries, indicating the variation across sectors[2].

Table 18: Advertising to Sales Ratios for Selected Products, Retail Stores and Services

Commodity or Class of Business	Average Ad Dollars as Percentage of Sales	Commodity or Class of Business	Average Ad Dollars as Percentage of Sales
Air Courier Services	1.2%	Household Appliances	1.5%
Amusement and Recreation Services	5.2%	Household Audio and Video Equipment	6.9%
Apparel and Accessory Stores	3.6%	Household Furniture	4.3%
Appliance and Electronics	Not noted	Insurance Agents, Brokers and Service	1.0%
Appliance Dealers	2.2%	Investment Advice	1.9%
Electronics Dealers	3.7%	Jewelry Stores	5.1%
Appliance and Electronics Dealers	2.7%	Leather and Leather Products	3.9%
Auto Dealers, Gas Stations	.9%	Legal Services	6.4%
Auto and Home Supply Stores	1.2%	Lumber & Other Building Materials	1.1%
Beverages	9.2%	Malt Beverages	8.5%
Bicycle Dealers	2.8%	Membership Sports & Recreation Clubs	5.8%
Books, Publishing & Printing	4.5%	Motion Picture Theatres	1.5%
Building Materials, Hardware, Garden(Retail)	3.2%	Musical Instruments	1.5%
Cable and Other Pay TV Services	7.7%	Office Furniture (excluding Wood)	0.8%
Carpets and Rugs	0.7%	Office of Medical Doctors	21.3%
Catalog, Mail-Order Houses	6.4%	Ophthalmic Goods & Services	4.9%
Child Day-Care Services	1.7%	Paints, Varnishes, Lacquers	1.2%
Computer and Office Equipment	0.8%	Perfume, Cosmetic, Toilet Preparations	7.4%
Convenience Stores	0.3%	Photographic Equipment & Supplies	4.7%
Department Stores	3.6%	Racing including Track Operations	2.8%

Table 18 cont'd

Drug and Proprietary Stores	0.8%	Radio, TV and Consumer Electronics Stores	3.2%
Educational Services	6.2%	Real Estate Agents & Managers	4.6%
Engineering, Accounting, Research Management and Related Services	0.3%	Restaurants	
Family Clothing Stores	2.4%	Security Brokers and Dealers	3.8%
Furniture Stores	5.9%	Shoe Stores	2.5%
Grocery Stores	1.0%	Skilled Nursing Care Facilities	0.5%
Hardware, Plumbing, Heating Equipment	0.6%	Sporting Goods Stores	
Hardware Stores		Security Brokers and Dealers	3.8%
Hobby, Toy and Game Shops	1.8%	Television Broadcast Stations	9.3%
Home Centers		Tires & Inner Tubes	2.0%
Home Healthcare Services	0.3%	Tobacco Products	4.0%
Hospital and Medical Service Plans	0.4%	Variety Stores	0.9%
Hospitals	0.2%	Video Tape Rental	3.5%
Hotels and Motels	2.3%	Women's Clothing Stores	2.8%

Impact on Decision Making

Typically, a lower advertising to sales ratio is better than a higher one, because if the marketer only had to spend 1% or 2% to generate a substantial revenue stream, then that implies the advertising was probably very effective in convincing the target audience. The word "probably" in the preceding sentence is important because we cannot conclusively infer that the low advertising to sales ratio means the ads were effective. It could be that there was a "natural" level of interest and buyer attraction to the company's products anyway, and that the same, or nearly the same, sales level may have been achieved with little or no advertising (although that is unlikely to last for very long).

As Table 17 indicates, there are differences among industries, due to the unique competitive characteristics of each industry. The auto industry, particularly in the U.S., spends 1–2% of sales on advertising. While that is obviously a low percentage, it is often in conjunction with aggressive promotional programs at the dealer level. This can include reduced financing, discounted pricing and gift giveaways or special upgrades for same day purchases, each serving as an inducement to purchase. Business products, such as enterprise hardware, are not advertised as much as consumer products. Marketers focus more on relationship development, value-added services such as additional hours of engineering support, and even user-group seminars to promote their products. Interestingly, Starbucks, the global coffee brand, is rarely if ever advertised. Instead, their stores serve as their primary marketing vehicle. Yet few would argue that they have been quite successful despite the absence of conventional advertising approaches.

Total advertising expenditure and total sales will both be measured in the income statement. Sometimes income statements capture marketing expenses in one or two general categories. If so, then simply review the marketing department budget for the detail on total ad dollars spent. Updated industry ad to sales ratio data can be found in financial institution reports such as Dun & Bradstreet and ad industry reports such as the one above from AdAge.

Endnotes

1 AdAge Global Marketing 2004 Report

2 http://www.news-record.com/advertising/advertising/ratio.html

Sources

Davis, J. *Magic Numbers for Consumer Marketing*. Singapore: John Wiley & Sons (Asia) Pte Ltd., 2005: pp.231-236.

Schonfeld & Associates. Advertising Ratios and Budgets, June 2003

North American Retail Dealers Association. Cost of Doing Business Survey Report, 2001

National Bicycle Dealers Association. The Cost of Doing Business Survey Report, 2003

National Retail Hardware Association. Cost of Doing Business Survey Report, 2002

National Restaurant Association. Restaurant Industry Operations Report, 2002

National Sporting Goods Association. Cost of Doing Business Survey Report, 2002

Reach 40

Measurement Need

Advertising is designed to appeal to a particular target audience. At a minimum, marketers want to know the size of the audience reached at least once during an ad campaign.

Solution

Reach is the number or percentage of people in the target audience reached by a single exposure (ad/commercial) in a specified period of time. Within this, it is important to clearly define what exposure is. An exposure is defined as an opportunity for members of the target audience to see or hear a particular ad. This does not mean that the target audience actually sees or hears the ad. For example, your company may advertise on television, but that does not mean that the target audience sees it.[1] When a member of the target audience actually sees or hears an advertising message, then this is known as an impression. Internet advertising refers to this as a view.

As a brief illustration, assume that there are ten households in a particular market. Five of the households are exposed to a company's advertisement one or more times. Since the total market is ten households, and five are exposed, the reach is 50%.

Impact on Decision Making

Knowing reach enables marketers to more effectively select the media vehicle that best captures the target audience they seek. The actual reach data may vary depending on the time of day and the program (if it is broadcast) or the content (particularly with print publications), so marketers must decide what is the most effective reach they can achieve for the proposed investment.

Reach would be incorporated in a description of the proposed advertising campaign, including the target audience, the creative content, the media vehicle, and the costs.

Media companies usually have media kits that provide data on reach, as well as other target audience profile demographics including age, income and race. Media companies include television and radio stations, magazine and newspaper publishers, outdoor media (billboards), and online portals.

As described at the beginning, reach does not actually measure impressions, only that the person was in the environment of the message. An ad in a magazine counts as an exposure to everyone receiving the magazine whether or not they saw the ad. A 30-second TV commercial counts as an exposure even if the person left for the kitchen during the ad. Therefore reach must be used cautiously. Some people recommend reducing the reach number by the probability that the ad was actually seen.

Reach is a decision about how many persons in the target market should be reached by an exposure one or more times. A company may prefer to use its money to reach a smaller percentage of the target market with a greater frequency. Much depends on the product and on an estimate of how many exposures are necessary to register an actual impression.

Reach is set during the marketing planning process. Marketers would either contact media companies directly, or use an ad agency, to learn about each media vehicle's reach statistics. Reach is an estimate that one must use cautiously. Media people will generally estimate reach on the high side (because they can charge more), but they are supposed to observe rules for estimation set by the Advertising Research Foundation.

Endnote

1 Adapted from the Definitions section of the American Marketing Association web-site, www.marketingpower.com

Sources

Davis, J. *Magic Numbers for Consumer Marketing*. Singapore: John Wiley & Sons (Asia) Pte Ltd., 2005: pp.237-238.

http://www.investorwords.com/4049/reach.html

Doyle, C. *Collins Internet-Linked Dictionary of Marketing*. HarperCollins Publishers, 2003, 2005: p.275.

Frequency 41

Measurement Need

When allocating their advertising dollars, marketers and/or their ad agency will have to also decide how frequently an advertisement can and should run.

Solution

Frequency describes the number of times an average member of the target audience is exposed to the same ad, commercial or program over a given period of time. To illustrate, if the five homes reached in the reach example (Chapter 40) saw a company's ad an average of three times, then the frequency would also be three.

Impact on Decision Making

Frequency is determined by marketers when considering their advertising budget allocations, based on media kit frequency pricing. Each media vehicle (radio, television, Internet, print) provides price reductions as more advertising exposures are purchased. But frequency is not a statistic found in media kits. It is determined by the marketer. If the same ad is placed in *Time* magazine in two out of the four issues that month, then the frequency is two for that month.

For example, popular U.S. television programs shown during prime time (considered 8-11pm on the east and west coasts and 7-10pm in the mid-west, when families are most likely to be home watching television) charge premium prices, even with frequency discounts, reflecting the size and characteristics of the target audience viewing the program. This is also true for radio advertising, when peak drive time (the busiest times of day—early morning and late afternoon—when automobile commuters are going to and heading from work) generally commands higher pricing than off-peak time slots. Print publications vary their pricing based on frequency as well. An ad that runs once is more expensive on a per-insertion basis than if the ad was run several times in either the same or multiple issues. Furthermore, location within the publication influences price, with locations such as inside covers or the back cover considered more valuable and, therefore, more expensive.

Similar to reach, frequency is used primarily in the marketing planning process. The real issue facing a marketer is how to split a given budget between reach and frequency. Alert marketers will carefully consider what they expect to accomplish with their advertising expenditures, which will help them determine the allocation between reach and frequency. If the objective is merely to create awareness, then a marketer may choose an advertising media that reaches the broadest possible audience. However, a healthy dose of caution is necessary here. Reaching a broad audience once may prove to be a waste or misuse of budget money. Part of marketing's role is to develop and nurture relationships with the company's target audiences. It is quite challenging to develop a relationship based on one exposure, even if it has a broad reach. A rare exception does occur, such as Apple Computer's famous "1984" television commercial, which was shown only once, during the Super Bowl football game (the championship game of professional football in the United States). This commercial launched the original Macintosh computer and it created a strong word of mouth "buzz" for Apple for several years afterward. But that is a very risky use of budget money for most companies (although many have since tried similar single-exposure campaigns on the Super Bowl and other major events). It places enormous emphasis on developing a message with widespread and lasting appeal, yet consumers can be quite unpredictable in responding to specific advertising messages, and knowing when a message has such a strong appeal is probably more art than science. Furthermore, it is incumbent that the marketer select the right media vehicle for this single exposure, otherwise the message may be completely ignored (recall the difference between exposure and impressions in the chapter on Reach).

To maximize limited budget resources, a marketer may instead consider repeating advertising messages to build the potential for lasting memory (see the chapters on Brand Recall and Brand Recognition, since they relate to this). But repeating messages is only part of the solution. Marketers must still ensure the message is targeted to the right audience, is relevant to their needs, and is capable of positively affecting consumer perceptions of the product or brand being advertised. While there is no single approach that guarantees that an advertising campaign will be successful, many companies test their messages with focus groups (randomly or pre-selected small groups of consumers). This test usually involves exposing the focus group to the advertising message, then having a trained facilitator encourage the participants to describe their reaction. Professional market research firms can be hired to assist in this process.

Market testing of advertising messages is not free and must therefore be included in the marketing budget. The marketer's job is not easy. He or she must determine what they wish to accomplish (in terms of reach, frequency and customer relationship development), identify the target audience, develop appropriate messaging, possibly test market the campaign, and then roll it out.

Endnote

1 Adapted from the Definitions section of the American Marketing Association web-site, www.marketingpower.com

Sources

Davis, J. *Magic Numbers for Consumer Marketing.* Singapore: John Wiley & Sons (Asia) Pte Ltd., 2005: pp.239-240.

http://www.investorwords.com/4049/frequency.html

Doyle, C. *Collins Internet-Linked Dictionary of Marketing.* HarperCollins Publishers, 2004, 2005: p.149.

Gross Rating Points 42

Measurement Need

When marketers advertise their company's product, particularly on television in the U.S., they want to know the size of the audience. If the media used is not television, then marketers want to know the equivalent advertising weight for the chosen marketing vehicle.

Solution[1]

Gross rating points (GRP) are an aggregate measure of the total amount or volume of advertising exposures a media campaign will generate via specified media vehicles (often television or radio, although newspapers use it as well) during a specific time period. In broadcast advertising, each GRP is equal to an advertising audience size of 1% of the total potential audience for a given media vehicle.

In mathematical terms, it is the product of reach (the number or percentage of people in the target audience reached by a single exposure) times frequency (the number of times the target audience is exposed to the same ad, commercial or program). GRP is represented by the following formula:

$$GRP = Reach \times Frequency$$

As a brief illustration, if your company chose to run a television advertisement at the World Cup Finals and 60% of the world's population was viewing, then the reach would be 60. Let's further assume that the same ad is run on other programs, creating a total combined reach of 75%. If the ad is run three times (frequency), then the total GRP is 225.

$$GRP = 75 \times 3$$
$$= 225$$

Impact on Decision Making

GRP is a cumulative measure of individual rating points used to measure the exposure of specific marketing campaigns or programs. As a gross measure, it includes audience duplication, which refers to the number of people or households exposed to a particular ad multiple times. Duplication is important to note because GRPs can, and often do, exceed 100% of the target population. This duplication can mislead marketers to believing that GRPs are a clear measure of impact when, perhaps more precisely, they measure exposures. A truer measure of impact would be any change (ideally, an increase) in sales resulting from the exposures.

If a marketer knows that the target audience needs to be exposed to the marketing campaign five times before they decide to purchase, and he/she wishes to reach 50% of the market with this campaign, then the marketer would need a media schedule that would give at least 250 GRPs (reach =50%, frequency = 5 times; 50 x 5 = 250). It is very important for marketers to review each marketing vehicle to determine its specific GRP so that the total marketing campaign can be effectively maximized to achieve overall campaign goals.

As with reach, the data to determine GRP is found in the media kits of the selected advertising vehicles. Radio, television, print and online media sources provide data describing their target customers in demographic and, increasingly, psychographic terms. These customer profiles help advertisers decide if the target audience of the proposed media vehicle is suitable for their marketing needs. The media companies use the data to defend their pricing strategies, charging different prices depending on the size and location in the publication or the time of day and length for broadcast vehicles.

GRP is used in both marketing planning and performance review. In measuring the effectiveness of their marketing campaigns, marketers would be wise to take the added step of comparing the media kit data to the actual GRP performance for the medium used, to determine any variance, either better or worse, from the marketing plan. The actual performance data is based on audited "post-buy" information, usually collected by a third party market research firm to measure each of the media companies in the specific market or vehicle chosen.

Using reach, frequency and GRP together, let's assume there are ten households in a specific market. In this market there are also two television channels—Channels A and B. Your company has decided to run a television advertisement on both channels. Six of the ten households watch Channel A and two of the ten households watch Channel B. During the course of the working week (Monday-Friday), the ad runs on the following schedule:

- Monday = 3 x
- Tuesday = 2 x
- Wednesday = 3 x
- Thursday = 1 x
- Friday = 2 x

Reach, GRP and frequency are as follows:

- Reach = 80%
  - each house represents 10% of the selected market and eight households watch either of these channels (8 × 10% = 80%)

- GRP = 140
  - each house is 10% of the market, therefore each time the ad runs it represents a rating of 10.

Monday = 30 rating

Tuesday = 20 rating

Wednesday = 30 rating

Thursday = 10 rating

Friday = 20 rating

Total   110 GRPs

- Frequency = 13.75 (110 GRPs / 8 households = 13.75)

Once marketers know their marketing objectives, along with their budget constraints, they can then determine the media vehicles that are most appropriate. Reach, frequency and GRP are useful measures that help a marketer evaluate the effectiveness of their final media decisions. Before evaluating the appropriateness of a particular media choice, a marketer needs to be clear on the kind of product they have, the marketing objectives required and the target audience they wish to reach. For example, newer products usually require greater emphasis on building awareness, which may dictate a higher frequency of exposure than needed by more mature products. Therefore, the marketer's objectives will be different in the early stages of a product's lifecycle versus later stages. In fact, the product lifecycle is an important influence on the marketing choices made and, consequently, the specific media needed. Figure 14 illustrates the point.

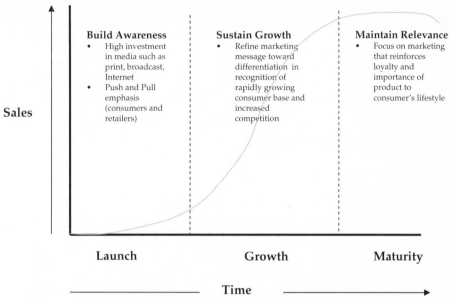

Figure 14: Product Lifecycle Stage Impact on Marketing Choices

This graph is a variation on the classic "S" curve (the name is derived from the shape of the curve) that illustrates the product lifecycle. While an overall marketing campaign for a product will likely have a long-term objective (such as to achieve 50% market share) and theme (for example, to be recognized as the most reliable), a product evolves over time from being unknown to, ideally, being well known. Each of the stages shown above will have different marketing objectives and, consequently, different media will be needed. Gross rating points will vary at each stage as well, reflecting the evolving marketing campaign.

Media choices will also be influenced by the kind of product, such as whether it is a simple product like soap, or a complex product like enterprise software. Complex products may require a higher frequency than simpler ones because they take longer to explain and to facilitate understanding. Furthermore, the specific media will vary as well. The marketing of complex products is likely to be more effective in information-intensive media, such as print ads in vertical trade media (versus using billboards, for example, since they tend to be better for simpler products and messages). Different geographic markets also affect media choices. The developing markets in Southeast Asia may not be familiar with a particular company's products, even if that company is well-known elsewhere. This may influence marketers to increase the frequency so as to ensure the target audience is sufficiently exposed to the message. Cultural differences will also affect a marketer's choice of media vehicle, frequency and reach.

Finally, the quality of the exposure is another important consideration when interpreting GRPs. A marketer needs to be aware that the target audience may "see" an ad, but may not be listening to the description or reading the content. Therefore, subtle messages may be missed by the target audience. This is an issue if a marketer discovers that a campaign with high GRPs, that looked strong on paper, actually yields a low return in terms of sales generated or negligible market share increases. Marketers will then need to review the relevance of the campaign content, the creative execution and even their understanding of the target audience to determine why a campaign may not achieve targeted results.

Endnote

1 Davis, J. *Magic Numbers for Consumer Marketing.* John Wiley & Sons (Asia) Pte Ltd., 2005: pp.241-242.

Sources

http://www.nielsenmedia.com/ratings101.htm

http://www.mediacampaign.org/publications/message99/2_5.html

Doyle, C. *Collins Internet-Linked Dictionary of Marketing.* HarperCollins Publishers, 2003, 2005: p.154.

Best, R.J. *Market-Based Management: Strategies for Growing Customer Value and Profitability.* New Jersey: Pearson Education, 2005: p.308.

Cost Per Gross Rating Point

Measurement Need

Advertisers plan their broadcast media buying based on target audience statistics of the proposed media vehicle and also gross rating points (GRPs—see Chapter 42). Their final media choice will be affected by the budgeted dollars available for that media, so marketers need to measure the cost per gross rating point, or cost per point (CPP).

Solution[1]

The formula for CPP is:

$$CPP = \frac{TC_{at}}{GRP_{Tt}}$$

Where

CPP = cost per gross rating point

TC_{at} = total cost of selected advertising in time period t

GRP_{Tt} = total gross rating points during time period t

CPP tells advertisers how much it will cost to reach one rating point (1% of the market). In Chapter 42, we illustrated GRPs using a hypothetical World Cup example. In that example, a company's advertising choice yielded a GRP of 225. If the cost for television ads during the World Cup was $100,000, then the CPP is $444:

$$CPP = \frac{\$100,000}{225}$$

$$= \$444$$

Impact on Decision Making

CPP helps marketers compare media options to determine those that yield the best cost per gross rating point. Cost alone will not determine the decision, as marketers also must consider target audience profiles of the various media choices, overall pricing differences that may allow better placement (such as a better time slot) and higher frequency (see Chapter 41) on certain media options (perhaps because that particular media is rated lower than the others. U.S. readers will note the regular ratings battles among the major networks ABC, CBS, NBC, CNN and Fox). CPP is a good measure of advertising efficiency, assuming common media are being compared (comparing TV stations, for example). CPP serves a dual measurement purpose: evaluative—comparing two or more media choices; and planning—helping advertisers plan the ideal media mix based on available budget, media audience profile, and time slot placement.

Endnote

1 Formula derived from Imber, J. and Toffler, B. *Dictionary of Marketing Terms*. Barron's Educational Services, Inc.. 2000: p.143.

Sources

Davis, J. *Magic Numbers for Consumer Marketing*. Singapore: John Wiley & Sons (Asia) Pte Ltd., 2005: pp.243-242.

Museum of Broadcast Communications, http://www.museum.tv/archives/etv/C/htmlC/cost-per-thou/cost-per-thou.htm

American Marketing Association: http://www.marketingpower.com/content17783.php

Sales Premiums 44

Measurement Need

When planning growth opportunities, marketers need to determine how to generate new or renewed interest in their products. This effort includes considering the advantages and disadvantages of offering a gift or bonus if the consumer chooses to purchase, versus advertising.

Solution

There is no formula for sales premiums. Their usage is one of many tools marketers use to influence sales of a key product or service. The use of sales premiums must be evaluated with the same scrutiny used to determine the attractiveness of advertising, direct mail or promotional discounts since each of these, while inspiring an increase in sales, incurs additional costs and, therefore, reduces margins.

Sales premiums are promotional items given to prospective customers as an incentive to purchase a product or service. Examples include coffee mugs, pens, t-shirts, Post-it® pads, mouse pads, glow sticks, magnetic business cards, toasters and more. The limit is the imagination of the marketer and the relevance to the target product to be sold. Marketers use messages like "Free Gift with Purchase" to generate interest in the product and its corresponding sales premium.

Marketers should calculate a break-even units-sold level without the sales premium, then factor in the cost of the premium to determine the new break-even level. If the marketer's judgment suggests that the break-even level is achievable with the inclusion of the sales premium, then it should be used.

Impact on Decision Making

Years ago, some banks in the U.S. would offer a free appliance (such as a toaster) as a premium or incentive to attract new customers. The appliance cost the banks little if a customer actually opened an account and stayed with the bank for a minimum period of time, during which the bank could generate income from fees, interest charges and other services used by the customer. The upfront cost was higher than the initial benefit because there was not a one-to-one relationship between the number of appliances acquired on behalf of the promotion and the number of new customers who opened an account directly as a result. Nevertheless, this form of sales premium served to bring in customers.

More recent examples include video-game consoles and bundled games. The product to be sold is the console, but the bundled games are the premium added to encourage purchase. The games provided free with purchase are rarely the most popular games. But the premium succeeds because a customer that acquires the console (and the free game) learns he or she enjoys playing and returns to the retailer to buy more games. The marketer effectively creates an ongoing revenue stream from each customer acquired by this program, assuming the customer is a dedicated gamer. The reason is simple: the premium game inspired the purchase of the console; playing the console then inspired the purchase of more games; as new games are subsequently introduced, customers' desire for these grows as well and leads to more purchases. Furthermore, premiums can be useful in attracting "premium customers"—customers who become loyal to the product or company. The marketer's challenge is forecasting demand accurately enough to "know" that the cost of the premium is paid for by the sales of the targeted product—hence the need to calculate break-even before the promotion runs.

Sources

American Marketing Association: http://www.marketingpower.com/mg-dictionary-view2483.php

Imber, J. and Toffler, B. *Dictionary of Marketing Terms*. Barron's Educational Series, Inc., 2000: p.433.

Kotler, P., Siew, M.L., Swee, H. A. and Tan, C.T. *Marketing Management: A Strategic Perspective*. Prentice Hall Pearson Education Asia Pte Ltd., 2003: p.654.

Davis, J. *Magic Numbers for Consumer Marketing*. Singapore: John Wiley & Sons (Asia) Pte Ltd., 2005: pp.207-212.

Promotion Profit[1] 45

Measurement Need

Marketing promotions are designed to increase sales over the duration of the promotion, with the hope that some of the customers acquired from the promotion become loyal over the long-term. Since promotions convey special offers, such as limited time discounts, sales volume will increase, but margins on each product sold will decrease. Marketers need to measure the profit resulting from their promotional campaigns.

In an article from the *California Management Review* entitled "The Three Faces of Consumer Promotions", the authors persuasively argue that promotions work in three ways:

1. Economic value: the value resulting from the discount

2. Information content: the message implied by the discount. This can be positive or negative to the consumer. Perhaps a discount is seen as an offer to try a new product. Alternatively, the consumer may see the discount as a ruse to sell older or lower quality products

3. Affective appeal: the feeling aroused by the discount

Solution

The formula for promotion profit is:

$$PP = \{U_{id} \times (M_r - D)\} + \{U_i \times M_r\} - \{U_{bd} \times D\} - C_p + (\pm CE)$$

Where

PP = promotion profit

U_{id} = incremental units sold on deal

M_r = margin r

D = discount

U_i = undiscounted incremental units sold

U_{bd} = base units sold on deal

C_p = promo costs

$\pm CE$ = positive vs. negative carryover effects

The first group of variables, $\{U_{id} \times (M_r - D)\}$, measures the additional profit made from incremental sales due to the promotional discount. The second group, $\{U_i \times M_r\}$, measures the incremental sales of units at the regular price. The third group, $\{U_{bd} \times D\}$, measures baseline sales sold at the discounted price. The fourth variable, C_p, measures the cost of the promotion, and the final group, $(\pm CE)$, measures the net value of any positive carryover effects over negative carryover effects. Carryover effects are the feelings consumers have from taking advantage of the deal: fortunate versus skeptical, for example.

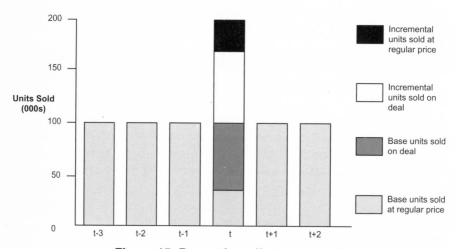

Figure 15: Promotion effect on sales[2]

The graph illustrates an increase of 100,000 units sold during the promotion period (assume one week). A total of 100,000 units were sold in each of the non-promotion weeks. While the promotion increased units sold, the next step is determining if the promotion was profitable. The authors state that the face value of the promotion was $0.50, versus the regular $0.80 margin. Per the chart, incremental unit sales at the discounted price totaled 70,000 units, creating a $21,000 profit (70,000 units × $0.30. Sales from baseline units sold on discount resulted in a $30,000 reduction below normal dollar volume since 60,000 units were sold at the promotion's face value of $0.50 (a loss since the baseline level of dollar sales without the discount would have been $0.50 per unit higher). So the promotion did not make an economic profit since the 70,000 units of incremental sales resulted in a $21,000 profit, yet the 60,000 units of baseline sales were at a $30,000 loss. Looking at the top bar of the chart during time period t, incremental unit sales at regular prices totaled 30,000, creating a $24,000 profit for those units (30,000 x $0.80 {the full margin}). The end result is a $15,000 profit before promotion costs and any positive/negative carryover effects:

$$PP = \{70,000 \times (\$0.80 - \$0.50)\} + \{30,000 \times \$0.80\} - \{60,000 \times \$0.50\} - C_p + (\pm CE)$$

$$PP = \{70,000 \times \$0.30\} + \$24,000 - \$30,000 - C_p + (\pm CE)$$

$$PP = \$21,000 + \$24,000 - \$30,000 - C_p + (\pm CE)$$

$$PP = \$45,000 - \$30,000 - C_p + (\pm CE)$$

$$PP = \$15,000 - C_p + (\pm CE)$$

Impact on Decision Making

An interesting aspect to this analysis of promotions is the differences between incremental and baseline sales at both the discounted and regular prices. Promotions should generate additional sales volume, but the greater challenge is doing so profitably. The analysis indicates there is a baseline (or steady state) level of sales that occurs every week, irrespective of promotions. When a promotion runs, baseline sales are then divided into regular price sales and discount price sales, resulting in a loss over what would have occurred during a normal, non-promotion cycle. Incremental sales can determine whether the promotion effects resulted in a profit or loss since they, too, are comprised of regular and discounted sales. Marketers must account for these different sales groups when planning promotions. If their planning indicates a positive outcome, as shown here, then the promotion can go forward. Actual results will inevitably differ from plan, so the marketer should review the actual promotion results with the same analytical rigor applied in the planning stages.

Marketers will gain insight into the economic effects of promotions, while also gleaning some of the psychological impact, since the promotion alters buying patterns from baseline performance. The challenge is for marketers to gather information on sales performance trends, knowledge of their target customers and their potential response to the promotion, and reasonable judgment about the after-effects of any promotion. This analysis is a blend of art and science that is the core of marketing decision making.

Endnotes

1 Grande, H., Inman, J.J. and Raghubir, P. "The Three Faces of Consumer Promotions". *California Management Review*, Vol. 46, No. 4 Summer 2004: pp.30-34.

2 Ibid., p.32.

Response Rate 46

Measurement Need

Companies face increasing pressure to improve efficiency and reduce costs. Senior management expects marketing management to provide more relevant and direct information on the investment return from each marketing communications campaign conducted. However, this is impractical and ill advised since the purpose of many marketing activities is to shape perceptions through large scale advertising and marketing communications campaigns. Nevertheless, many of marketing's activities, including direct marketing, can be measured. Measurements can be made with a higher degree of precision if ad campaigns are properly coded and the ensuing responses are correlated back to the originating campaign.

One of the marketing areas where more accurate measurement is feasible is direct marketing campaigns (such as direct mail or online permission marketing). Marketers want to measure the total number of advertisements (or mailers, or offers) they send and compare it to the number of customers who responded by clicking through or, best of all, actually purchasing. Marketers want as high a correlation as possible between total advertisements and the total number of customers who responded to the ads.

Solution[1]

The response rate refers to the percentage of people who respond to an offer relative to the number of people who received the offer. The following formula captures the key variables:

$$R_r = \frac{P_r}{P_e}$$

Where

R_r = response rate

P_r = number of people who respond to your ad

P_e = number of people exposed to your ad

If a company targets 10,000 people in its direct marketing campaign and receives 200 responses, then its response rate is:

$$R_r = \frac{200}{10,000}$$

$$= 2\%$$

Impact on Decision Making

The response rate is a basic measure that can indicate the percentage of people who find the offer attractive. If they respond, then this can lead to purchase, but it is not a guarantee. Turning direct marketing responses into actual purchasers is described by the conversion rate in Chapter 47. A response may also be a request for additional information. This depends on the wording in the offer. If it is clear to recipients that they will somehow benefit by responding (such as a price discount on a favorite product, or a free gift with purchase), then the chance of converting them to actual buyers increases. However, if the offer is somewhat vague, such as describing a "hot new feature" but no other benefit or clear relevance to the target customer, then a lower purchase rate is likely.

Direct marketing has proven over the years to be most successful when it is offering a tangible benefit that can be easily obtained, in contrast to developing general awareness which tends to be accomplished more effectively by broadcast advertising. Direct marketing also works well for shorter-term promotions aimed at increase immediate demand and revenues. Classic marketing theory suggests that if you can convince customers to buy your product, then you have a better chance of making them loyal customers. Of course, that is dependent on your commitment to quality, service and products that are relevant. That is not as easy as it sounds.

Marketers need to be aware that response rates vary depending on the direct marketing vehicle used. The following table[2] from the Direct Marketing Association lists the average response rates by media. For the curious reader, the revenue per contact refers to the actual dollars of sales generated from each buyer, promo cost per contact describes the average cost to reach the individual target customer, and the ROI index is the ratio of revenue per contact to promo cost per contact.

Table 19: Response Rate ROI Index

Media	Revenue Per Contact	Promo Cost Per Contact	Average Response Rates	ROI Index
Telephone	$45.37	$2.50	5.78	18.20
E-Mail	$1.60	$0.10	1.12	16.00
Dimensional Mail	$14.16	$0.91	2.30	15.30
Direct Mail	$11.36	$0.56	1.88	14.90
Newspaper	$0.45	$0.05	0.09	8.80
Coupons	$1.50	$0.23	1.65	6.50
Catalog	$1.48	$0.69	2.18	6.40
Inserts	$0.49	$0.14	0.45	3.50
Magazine	$0.22	$0.11	0.13	2.00
FSIs	$0.12	$0.07	0.13	1.60
Radio	$0.08	$0.07	0.10	1.20
DRTV	$0.02	$0.03	0.04	0.70

As Table 19 indicates, the revenues received, costs and response rates vary significantly depending on the media selected. Direct marketing is an effective tool when marketers and management establish clear objectives about the purpose of the campaign, design an offer that is relevant to the target audience, and set a time limit in which the offer will remain valid. Direct marketing is generally ineffective for general awareness building, primarily due to the higher per person cost versus broadcast campaigns that can reach many times more people. Therefore, marketers should resist creating awareness-building direct marketing programs to the general population, since they tend to yield a low response. A proven in-house list of target customers is an ideal audience, since they are already familiar with the company and its products. A third-party list can be quite good, if the marketer understands her target audience clearly and if the third-party vendor has a reputation for providing high-quality names. But a good customer list is only one step towards an improved response rate. Marketers must combine this with a relevant message and the best media to reach the target customer most effectively.

The target audience names come from the marketer's database, a third-party database, or a combination of these two. The numbers in the formula are derived from the marketer's own statistics based on their specific direct-marketing objectives and activities. If the marketer's goal was to generate 400 favorable responses from the 10,000 people reached in the initial target audience, then the 2% response in the example is low. If the goal is a higher response rate, then marketers should use a reputable list comprised of either current or previous customers, or a list of customers who appear to fit the target audience profile.

Endnotes

1 Davis, J. *Magic Numbers for Consumer Marketing*. Singapore: John Wiley & Sons (Asia) Pte Ltd., 2005: pp.241-242.

2 "2004 Response Rate Report"by the U.S. Direct Marketing Association

Sources

http://www.the-dma.org/cgi/dispnewsstand?article=2891

http://www.dbmarketing.com/articles/Art108.htm

http://www.marketingprofs.com/2/62percent.asp

Conversion Rate

Measurement Need

Marketers want to measure how many of the customers who responded to an ad or promotional offer convert to purchasing customers.

Solution[1]

The conversion rate is the percentage of prospective customers or visitors (to a website) who both respond and buy a company's products and services.

$$C_r = \frac{P_b}{P_r}$$

Where

C_r = conversion rate

P_b = number of people who both respond and buy

P_r = number of people who respond to your ad

In Chapter 46, we introduced the response rate and cautioned that customers who respond to a direct marketing campaign are not necessarily buyers yet. Continuing with Chapter 46's example, if 75 of the 200 responses actually buy the product, then the conversion rate is 37.5%.

$$C_r = \frac{75}{200}$$

$$= 37.5\%$$

Impact on Decision Making

Without question, companies should strive for a high conversion rate, because this is an indication that their offer was attractive enough to both warrant a response and a purchase. Achieving a high conversion rate depends on many variables, including the relevance and appeal of the offer to the target customer, how easily accessible the offer is, the visual design, appropriate price, and how it compares to competing offers. With this list of qualifiers, it does appear to be a daunting task to develop a successful campaign. But that is the beauty of marketing—it is part art and part science. Marketers must be able to balance the quantitative performance demands with the qualitative aspects of sound judgment. Additionally, marketers must market their plans and ideas inside their own organizations if they want to achieve internal support and, consequently, deliver on the promises their programs make to the marketplace.

Similarly to the response rate's limitations, the conversion rate is highest when the marketer is exceedingly clear in his objectives, target audience identification and message design. An appropriately chosen direct marketing media is also important. To achieve high conversion and response rates, marketers must exercise surgical precision in their marketing efforts and resist the temptation to develop a one size fits all campaign. By using direct marketing for its intended purposes—to build either a relationship with loyal customers or general short-term increases in sales through promotional offers—the resulting rates will likely satisfy the marketing campaign objectives.

The data for the number of people who actually buy will be captured in the company's chart of accounts on a regular basis (daily if online, or weekly/monthly for other retailers). More specifically, it will be contained in the customer accounts summary (or its equivalent), either in the sales department, customer service or a similar order-taking department. A sophisticated marketing operation will also keep track of customers who bought products as a result of any direct marketing campaign by putting a reference code in the campaign message asking consumers to mention the code to receive the special offer. Similar types of reference tags can be used to track response to specific campaigns.

Endnote

1 Davis, J. *Magic Numbers for Consumer Marketing.* Singapore: John Wiley & Sons (Asia) Pte Ltd., 2005: pp.268-269.

Sources

Doyle, C. *Collins Internet-Linked Dictionary of Marketing*. HarperCollins Publishers, 2003, 2005: p.104.

http://www.marketingprofs.com/2/ignoremarketing.asp

Direct Mail Revenue Goals[1] 48

Measurement Need

The Four Ps of the marketing mix—product, price, place, promotion—are useful to marketers as planning frameworks when preparing to enter the market with new or improved products. The marketing activities marketers choose are designed to improve the company's competitive performance, including increasing growth. When marketers use direct mail, it is done to reach a specific target segment with a clear message and/or offer that inspires the prospective customer to respond by purchasing. When a direct mail campaign is designed to produce a certain level of new revenue, the marketer needs to ascertain how many mailers must be sent to achieve the revenue goal.

Solution

Direct mail revenue goals measure the effectiveness of the marketer's direct mail advertising by setting a revenue target, then determining the number of direct mail pieces that need to be sent to achieve that target.

$$DM = \frac{R_t}{S_a \times R_r \times C_r}$$

Where

DM = number of direct-mail pieces

R_t = revenue target

S_a = average sale

R_r = response rate

C_r = conversion rate

Let's assume a retail marketer whose company sells toys is interested in increasing its revenue by $40,000 and she wants to know how many direct-mail pieces to send to achieve the revenue target. She knows from experience that out of 200 customers who visit the store each day, 150 buy products. This gives her a conversion rate of 75% (for more on this, see Chapter 47 about the conversion rate). Those who buy spend an average of $30. The marketer has done her homework on the industry and knows that the average response rate is 2% for direct-mail campaigns promoting toys.

$$DM = \frac{\$40,000}{\$30 \times 0.02 \times 0.75}$$

$$= 88,889 \text{ pieces}$$

If this marketer is quite clever, she might be able to create a message that is so compelling that it increases the response rate to 5%. This improvement would decrease the number of mailing pieces she needs to send to 35,555 pieces, which would also reduce the amount of money she would have to spend on printing and postage.

$$DM = \frac{\$40,000}{\$30 \times 0.05 \times 0.75}$$

$$= 35,555 \text{ pieces}$$

Impact on Decision Making

The benefit of direct mail revenue goals is that they help marketers set specific revenue and resulting cost targets for a given campaign. In the case of the example used above, another benefit is that the retailer gains 1,333 new customers ($88,889 \times 0.02 \times 0.75$) who might develop long-term loyalty. While this particular campaign may produce the $40,000 revenue increase the marketer is seeking and convert those buyers into loyal customers over the long-term, it also has the potential to convert those who do not initially respond into future customers. Since they are now aware of the company and its products, they add to the retailer's customer foundation and create, in effect, an ongoing customer revenue stream.

These benefits are partly due to direct mail's effectiveness as a marketing tool that generates a specific response from target customers based on crafting a relevant offer. Marketers can set a revenue target and can expect to generate measurable results tied specifically to the campaign. This degree of measurement precision is harder to achieve with general awareness marketing, like television or radio broadcast ads, because they are designed to develop an image rather than inspire a call to action for customers.

Direct mail revenue goals are a useful measure for specific campaigns, but ongoing success with this format requires marketers to have unique offers each time that are relevant to the target customer's needs and are consistent with their company's strategic objectives. Since direct mail is often used for promotional offers, it is challenging for companies to regularly offer limited time period discounts without the risk of training their customers to always wait until the next price promotion. Furthermore, frequent promotions may erode brand value at both the product and corporate level if done too frequently.

Direct mail is also used to develop a one-to-one dialog with loyal customers, enabling marketers to tailor their messages accordingly. While customer loyalty is certainly an important goal for most companies and marketers, actually developing it requires more than setting revenue targets for specific loyalty-building campaigns. The message to loyal customers must resonate with them, suggesting to them that the company truly understands their needs and, perhaps even more importantly, that their continued loyalty is appreciated. As with many other marketing metrics, the measurement is the easy part. The development of the right strategy and campaign that yields the desired results is quite challenging, however.

Marketers may be tempted to adjust the metrics in the formula to fit their revenue goals, irrespective of industry or competitor response and conversion rate averages. The challenge is remaining realistic about the expected performance of a campaign, since its success depends on many factors: the right target audience; a well-conceived campaign and message; imaginative creative design; a product that the customer wants; and the right offer. These various criteria are critical components of the marketer's overall plan. Yet even if these are each executed flawlessly, there is still the chance that the target audience will not respond as expected, since it is quite difficult to predict actual behavior. Therefore, marketers are encouraged to review past campaigns and those of competitors to determine the strengths and weaknesses of each marketing program.

These statistics are found in specific reports within the marketer's company. For example, revenue targets are usually established at the corporate level, then translated into more specific targets for each product line or retail outlet. Average sales statistics will be based on company averages and, while possibly found in end of year financial statements, are more likely to be contained in the product line or per-store profit and loss reports as a footnote measure. Chapters 46 and 47 provide guidance on the response rate and conversion rate statistics, respectively.

Endnote

1 Egelhoff, T. "Direct Mail: Why it Works and How to Use It". www.smalltownmarketing. com.

Source

Davis, J. *Magic Numbers for Consumer Marketing*. Singapore: John Wiley & Sons (Asia) Pte Ltd., 2005: pp.270-272.

Direct Mail Profit Goals[1]

Measurement Need

When setting a direct mail campaign profit goal, a marketer will need to estimate the number of direct mail pieces that need to be sent to achieve the goal.

Solution

The formula for direct mail profit goals uses target profitability levels to help marketers determine the number of direct mail pieces that need to be sent. The formula is nearly identical to that for direct mail revenue goals, except that the denominator includes the target profit percentage, as follows:

$$DMPG = \frac{R_t}{S_a \times P \times R_r \times C_r}$$

Where

$DMPG$ = direct mail profit goals

R_t = revenue target

S_a = average sale

P = profit goal in percentage terms

R_r = response rate

C_r = close ratio

Continuing with the example of our marketer selling toys from Chapter 48, let's assume that her target profit margin is 30%. This factor is added to the formula as follows:

$$DMP = \frac{\$40,000}{\$30 \times 0.30 \times 0.02 \times 0.75}$$

$$= 296{,}296 \text{ direct mail pieces}$$

The impact of this on the cost of her mailing campaign is significant. If, as we discussed in Chapter 48, the marketer were to create an offer that would yield a 5% response, then it reduces the size of the required mailing to 118,519 pieces to achieve the same profit target.

$$DMP = \frac{\$40,000}{\$30 \times 0.30 \times 0.05 \times 0.75}$$

$$= 118{,}519 \text{ direct mail pieces}$$

Impact on Decision Making

The benefits and risks are similar to those with direct mail revenue goals. Whether or not a particular profit goal is feasible for a given business will be partly determined by a profitability analysis for its industry and a keen knowledge of the competitor dynamics.

Establishing profit goals is an important aspect of any business, and it is increasingly important to marketers. While a marketing campaign may generate revenue, the challenge is whether it is profitable. Marketers determine spending allocations based on overall company goals and specific product budgets. For a new product launch, a marketer may decide that revenue generation is more important than profitability, driven by the goal to develop awareness quickly. This may even be acceptable for several concurrent marketing programs within the context of an overall marketing plan, since a profitable performance for the entire company is generally more important than success with any specific product line. However, marketers must think carefully how to transition from revenue growth to profit growth as products mature and customers change. The direct mail campaign should include profit targets as a result.

Endnote

1 Egelhoff, T. "Direct Mail: Why it Works and How to Use it". www.smalltownmarketing.com.

Source

Davis, J. *Magic Numbers for Consumer Marketing*. Singapore: John Wiley & Sons (Asia) Pte Ltd., 2005: pp.272-274.

Direct Mail Gross Profit[1]

50

Measurement Need

Chapter 49, Direct Mail Profit Goals, showed how to calculate the number of direct mail pieces needed to achieve a specific profit goal. Alternatively, marketers might select a specific number of mail pieces to be sent, perhaps based on response rates for their business. So they need to determine if a campaign of a certain size will produce a gross profit.

Solution

This calculation tells you whether your direct mail campaign produces a positive gross profit.

$$P_g = DM \times P \times S_a \times R_r \times C_r$$

Where

P_g = gross profit

DM = number of direct marketing pieces

P = profit goal in percentage terms

S_a = average sale

R_r = response rate

C_r = conversion rate

Let's plug in the numbers from Chapters 48 and 49, in which we used the example of the toy retailer:

$$P_g = 88,889 \times 0.30 \times \$30 \times 0.02 \times 0.75$$
$$= \$12,000$$

Impact on Decision Making

The marketer's gross profit looks quite good and, at this stage, it would indicate that she should go forward with the campaign. However, it would be smart for her and her team to check the net profit to ensure that this is the right move. This will be discussed in Chapter 51, Direct Mail Net Profit.

Positive gross profits are an important first step in determining the success of a direct mail campaign. Certainly, a marketer ought not to proceed with additional mailings of a similar design if this initial calculation reveals a loss.

Endnote

1 Egelhoff, Tom, "Direct Mail: Why It Works and How to Use It". www.smalltownmarketing. com.

Source

Davis, J. *Magic Numbers for Consumer Marketing*. Singapore: John Wiley & Sons (Asia) Pte Ltd., 2005: pp.274-276.

Direct Mail Net Profit[1]

51

Measurement Need

Continuing our direct mail measurement, the marketer needs to determine net profitability from the direct mail campaign.

Solution

Net profit is gross profit minus operating expenses. Calculating this helps you determine if your direct mail campaign produces a positive net profit. This is virtually identical to the formula for direct mail gross profit, with one new component—operating expenses (cost of direct mail campaign, in this case):

$$P_g = DM \times P \times S_a \times R_r \times C_r - C_{dm}$$

Where

P_g = gross profit

DM = number of direct marketing pieces

P = profit goal in percentage terms

S_a = average sale

R_r = response rate

C_r = conversion rate

C_{dm} = cost of the direct mail campaign

Using the same numbers as before, let's now include the cost of the direct mail campaign. In this case, the toy marketing manager outsourced the design and printing work, which cost her $8,000.

$$P_g = 88{,}889 \times 0.30 \times \$30 \times 0.02 \times 0.75 - \$8{,}000$$
$$= \$4{,}000$$

Impact on Decision Making

Our toy marketing manager now knows that her campaign estimates indicate she will produce a net profit. The point to this particular sequence is to demonstrate the various levels of analysis needed to determine the efficacy of a direct marketing campaign. Numerous factors are within the direct control of any company: goals, size of mailing list, content of the offer and industry metrics. The harder area to control is consumer behavior. There is no guarantee that, despite analytical rigor and an elegant business plan, customers will respond as hoped. But knowing this can help marketers develop a certain creativity and patience in their marketing efforts. Doing so will enable marketers to learn which activities work best, as well as those that missed the mark.

Endnote

1 Egelhoff, Tom, "Direct Mail: Why It Works and How to Use It". www.smalltownmarketing.com.

Source

Davis, J. *Magic Numbers for Consumer Marketing*. Singapore: John Wiley & Sons (Asia) Pte Ltd., 2005: pp.241-242.

Direct Mail ROI[1]

52

Measurement Need

As with many proposed expenditures, a company's leaders want to know the return on investment for a given project. Direct mail's potential as a one-to-one marketing tool can be powerful, but years of "junk" mail (and now "spam"—the online equivalent) have jaded consumers, resulting in mailers being thrown away by the target audience before being read. Marketers know that response rates can make or break a marketing campaign, and to justify the risk to senior management, marketers need to measure the investment return.

Solution

Direct mail ROI is the return on your direct mail investment.

$$ROI = \frac{((DM \times R_r \times C_r \times S_a) - C)}{C}$$

Where

DM = total number of direct-marketing pieces sent

R_r = response rate

C_r = conversion rate of people who actually made a purchase

S_a = average sales per purchase

C = total cost of direct-mail campaign

Let's assume our toy marketer from Chapters 48-51 has decided to market a premium specialty toy by sending direct mail pieces to 250,000 target customers at a total cost of $200,000. The marketer's research indicates that specialty direct mail campaigns such as this tend to get a very high response rate of 25%. Of the 250,000 people targeted, the marketer anticipates that 62,500 will respond and that many more consumers will visit the website and buy merchandise. The toy company expects 10% of the respondents, 6,250 people, to convert to sales. Furthermore, based on previous direct mail experience with similar toy products, the average amount spent per customer is $100. The calculation is as follows:

$$ROI = \frac{((250,000 \times 0.25 \times 0.10 \times \$100) - \$200,000)}{\$200,000}$$

$$= 213\%$$

This campaign's return on investment is 213%, certainly a substantial and positive result.

Impact on Decision Making

As with any ROI calculation, direct mail ROI will provide marketers with an indication of the success of a particular investment. In this instance, we examined an expected mailing, response and conversion. The final test would be to revisit this ROI after the event and compare the projected and actual performance results. But from these preliminary forecasts, it is apparent that this is an attractive marketing opportunity. There are online ROI calculators that marketers can use specifically to assess direct mail performance, including:

- The American Marketing Association http://www. marketingpower.com/content2806C4842.php.

- The Schraff Group http://www.schraff.com/adv/helpdesk/direct_ response_roi_calculator.php

- Contemporary Communication Specialists http://www.mailcci. com/direct_mail_ROI.asp

- Marketingprofs.com http://www.marketingprofs.com/2/ directmailreturn.asp

Marketers do not have the luxury of telling their bosses to approve spending requests for marketing programs, unless the program can demonstrate a reasonable ROI before the budget money is approved. Direct marketing return on investment is a good tool to use to review the potential return of a future campaign. It is, of course, even better if the marketer uses post-campaign actual numbers to review the true success. As cautioned throughout this book, the success of any marketing program will depend on many factors beyond the control of the formulas that measure performance. Marketers must make the effort to understand their target customers as thoroughly as possible so that the best possible campaign can be designed. Doing this increases the chances of the marketing program's success.

As with the marketing metrics concerned with direct marketing, the data quality for understanding ROI depends on the direct mail list being used (in-house, third-party, random), and the number of responses will usually depend on how many pieces are mailed and the offer described in the direct mail piece. Also, the response and conversion rates depend on the promotional offer and, to a lesser extent, industry trends. In each case, these rates will vary, so marketers should know the benchmark metrics for their industry, and their company's objectives, in advance. This knowledge will make it is easier to measure success once the campaign is under way.

Endnote

1 Marketingprofs.com http://www.marketingprofs.com/Faqs/showfaq.
   asp?ID=137&CatID=10

Source

Davis, J. *Magic Numbers for Consumer Marketing*. Singapore: John Wiley & Sons (Asia) Pte Ltd., 2005: pp.278-280

Click-Through Rates

Click-Through Rates   53

Measurement Need

Marketers want to learn whether their online advertising is generating interest with Internet users. Online advertising typically uses banner ads, interstitials and links (such as those found on Google search pages). Banner ads are simple online graphic ads with one or two lines of copy, similar to a conventional banner. Interstitials are online ads that are longer in content and larger in size than banners. They usually appear between content pages as a user is clicking from one section to the next. Pop-up ads are another form of interstitial.

Solution

The click-through rate measures user response to online advertising and is calculated with the following formula:

$$CTR = \frac{C_a}{V_a} \times 100\%$$

Where

    CTR = click-through rate

    C_a = number of clicks on an advertisement

    V_a = number of views of an advertisement

A banner placed on Amazon.com and viewed by 100,000 people, may be clicked by 3,000 people. The click-through rate is 3%.

$$CTR = \frac{3,000}{100,000} \times 100\%$$
$$= 3\%$$

Impact on Decision Making

Marketers must be clear on what click-through rate measures. It measures people who clicked on a specific ad that routed them to a different website. For the marketer working for the firm that placed the online ad, they need to separate total visits to their site from those who visited as the result of specifically clicking on the ad. The latter will be a smaller number, but it will also suggest whether this form of advertising is yielding the results sought.

One of the benefits of online advertising is the immediate feedback it provides marketers. If the ad is promoting a special offer to those who respond, then it is quite easy to track those who click on the ad, visit the site and buy something as a result (the conversion rate)—not just on the day, but to the hour and minute of the response. Marketers can then gauge the response rates to determine the best times to advertise online. Of course, each site, such as Yahoo! or Amazon.com, has its own advertising rates for these ads, and these are tied to the programming schedule of the ads, with more popular web pages and times of day more expensive on a per click basis. Web tracking software comes with most website development packages, or from Internet service providers (ISPs) or can be easily coded by website developers.

Online advertising responses have become less effective in recent years, as the Internet has matured and regular users grow increasingly weary of pop-ups, floating banners and interruption ads that disrupt a web user's enjoyment of the Internet. The biggest challenge is converting the click-through rate into purchasing customers. Despite the significant advances in marketing communication options available to companies today, similar challenges confront electronic advertising as have confronted print and direct mail advertising for decades: how to generate a high response and a high conversion rate.

Source

Adapted from: http://www.marketingterms.com/dictionary/clickthrough_rate/

Gross Page Impressions (or Gross Page Requests)

54

Measurement Need

The Internet has become a key vehicle in a marketer's communications "tool box". It can be used for a wide range of functions, from a general information source, much like an electronic brochure, to a product-delivery service (software downloads, for example). Unlike print ads placed in different publications, which are difficult to measure beyond general circulation numbers, the Internet's electronic foundation allows for easy measurement across many different criteria. Overall, marketers want to measure whether their website is even being used and, if it is, how frequently.

Solution

Gross page impressions (GPI) measures a website's total traffic volume. It is the number of times any person has accessed a website, irrespective of repeat visits or unique visitors.[1] Website traffic data can be collected from web server logs, which are software programs that automatically record each and every website visit.

Impact on Decision Making

GPI is useful information for starting an analysis of marketing vehicle usage as it will suggest to marketers whether their website is generating much interest from the market overall. However, it does not reveal any specifics about the users or their web surfing choices (web surfing describes a user's online search across the Internet as they move from page to page and website to website). If marketers want more in-depth information, a third party market research firm, such as an audience measurement company, could assist. For example, marketers may want to determine the advertising potential for their website based on the traffic visiting it; using that data to sell the attractiveness to potential advertisers. GPI is a helpful measure to show potential advertisers the number of people visiting the website. Of course, many other variables will be important to advertisers, but GPI is a good starting point.

Endnote

1 www.online-publishers.org

Cost Per Click 55

Measurement Need

Each advertising medium has different pricing and payment conventions. In print and broadcast advertising, for example, cost advertisers less as they buy more print ads or airtime. Payment is usually upfront, meaning that the advertisement will not be placed until the advertiser has paid the media vehicle in full for the use of that space.

Web advertising is most often in the form of banners, interstitials and links (referenced in Chapter 53, Click-Through Rates). Marketers know how to measure the effectiveness of these ads using click-through rates, so now they must determine how to measure the cost of these ads.

Solution

Cost per click is the price paid for an Internet advertisement on a per click-through basis. Websites that offer online advertising have simple pricing structures. For example, consider a campaign where payment is based on the number of times a banner is clicked. Clicks are sold for $0.10 per click. Hence, if there are a thousand clicks per week on the banner, the total amount payable to the website for that week would be $100.

Impact on Decision Making

Advertisers must weigh costs with each media vehicle chosen. Online advertising is a simple approach, although the costs are not always obvious, since predicting the actual number of user click-throughs is difficult. Advertisers have faced the unfortunate side-effect of competitors who repeatedly click the online ad, just to increase the cost. Since per-click pricing is relatively cheaper, a competitor has to be devoted and persistent to drive up the costs. Fortunately, most websites have software tools that can determine if click-throughs are following a repetitious pattern, so that advertisers don't pay for these types of clicks. Marketers should ensure the website they have chosen has user statistics that provide guidance on the audience type. This helps marketers determine if the site reaches the desired audience.

Source

Adapted from: http://www.marketingterms.com/dictionary/clickthrough_rate/

Cost Per Action

Measurement Need

Cost per click (Chapter 55) charges per user click whether or not a paying transaction ultimately occurs. Senior management may find cost per click's lack of a guaranteed transaction too imprecise to justify their advertising expenditure; therefore, marketers need to demonstrate a stronger correlation between advertising and final sales.

Solution

Cost per action is based solely on specific results, such as sales or registrations[1] that are converted from user clicks. The website owner takes most of the advertising risk since their commissions depend on good conversion rates that translate into sales.

Let's assume your company pays $0.10 to a website for every completed transaction (and not per click) coming from a banner ad. If one thousand people visit your website daily, one hundred click on the banner and ten buy a product, then the cost of advertising on the website would be $1 per day ($0.10 $\times$ 10 sales).

Impact on Decision Making

For website owners, the decision to charge for completed transactions versus per clicks is a higher risk strategy, but it will also build confidence with customers because a cost per action payment system suggests you are willing to support your website audience claims, since you receive no payment until a transaction is completed.

For advertisers, a cost per action approach will cost more per click since you are paying for a revenue-generating result. But your marketing and senior management will likely be happier since the cost is directly related to a positive financial result.

Source

Adapted from : http://www.marketingterms.com/

Cost Per Sales Dollar 57

Measurement Need

Credit sales occur both online and at the retail level. Since credit purchases are cashless, mechanisms exist to verify that the buyer has the funds (known as a credit limit) and that the seller can accept the electronic funds transfer once the transaction is approved. The benefit to sellers is that credit transactions are credited directly into their bank accounts once the buyer is approved. However, this costs the seller processing fees since the credit issuers charge sellers for the convenience and security of electronic transactions. Another form of credit sale is the individual account established between sellers and buyers whereby sellers provide buyers a specific credit limit that allows the buyers to acquire products now and pay for them in the future, based on a regular billing cycle (usually monthly). Credit sales can turn into bad debt if a buyer does not pay his bills, costing the sellers a collection fee, which raises the cost per sale. Sellers, therefore, want to measure the cost per sales dollar of each credit sale.

Solution[1]

Cost per sales dollar is measured as follows:

$$C_{SD} = \frac{C_{oi}}{S_{ci}}$$

Where

C_{SD} = cost per sales dollar

C_{oi} = total departmental operating costs in period i

S_{ci} = total credit sales in period i

To illustrate, let's assume that a food supplier receives an order from a grocery customer for five cases of canned peaches. The supplier sends the five cases to the retailer, along with a bill with net 30 terms (meaning that the retailer must pay the bill within 30 days or an interest penalty will be charged in addition to the principal amount owed). If the retailer does not pay, then the supplier incurs collection costs from the effort to retrieve payment, ranging from a simple letter (the cost of the labor, letterhead and postage) to the retention of a collection agency at a substantially higher cost. In a one-year period, the departmental operating costs incurred to collect credit sales can be significant. Total departmental operating costs are the sum of annual fixed and annual variable costs. In our example, the supplier's costs are as follows:

$$\text{Annual Fixed Cost} = \$\,80,000$$

$$\text{Annual Variable Cost} = \$\,70,000$$

Therefore, total departmental operating cost are $150,000. If the annual revenue expected by the food supplier is $200,000, then we can calculate the cost per sales dollar:

$$C_{SD} = \frac{\$150,000}{\$200,000}$$

$$= \$0.75$$

It costs our food supplier $0.75 per dollar of credit sales generated.

Impact on Decision Making

Marketers want to minimize the costs per sales dollar for a simple reason: profits improve as the costs decline. A high cost per sales dollar may not necessarily be cause for alarm, however. Industry practices may impose a higher cost structure, so your company should compare its costs to those of the competition to determine if the result is within reason for the industry. However, marketers would be well-served by understanding the sources of the higher costs before concluding that it is acceptable to be at cost parity with the competition. Perhaps the industry is in decline and arcane practices need to be phased out.

The sources of the costs are more than the processing and collection fees. Marketers must step back and review the entire customer selection process. High costs may indicate changing segment and customer needs. High costs may also suggest that a more effective customer audit process is needed to determine the highest quality customers that pay on time versus those that are regularly late. Even marketing's communications efforts may need revamping since high costs may signal that customers are not clear about payment terms. Higher costs could also result from mislabeled or inaccurate billing, perhaps resulting from hastily prepared invoices or unclear writing from the salesperson. Finally, high costs may also indicate unevenly enforced policies, allowing customers to infer that the supplier is relaxed about payment terms. Each of these scenarios suggests potential problems, even if the industry norm indicates otherwise.

Endnote

1 Adapted from "http://www.crfonline.org/orc/ca/ca-7.html"

Sources

https://www.agecon.purdue.edu/planner/resources/breakeven.pdf

http://kevinchen.nease.net/dissertation/DISSERTATION.pdf

Hits   58

Measurement Needed

Website providers seek to measure the number of times a server is accessed.

Solution

Hits are a gross measure of the number of files sent to a web server, resulting from a website visitor's request for a particular web page. Web pages are composed of several files, including the page, an image, a graphic, an audio file or any similar web page component. If a web page has four banner ads, two graphics and an audio file, then when the visitor requests that page, the total number of hits is eight (the web page itself is included). Readers must understand that hits are *no longer* considered a valid measure of website traffic, although they are often mistakenly defined as such.

Impact on Decision Making

In the early days of the commercial Internet (the 1990s), hits were considered a good measure of traffic flow. However, in more recent years the term has become less meaningful as newer, more sophisticated measures have emerged that help advertisers and web page providers determine usage more effectively. As a crude, generic overview of gross traffic flow, hits may still be of use to certain websites. However, marketers generally need more precise measures and, in fact, will be considered uninformed if they suggest that the term has any real value or meaning today.

Sources

http://www.marketingterms.com/

http://www.webopedia.com/TERM/H/hit.html

http://en.wikipedia.org/wiki/Hit

http://www.marketingpower.com/mg-dictionary-view3512.php

Pay Per Lead 59

Measurement Need

Marketers obtaining customer leads online need a payment method for each lead acquired.

Solution

Pay per lead simply describes an online payment method in which payment is based on actual, qualifying leads generated by a website or an advertisement on a website.

Assume, for example, that your company attracts 10,000 visitors per day to its website, 1,000 of which click on a banner ad promoting the advertiser's website and, of those, 100 register on the destination website. Then your company, as the publisher of the website on which the banner ad was placed, will be paid for the 100 leads that were generated.

Impact on Decision Making

An advantage of website advertising is the measurement precision that allows marketers to know the details of their customers' website behavior (their page selection, length of time on each page, links clicked, repeat visits, etc.). Qualified leads are any marketer's desire, as long as the overall revenue generated from qualified leads that turn into sales is not exceeded by the cost. A sizable and growing challenge with online advertising is getting website visitors to pay attention to ads since, over the past several years, online advertising effectiveness has declined (although it can still be very cost effective compared to traditional advertising forms). As with any marketing communication, the key to success is identifying the right need, the right audience, the right message and the right website. Even then, success is not guaranteed.

For the website publisher, pay per lead is similar to cost per action, since customers of your site will have greater confidence if you charge them only for actual qualifying leads, based on actual registrations. These registrations are important to the advertiser since customers who register are giving their approval to be contacted in the future, qualifying them as viable prospects.

Pay per lead can be unreliable due to the potential for fraud. Website publishers may generate false leads on the destination website through the use of programs called robots. Activity-based filtration (ABF) is a tool marketers can use that analyzes website log files to identify activity suspected to be robot-generated. ABF should be conducted periodically to check questionable activity.

Sources

http://www.marketingterms.com/

http://en.wikipedia.org/wiki/Affiliate_marketing

http://www.marketingpower.com/mg-dictionary-view3541.php

Brand Equity 60

Measurement Need

To paraphrase Peter Drucker, the purpose of a business is to create customers, and marketing is a key activity that adds value in this effort. In creating customers, marketing can guide the business's managers to develop more distinctive products, more sophisticated communications and a highly differentiated position in the market through research and understanding of customer needs. Increasing emphasis is placed not just on the return on investment for each marketing program, but the total value marketing adds to the business.

Brands have become more than names; they have become strategic assets that distinguish companies and their offerings from their competitors. Typically, better known companies and products tend to command higher valuations and prices than their lesser-known competitive counterparts. It is important that this value is measured. Therefore, marketers need to determine the value that a brand contributes to their company and/or products beyond book value.

However, the challenge for marketers is that measuring brand equity has many approaches. This is partly due to the intangible value associated with the concept of "brand". Interbrand, a global brand consultancy, uses a proprietary methodology, the results of which are popularized in their annual Global Brands Scorecard study, conducted with, and published by, *BusinessWeek Magazine*. Their approach values assets based on how much they are projected to earn in the future.[1] The challenge is clearly identifying and valuing the intangible factors that are the sources of brand equity. Products often elicit an emotional response from consumers ("that car is so *cool!*"), or images are conjured when particular companies are mentioned ("they are really innovative"). These responses reflect the reputation of the entity. But what is the value of this reputation? It is not an easy question to answer, but there are techniques that provide guidance. Two of them will be discussed here.

Solution

Approach 1[2]

Roger J. Best, Emeritus Professor of Marketing from the University of Oregon, views brand equity as the analog to the owner's equity in the balance sheet, except that brand equity is determined by subtracting brand liabilities from brand assets. He suggests two useful scorecards, one measures brand assets and the other measures brand liabilities.

Brand Assets

Best sees brands as comprised of five primary assets:

1. *Brand Awareness*: how aware are consumers of your company and/or its products?

2. *Market Leadership*: what is your market share?

3. *Reputation for Quality*: are you perceived as offering superior quality?

4. *Brand Relevance*: are your products relevant to the consumers you target?

5. *Brand Loyalty*: do customers stay with your products over time?

He suggests companies compare their brand to that of the average brand in their market by scoring each of the five brand asset categories using a 20 point scale, with a maximum possible score of 100. Marketers can assess their brand relative to the average competitor and derive a score that indicates the relative strength of the brand. Figure 16 shows brand asset scorecard.

Brand Assets	Below Average (0)	Somewhat Below (5)	About Average (10)	Somewhat Above (15)	Top Performer (20)	Brand Asset Score
Brand Awareness						
Market Leadership						
Reputation for Quality						
Brand Relevance						

Brand Loyalty						
Total Brand Assets						

Figure 16: Brand Asset Scorecard

Brand Liabilities

To complete the analysis, Best offers a similar framework with five liabilities:

1. *Customer Dissatisfaction:* how high are customer complaint levels?

2. *Environmental Problems*:* are your environmental practices poor?

3. *Product or Service Failures:* is product quality low?

4. *Lawsuits and Boycotts:* is your company facing legal problems?

5. *Questionable Business Practices:* are there ethical lapses?

*Corporate social responsibility (CSR) is increasingly important as a determinant of reputation. Does your company ignore the communities in which it operates?

Similar to brand assets, marketers would want to score their companies and/or products on Figure 17.

Brand Liabilities	Below Average (0)	Somewhat Below (5)	About Average (10)	Somewhat Above (15)	Top Performer (20)	Brand Liability Score
Customer Dissatisfaction						
Environment						
Product Failure						
Lawsuits						
Questionable Practices						
Total Brand Liabilities						

Figure 17: Brand Liabilities Scorecard

The final step is to subtract brand liabilities from brand assets. The difference is brand equity. Best provides a useful diagram to illustrate the methodology:

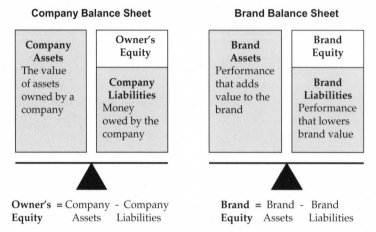

Figure 18: Brand Balance Sheet and Brand Equity

Approach 2[3, 4]

Using a somewhat similar approach, Deborah MacInnis, Professor of Marketing at USC's Marshall School of Business, and C. Whan Park, the Joseph A. DeBell Professor of Marketing at USC's Marshall School of Business, describe brand equity as "the financial value of brand reflecting its efficiency in attracting and retaining customers." They suggest evaluating brand equity as one would evaluate other financial variables. The key difference from Roger Best's approach is that MacInnis and Park suggest that equity has a very specific meaning based on financial valuation techniques and, therefore, should not be subjected to the uncertainties associated with intangibles like consumer perception since those are harder to quantify. As Best's approach illustrated, intangibles are an important factor. Conversely, MacInnis and Park believe it is very hard to place a value on one's perceptions (as one example of an intangible) since they are highly subjective.

MacInnis and Park suggest brand equity be examined from both the revenue and costs sides of the business. Since a key purpose of business is to attract and retain customers, establishing a price that customers find attractive will influence the quantity purchased and, ultimately, the overall revenues generated. Assuming a company's brand has value (compared to the competitors'), then it stands to reason that the brand can command not only a higher market share at equivalent prices, but disproportionate revenue increases at lower prices. Therefore, any brand equity measure should include:

$$R = P \times Q_{ne}$$

Where

R = revenues

P = price

Q_{ne} = quantity demand from new and existing customers

Second, the investments made to develop the customer base affect brand equity. Strong brands should enable a company to develop its customer base more effectively (and, arguably, more efficiently) than lesser-known rivals. Therefore, the brand should provide leverage that makes customer acquisition less costly compared to competitors, since the well-known brand does not have to spend as much to acquire and retain customers. Over time, well-known brands ought to be able to develop their customer base at a lower per-unit cost than before, since the brand is better known than it was at the beginning, making the brand even more valuable to the company. Thus, as revenues increase and costs decrease due to the leverage provided by a strong brand, the brand equity should increase as well.

MacInnis and Park offer Table 20 to describe brand equity, comparing the industrial accounting method with the marketing accounting method described above. The similarity is obvious, and for those who seek a basic approach to brand equity based on financial and accounting techniques, this is a useful definition.

Table 20: Industrial and Marketing Accounting Systems

Industrial Accounting System	Marketing Accounting System
Total Revenues	Total Revenues
Cost of Goods Sold	*Total Marketing Costs*
Operating Profit	Magnitude of Brand Value
Marketing Expenses	*Cost of Goods Sold*
Contribution Margin	Contribution Margin

MacInnis and Park caution, however, that this initial brand equity effort is incomplete because it does not account for differences in different-sized firms with differing marketing costs. While brand value is important, it is equally important to determine the return on marketing costs to understand the efficiency of marketing investments. They illustrate this with the examples in Table 21.

Table 21: Measuring Return Marketing Costs

Case 1	Company A	Company B
Total Sales	$2,000,000	$3,000,000
– *Marketing Costs*	$1,000,000	$2,000,000
Brand Value	$1,000,000	$1,000,000
Operating Margin	$1,000,000	$1,000,000
/ Marketing Costs	$1,000,000	$2,000,000
Return on Marketing Costs	1.0	0.5

Case 2	Company A	Company B
Total Sales	$2,000,000	$1,250,000
– *Marketing Costs*	$1,000,000	$ 500,000
Brand Value	$1,000,000	$ 750,000
Operating Margin	$1,000,000	$ 750,000
/ Marketing Costs	$1,000,000	$ 500,000
Return on Marketing Costs	1.0	1.5

The two cases are excellent and useful, if somewhat simple, illustrations of how measuring value only tells part of the brand equity story. While a strong brand can certainly return a premium value compared to competitors, it is even more helpful to know how efficient you are with the marketing investments that helped create the enhanced value in the first place.

Brand values may be similar, such as in Case 1, but the return on marketing costs indicates that Company A had a higher return on its marketing than Company B, indicating that it was more efficient with its marketing expenditures. In Case 2, Company A was less efficient with its marketing than Company B, even though A had a higher overall brand value. You can easily extrapolate that Company B is likely to overtake Company A in brand value one day if it continues with its marketing efficiencies.

The return on marketing costs is reflected by the formula:

$$ROMC = \frac{V_b}{C_m}$$

Where

$ROMC$ = return on marketing costs

V_b = brand value

C_m = marketing costs

Using the formula to verify the results in Case 2, we have the following:

$$\text{Company A's ROMC} = \frac{\$1,000,000}{\$1,000,000}$$

$$= 1.0$$

$$\text{Company B's ROMC} = \frac{\$750,000}{\$500,000}$$

$$= 1.5$$

As MacInnis and Park describe, when two companies have the same brand value but different return on marketing costs, as shown in Case 1, then the efficiency of the marketing dollars used becomes a key part of the brand equity analysis, with higher brand values resulting from more efficient marketing expenditures.

Marketing efficiency uses the same variables as brand value (revenue and marketing costs) but calculates the result differently. As shown in both Cases 1 and 2, brand value is the difference between total revenues and total costs. Marketing efficiency equals total revenues *divided* by total costs. A higher ratio signals more efficient marketing and improved brand equity. Marketing efficiency can be shown as:

$$M_e = \frac{R}{C_m}$$

Where

M_e = marketing efficiency

R = total revenues

C_m = marketing costs

With marketing efficiency known, the brand value can be updated. Interestingly, MacInnis and Park note that despite the same variables being used to determine both marketing efficiency and brand value, the two measures are "not always positively correlated". This may be because the marketing dollars expended did not lead to financial improvement for the brand, even though the revenues may have increased (i.e. promotional campaigns offer reduced prices which may drive increased sales but at reduced margins, and at the risk of some dilution of the brand's image). MacInnis and Park offer the following formula to calculate the change in brand value with the marketing efficiency included:

$$CBV = \frac{M_e \times R}{1 + M_e}$$

Where

   CBV = change in brand value

   M_e = marketing efficiency

   R = total revenues

Using Company A in Case 2 as an example, we can calculate the following:

$$M_e = \frac{\$2,000,000}{\$1,000,000}$$

$$= 2.0$$

$$CBV = \frac{2.0 \times \$2,000,000}{1 + 2.0}$$

$$= \$1,333,334$$

Finally, MacInnis and Park mention that this analysis is useful if you are evaluating the same brand in the same industry. But if your objective is to compare the equity of your brand with that of another in a different industry, then they suggest adjusting the formula to reflect differing growth rates in each industry. The rationale is that growth rate differences between industries can distort brand-to-brand comparisons. One industry may be growing overall and, thereby, lifting the brand equity value of all companies within (a crude example would be the dot.com mania of the late 1990s), while the value of equity for a brand being compared from another industry may be negatively affected by a slowdown in its industry (the U.S. auto industry, for example). In either case, individual brand equities are being distorted by larger industry forces. Therefore, adjusting the formula by adding growth rates would be useful:

$$CBV_{gr} = \frac{M_e \times R}{1 + (1 + gr) \times M_e}$$

Where

   CBV_{gr} = change in brand value including growth rates

   M_e = marketing efficiency

   R = total revenues

   gr = growth rates

Completing our Company A in Case 2 example, we get the following:

$$\text{CBV}_{gr} = \frac{2.0 \times \$2,000,000}{1 + (1 + 0.10) \times 2.0}$$

$$= \frac{\$4,000,000}{3.2}$$

$$= \$1,250,000$$

Impact on Decision Making

Both approaches borrow from classic accounting techniques and, consequently, serve as useful devices to illustrate the concept of brand equity. They also demonstrate some of the differences in determining brand value. Therefore, it is not possible to conclusively suggest that these approaches are the best models of brand equity.

As with any model, the challenge is in determining the best possible estimates. With MacInnis and Park, calculating the marketing efficiency, or the ROI on marketing costs, is affected by a few not entirely controllable factors: the response of customers to a marketing communications effort; assumptions the company makes about its marketplace and its customers; and the reaction of competitors and how their strategies might impact on or even disrupt your plans. Roger Best's framework helps address the intangibles at a general level, but the question of a clear definition of each intangible's source of equity remains. Nevertheless, both approaches are useful guidelines.

There are several online sources available for those interested in learning more about brand equity:

- Futurebrand: www.futurebrand.com
- Interbrand: www.interbrand.com and www.brandchannel.com
- Brand Finance: www.brandfinance.com
- Landor: www.landor.com
- Young and Rubicam's Brand Asset Valuator: www.yrbav.com

Endnotes

1 "Global Brands". *BusinessWeek Magazine,* August 1, 2005.

2 Best, R.J. *Market-Based Management: Strategies for Growing Customer Value and Profitability.* Upper Saddle River, Pearson Education, Inc., 2005, 2004, 2000, 1997: pp.220-223.

3 MacInnis, D. and Park, C.W. "Making the Most of Your Brand: Leveraging Brand Equity Through Branding Strategies". www.marketingprofs.com, March 2004.

4 Davis, J. *Magic Numbers for Consumer Marketing.* John Wiley & Sons (Asia) Pte Ltd., 2005: pp.92-99.

Brand Premium 61

Measurement Need

Marketers spend their careers trying to convince the market that their products are different and offer unique value to customers. However, this is true only if customers recognize the distinction and, more importantly, view it as relevant to their needs. When a product's (or company's) unique value is clear and meaningful to the customer, then marketers can price the product at a premium level, versus the less-differentiated offerings from the competition. The challenge is determining what is "unique" and whether that uniqueness warrants a premium price.

Solution

A brand or price premium is the price that can be commanded above the "normal" price as a result of one or more distinctions: a strong brand name, recognized superior quality or performance, and a product with unique features or an entirely unique product.

While there is no single formula for premium, Cotton Inc., an organization devoted to promoting cotton-related products, described brand premium in the apparel market in their Winter 2003 newsletter *Textile Consumer* as follows[1]:

$$BP = P_{ab} - P_{ac}$$

Where

BP = brand premium

P_{ab} = average retail price of a branded apparel product

P_{ac} = overall average retail price for that apparel category

Thus, a branded apparel company that charges an average price of $100 for a men's dress shirt in a category where the average retail price is $60, commands a positive brand premium of $40.

$$BP = \$100 - \$60$$

$$= \$40$$

If that same company were charging $50 for their branded shirt and the average retail price for that category remained at $60, then the company would have a negative brand premium of −$10—an unenviable situation.

Impact on Decision Making

Brand premium is closely correlated with corresponding pricing strategies. Skimming, for example, is a price strategy pursued by marketers to charge the highest possible price for uniqueness or innovation relative to current substitutes. Skimming strategies are targeted to exclusive, high-end customer markets only, where there are a sufficient number of customers to sustain the business, but not so many as to attract competitors. Products with a superior image and reputation can be good candidates for skimming. Skimming pricing helps convey and reinforce a strong brand image and, overall, positively impacts brand equity.

The Cotton Inc. formula introduced earlier implied that a premium is simply the difference between a branded product's price and its lesser-known competitor's price. Finding this data is substantially harder than reviewing the prices of a few shirts at the local retail store. To fully understand brand premium, marketers must conduct research that targets consumer perceptions of their brand, preferably in comparison with competitors' brands. Factoring in reputation, perceived quality and relative market position will further sharpen the marketer's understanding of their brand's premium position. But it is important to recognize that these are qualitative assessments, with interpretation and judgment as guides, rather than rigorous quantitative precision in determining premium price.

While many pricing models are influenced by costs, premiums are affected more by brand image, reputation and equity. Specifically, the value of a brand directly affects the credibility associated with the premium charged for its products. Mercedes and BMW can charge a price premium for their cars because their brands are consistently associated with a higher perceived value. Saturn (from General Motors) is unlikely to have any credibility if it were to introduce a premium-priced car since this would be inconsistent with its image. Lexus was launched as a new brand, not linked to Toyota, in part due to the association Toyota generally had with entry-level and mid-market cars.

Rolex

Rolex is widely considered a top-quality watch. Despite the addition of gold and diamonds in some models, many of Rolex's components (the mechanisms that make the watch work) are very similar to those used in other watch brands, whether at the luxury or commodity ends of the spectrum. So what are Rolex customers buying? They are buying prestige, image, tradition, reputation and association with a socio-demographic audience that is among the top 1% of income earners.

How has Rolex been so successful in capturing this audience and in convincing them that its watches are worth the money? Certainly, Rolexes do have a reputation for quality—this has been true for decades. We never read about quality-control issues or product recalls from Rolex. Concomitant with quality is implied expertise in workmanship. Rolex has figured out over the years how to build an extremely reliable watch with nearly flawless components. Therefore, it is safe to assume that its reputation for quality is deserved. But does that justify its premium image and corresponding price? Rolex has been the favorite of "ultra-successful" people for years. This suggests they believe in Rolex's promise of quality, find its high-status image appealing, and are not disappointed by the product once they use it.

Clearly, quality is part of Rolex's premium, but so is its reputation for being worn by the most discriminating customers. Does that warrant its premium image? Psychologically, people like to associate with others similar to them, and/or aspire to be like other people whom they perceive as being successful. Rolex's customers get a psychological reward for wearing a Rolex. But beyond quality and discriminating customers, there are still other factors that contribute to Rolex's premium image: tradition and brand associations (golf, yachts, luxury cars) that serve to reinforce the reputation. While, separately, each of these may not justify Rolex's premium image, it is these ingredients that collectively create the premium image the company enjoys. The challenge, of course, is how to maintain this image.

Most of the great luxury brands took years to develop their reputations. Many great luxury brands are considered one-of-a-kind. The company's management must have tremendous focus, dedication and a clear understanding of the company's purpose and heritage to consistently uphold these values, especially in difficult business conditions. Furthermore, despite the tradition associated with many luxury products, tradition alone will not sustain them indefinitely. Rigorous work goes into the details of the world's leading premium products. The service at Four Seasons or Banyan Tree is the result of years of training of employees, devotion to mission, a clear understanding of customers and a commitment to retaining the best employees, who understand all of this. Similarly, the prestige associated with Rolls Royce and Rolex is the result of dedication to first-rate quality.

The bottom line is that these firms are passionately committed to protecting their reputations, retaining the absolute loyalty of their customers and maintaining the mystique of their products. It is part of their brand DNA.

However, maintaining a price premium is tricky for the same reasons that sustaining a premium image is challenging. It is very hard to actually know if the suggested premium price is going to be charged at the time of purchase. Branded products sold below full price risk dilution of their brand image. Yet not selling the product at all risks undermining the company's survival. Interestingly, there is no universal rule when it comes to price premium. While it is hard to recall an instance when there has been a Rolex "sale", Mercedes and BMW regularly offer financing or even direct-from-sticker discounts (despite their luxury positions). Each of these companies attracts a high-end customer and each has been largely successful in maintaining its image over time. But clearly each would suffer if a prolonged program of price discounting were codified.

Cunard[1] confronted this in the early 1990s following the first Gulf War. At the time, Cunard operated seven ships, five of which were five-star vessels and the other two four-star. Their premier ship was the Queen Elizabeth II, more commonly known as the QE2. Cunard had 50% of the five-star market but, for the first time in its 160-year history, it was facing dwindling demand and competitive discounting. Customers traveling on a Cunard ship expected and received an extraordinarily high level of service. However, increasing evidence suggested that the culture of cruising was changing and passengers were finding the more family-oriented atmosphere of the emerging cruise lines to be attractive. Cunard wrestled with this, and responded by offering premiums, effectively discounting their original service. These premiums came in several forms: a shopping spree at Harrod's; travel on the Concorde; reduced fares for the second passenger; and even a one-day sale. Fast forward to today and Cunard no longer operates the four-star ships. It focuses exclusively on five-star, ultra-luxury cruising with the newly launched Queen Mary 2 and the QE2. Sometime during the past decade Cunard concluded that protecting its prestigious upper-class legacy was more important than chasing the discounted four-star and family-cruise approaches.

In early 2006, Cunard's ship Queen Mary 2 suffered damage to one of its propellers, forcing a delay in its scheduled Latin American cruise. As the ship continued on its journey after repairs, it then announced the elimination of several ports of call along the way in order to make up time in the schedule. Passengers were incensed. After an initially slow response to its passengers, Cunard offered a 50% refund, but the announcement at sea and the subsequent poorly handled public relations had angered passengers who felt the refund was insufficient. Cunard eventually relented and agreed to a full refund for those who sought it. The question is whether this situation harmed Cunard's former superior reputation permanently, or temporarily. Either way, the worldwide media coverage tarnished Cunard's image for a few days[3].

Endnotes

1 http://www.cottoninc.com/TextileConsumer/TextileConsumerVolume31/1203TC.pdf

2 Greyser, S.A. and Young, R.F. "Cunard Line Ltd.: Managing Integrated Communications" Case # 9-594-046. The President and Fellows of Harvard College, 1994.

3 http://news.bbc.co.uk/1/hi/world/americas/4652724.stm

Source

Davis, J. *Magic Numbers for Consumer Marketing.* Singapore: John Wiley & Sons (Asia) Pte Ltd., 2005: pp.207-212.

Recall 62

Measurement Need

Advertising remains a successful and important marketing vehicle, despite significant changes over the past decade with the advent of the Internet, online advertising, exponential increases in available information at one's fingertips and increasingly fragmented customer markets. Advertising campaigns are usually run in blocks or time cycles (i.e. an ad runs for two months, stops for one or two months, then returns for two more months), with specific messages, imagery and themes repeated for finite periods of time before a new or revised campaign is introduced. The law of diminishing returns is a factor in these campaign changes since consumer interest dissipates over time when the same advertising theme is repeated. To keep consumer interest, marketers vary the message and approach, often supported by a time-tested concept. For example, Nike's "Just Do It" slogan has been used for nearly 20 years in a diverse range of advertising campaigns featuring different athletes, sports, and even lifestyle themes.

With these changes, marketers are interested in measuring if consumers remember a recently ended advertising campaign.

Solution

Recall is a test of overall brand awareness or of advertising impact. In brand awareness, recall refers to a situation where, given a product category, a consumer can name (or "recall") a brand or advertising campaign without further prompting. This level of awareness can suggest that a reasonably strong brand has been built over time.

There are two types of recall, which are easily measured with recall tests. Consumers are asked which brands in a particular product class (i.e. soaps) they recall, and their replies tend to fall into one of two categories (and sometimes both):

- Top of mind: the first brand recalled

- Dominance: the only brand recalled

In advertising, recall has a similar meaning, except that the consumer recall is triggered by reference to a particular media vehicle (television, radio, internet, print) within a pre-determined time after the ad has run or been shown. In this case, consumers are asked to recall advertising they have seen or heard in a given media vehicle. Within advertising recall there are two variations: aided recall, where some of the ad's elements are described without mentioning the product or company; and unaided recall, where no prompting occurs.

Recall is not a formula, but a question. Here are some examples (not exhaustive):

- Which brands in this product class do you recall?

- Please describe the most memorable ad from the last television show you watched.

- Do you recall an ad that had trumpet music and birds flying?

Recall is further divided into aided and unaided recall:

Aided recall: a research technique in which a person is shown an ad, product, brand name or trademark and asked to recall the previous time they saw it.

Unaided recall: respondents are asked to describe any product, advertising, brand name or trademark they recall seeing recently; perhaps on TV the previous night, in a recent print publication, or a retail store.

Much of the information gathered from these research techniques is qualitative and, therefore, harder to quantify. However, a good market researcher or marketing manager would, at a minimum, summarize the findings overall, then organize the answers into common themes. Repeated comments can then be tallied to indicate which consumer insights are most common and which are marginal or irrelevant.

Impact on Decision Making

Recall is a one-dimensional measure of advertising effectiveness, but it is not a measure of preference. Results from recall measures do not reveal whether a consumer prefers the products or if they have decided to purchase the products advertised, only whether consumers recall the advertising or product. Qualitative research, indeed even some quantitative research, is subject to bias and interpretation. This may discourage managers and CFOs from seeking absolute answers from their marketing department's communications programs. If so, then you need to adjust your expectations. Recall is a reasonable test of how successful your marketing efforts have been in building awareness. But an important question to remember is: what period of time are you evaluating? You may launch a marketing campaign and sales increase 25%. You may conclude from this that your campaign was the reason for the increase. But you might be wrong. The competition might have made a strategic blunder, causing customers to switch to your company. Or the marketing efforts of previous years might finally be bearing fruit, in which case your predecessors deserve at least some of the credit. So how will you know? The answer is: you won't, at least not perfectly.

Recall can also be the proverbial double-edged sword if your product becomes so popular that it is increasingly viewed as generic. Examples include:

- FedEx
- Rollerblade
- Windsurfer
- Aspirin
- Cellophane
- Kleenex
- Escalator
- Xerox

Recall can also result from a negative association, which means your product and/or company is at risk for being perceived poorly. Such associations can arise from many things, including:

- A bad meal at a restaurant
- Bad service at a hotel
- Poor customer service when returning a product to a retail store
- Product performance not delivering on promises implied by advertising

Companies risk developing negative recall results if their products or product associations (the extended touch points in the market where their product is represented) are controversial or offensive. Benetton has for years run advertising campaigns that tackle sensitive social issues in a direct, almost confrontational way, virtually daring consumers to use their products despite their bold messages. Nike, too, has courted controversy in the past with its athlete endorsements and outsourcing practices.

Recall can even affect entire industries. Prior to April 2000, it was considered glamorous to be working for a dot.com, irrespective of what it did or whether it actually made money. In the post-April 2000 world, dot.coms are often derided and labeled as the poster child of immature, poor businesses with bad planning and arrogant owners. Thus, while recall of dot.coms is quite high, it is not the sort of recall one would wish for.

Recall data is gathered through several different research techniques such as surveys, focus groups and interviews. The research can be conducted by an independent third-party market research firm, or through your own, in-house research project. In either case, survey design is important, as the way that questions are asked can affect how consumers answer. Focus groups must also be planned thoughtfully and led by an expert facilitator who can keep the discussion going and on track.

Sources

Doyle, C. *Collins Internet-Linked Dictionary of Marketing*. HarperCollins Publishers, 2003, 2005: p.275.

Davis, J. *Magic Numbers for Consumer Marketing*. Singapore: John Wiley & Sons (Asia) Pte Ltd., 2005: pp.105-108.

Ambler, T. *Marketing and the Bottom Line*. FT Prentice Hall, 2003.

Imber, J. and Toffler, B. *Dictionary of Marketing Terms*. Barron's Educational Services, Inc., 2000: pp.22, 561.

American Marketing Association: http://www.marketingpower.com/mg-dictionary.php?Searched=1&SearchFor=recall%20test

Recognition 63

Measurement Need

Advertising is designed to be memorable, whether the message is intended to introduce a new product, build awareness, or promote a limited-time offer. A measure of a company's advertising's effectiveness is whether consumers remember the company, ad or product when they are shown the ad again.

Solution

Recognition research asks: have you been exposed to this brand (or product, or ad campaign) before? This and similar questions are used to gauge the consumer's awareness.

Impact on Decision Making

Measuring recognition can reveal whether or not an advertising campaign is remembered by consumers. However, recognition is really the weaker cousin of recall, since it requires the consumer to be prompted directly with the name of the company, product or a description of the literal advertising message.

Note on Recognition and Recall

High recognition and low recall is not ideal when viewed through the lens of advertising effectiveness because it means consumers remember the ad, product or company only after being prompted. High recall is better. But high recognition and high recall is best, assuming the combination is a positive association, not negative. Niche brands tend to have high recall with loyal consumers, but low overall recall and recognition in the general market. The combination of high recall and high recognition can often result in positive feelings from consumers. Familiarity often leads to successful advertising and premium perceptions over less-known rivals. Of course, familiarity can also breed contempt or indifference from excessive message repetition or irritating advertising. Finally, since part of the reason companies market themselves is to build trust with consumers, their efforts to advertise and, thereby, attract attention often signal that they believe in their products and are willing to stand by them in public. At least, one hopes that is the case.

A key question marketers must consider is: What are good levels of recall and recognition? Both recall and recognition are measures of awareness, but is an awareness level of 30% good or bad? The answer depends entirely on the product and industry. For example, 30% awareness may be low if the metric is for a consumer products company with multiple brand names.

Of course, that is still somewhat vague, so let's look at a specific category: laundry detergent. Tide, from Procter and Gamble, is well known in most parts of the world. It is the category leader, and has been for years. In asking consumers if they can name a laundry detergent brand, Tide is likely to be one of several brands mentioned, indicating good recall. Alternatively, if consumers were asked if they have heard of Tide, the likelihood of "Yes" being the answer is also quite high, indicating high recognition. Both indicate a high level of awareness. But what is that level? Let's assume that the awareness level is 90%, which would mean that Tide is mentioned nine out of ten times in surveys that ask respondents if they can name a brand of laundry detergent (recall) or if they remember the brand called Tide (recognition). But what is the awareness level if respondents can name Tide seven times out of ten, but can remember it nine times out of ten when prompted? The answer is unclear, highlighting the challenge of precisely measuring awareness.

If a competitor's awareness level among consumers is 30% in this category, then clearly the competitor is cited and remembered less than Tide. Is 30% good? Compared to Tide, it is clearly not as good. Is 30% bad? Perhaps "bad" is an overstatement. This is somewhat specific to the context, and there is no set level that is considered a good level of awareness. When compared to Tide, this other brand, called Xtra Sparkle, does not generate the same level of awareness.

Alternatively, if Xtra Sparkle had been launched in the past year or two, then 30% awareness signals rapid growth and that Tide might have cause for concern. On the other hand, if Xtra Sparkle had been around as long as Tide, then its 30% awareness level would indicate that it is perceived as a distant competitor, far behind the leader.

This example is based on only one industry and one product category. Awareness in a niche or fragmented market may be entirely different. A 30% level might indicate a strong, market-leading competitor. The point is that measuring awareness is more complex than a simple measure of recall and recognition. The next question is: compared to what? Marketers must understand the business context in greater depth and determine if the results are consistent, extraordinary, or under-whelming for their industry.

In recent years the introduction of digital video recorders (DVR), such as that offered by TiVO, has provided consumers with the technology to fast forward through television commercials. Television networks and advertisers in the U.S. have been concerned about this technology since it gives more power to the consumer to control what they watch than ever before; certainly not desirable for the national networks which sell advertising time and want advertisers to know that their programming attracts the desired target customers. One concern is that the consumer's ability to fast forward or even eliminate advertising from their recorded programs means that products won't even have the chance to develop recall or recognition in the first place. However, new research by marketing research company Millward Brown, done cooperatively with ABC, CBS, NBC and CNN, shows that there "is no difference in advertising recall or ad recognition between digital video recorder (DVR) owners and non-owners for ads aired on network TV during prime time."[1] The report further states:

> *"DVR owners are not less engaged with TV ad viewing," said Michelle de Montigny, senior VP, Millward Brown Media Practice. "Consumers who own DVRs are more likely to pay attention to television during commercial breaks when viewing live and are less likely to be distracted by other activities that non-DVR owners get involved with."[2]*

The findings are intriguing since they imply advertisers have an opportunity to create different television ads that work better when fast forwarded. Marketers must weigh opportunities like this before concluding that television advertising no longer works. As with many new technologies, disruption creates challenges for established companies, but can present unique opportunities as well, for those who are resourceful.

Endnotes

1 Consoli, J. "Study: DVR Users Still Have Ad Recall". *Adweek Magazine*, April 7, 2006. http://www.adweek.com/aw/search/article_display.jsp?vnu_content_id=1002313860

2 Ibid.

Sources

Doyle, C. *Collins Internet-Linked Dictionary of Marketing*. HarperCollins Publishers, 2003, 2005: p.275.

Davis, J. *Magic Numbers for Consumer Marketing*. Singapore: John Wiley & Sons (Asia) Pte Ltd., 2005: pp.109-111.

Asia Market Rearch: http://www.asiamarketresearch.com/glossary/brand-recognition.htm

Wathieu, L."TiVo in 2002: Consumer Behavior", *Harvard Business School* #9-502-062, July 26, 2002.

Ambler, T. *Marketing and the Bottom Line*. FT Prentice Hall, 2003.

Usage 64

Measurement Need

Marketers identify needs, target specific customers, and position products accordingly. Products that offer demonstrable and distinctive added value to the customer can command premium prices. Therefore, marketers want to determine product usage at different prices.

Solution[1]

Usage is not a formula, but a framework for assessing the maximum financial benefits a company can produce while also yielding substantial value for the consumer.

Roger J. Best, in his book *Market-Based Management: Strategies for Growing Customer Value and Profitability*, provides an excellent example of usage (see Figure 19 on p.261). The subject is a hypothetical company that manufactures a new product that delivers more value to its customers at a lower cost, yet can also command a higher price, resulting in improved profits for the company. The value lies in the reduced installation, usage and maintenance costs for the customer, even with the higher price. The reason? The overall cost ("Lifecycle Costs", on Figure 19) to the customer is $125 cheaper, even though the retail price of the product itself is $75 higher. Look at the chart closely. The benchmark comparison describes the current product offering and associated costs: $500 for usage and maintenance; $200 installation; and $300 purchase price. Each of these is paid by the customer. The next bar in the graph shows that the new solution reduces installation, usage and maintenance costs ($500 versus $700 with the current solution), yielding a hypothetical maximum value of $500, assuming the new product is priced at zero. The final bar in the graph reflects the company's new product, priced higher for the unit (so the telecommunications manufacturer recaptures economic value), but lower overall when the other costs are included.

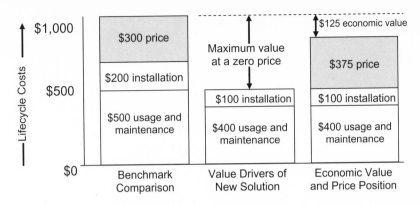

Figure 19: Economic Value of a Product

Impact on Decision Making

The benefit in this example is self-evident. By creating a new product with lower costs, yet also offering higher value, the marketer is able to command a premium price that also offers lower overall costs for the customer.

Usage analysis helps marketing planning efforts by visualizing the value associated with different products based on their lifecycle costs. Marketers can use this to analyze new products compared to older ones, as was illustrated above, or to compare their own product offerings to those of the competition, identifying opportunities and/or risks in the process. However, marketers must have a thorough understanding of their customers' needs relative to their product offerings, and those of the competition, if they are included, to determine where the value opportunities exist.

This analysis is also useful in matching products to different segments, based on their needs and usage. Some segments may use a product less, but expect the product to last longer as a result. They would opt for the lower-priced product, even if it has higher maintenance costs, since their costs are spread out over time versus up front. Conversely, higher usage segments may prefer the higher up front price in return for lower maintenance costs on the new product.

Source

Best, R.J. *Market-Based Management: Strategies for Growing Customer Value and Profitability.* New Jersey: Pearson Education, 2005: pp.106-107.

Transactions Per Customer

65

Measurement Need

Retailers want to know how many in-store potential customers convert to actual buying customers.

Solution[1]

Transactions per customer measures the percentage of potential customers that actually buy. The formula is:

$$TPC = \frac{T_{transt}}{T_{trafft}} \times 100$$

Where

TPC = transactions per customer

T_{transt} = total number of transactions in time period t (usually one day)

T_{trafft} = total customer traffic in time period t

For example, if you run a retail outlet and a particular day has customer traffic of 1,000 people, and the total transactions for that day is 100, then the TPC is 10%:

$$TPC = \frac{100}{1000} \times 100$$

$$= 10\%$$

Impact on Decision Making

TPC is a measure of a retailer's success in converting potential customers into actual buyers. Alternative terms are the "percentage yield rate" and/or the "walk to buy ratio", but each measures the same thing.

Generally, the higher the percentage, the more effective the retailer is at converting those who are merely browsing into paying customers. If the figure is low (a low figure will vary by store type, location, brand name and even economic conditions), then the retailer may need to review its marketing activities, including:

- promotions (the discounts are not attractive enough or the wrong products are being promoted)

- point of purchase materials (stocking may be low, the display may be poorly placed, or the design may be unappealing)

- merchandising (the look of the products on stores shelves and their location in the store may not appeal to customers or reflect how they walk through the store)

- general marketing activities (awareness-building brand development activities may not be consistently executed, print ads for specific products may be confusing or poorly executed, and the store location may be inconvenient).

The biggest challenge is measuring customer traffic since it is difficult to actually measure each individual potential customer unless a specific person(s) is devoted to counting customers for a given period of time, or a third party research firm is retained to conduct a customer count survey. There are automated tools that can count customer traffic as well, although these do not account for double counting (customers who visit more than once in the time period measured).

Finally, transactions are recorded on the cash register tapes (or hard drive, if it is a computer-based system), so these totals are more easily gathered than the customer traffic totals.

Endnote

1 Strategis: Canada's Business and Consumer Site http://strategis.ic.gc.ca/epic/internet/ inretra-comde.nsf/en/qn00027e.html

Returns to Net Sales

66

Measurement Need

Retailers strive to have high customer satisfaction. Returned products are an indication of possible customer dissatisfaction, so retailers seek to measure this occurrence.

Solution[1]

Returns to net sales (RTS) measures the value of products that are returned relative to net sales.

$$RTS = \frac{T_{rat}}{S_{nt}} \times 100$$

Where

RTS = returns to net sales

T_{rat} = total $ returns and allowances in time period t

S_{nt} = net $ sales in time period t

To illustrate, a retailer has total returns and allowances of $3,000 in a one-month period. During the same period, net sales are $100,000. RTS equals 3%:

$$RTS = \frac{3,000}{100,000} \times 100$$

$$= 3\%$$

Impact on Decision Making

A higher figure suggests that the retailer may have problems related to the quality of the products and/or a below average service experience (perhaps the customer was sold a product based on hard-sell tactics or misleading information). While it is generally challenging to have a 0% RTS (admirable though it may be), retailers want the lowest possible RTS figure, since returned products or allowances cost them money as well as harm their reputation.

Endnote

1 Strategis: Canada's Business and Consumer Site http://strategis.ic.gc.ca/epic/internet/inretra-comde.nsf/en/qn00027e.html

Transactions Per Hour 67

Measurement Need

Retailers juggle multiple responsibilities, including setting employee work schedules, buying the product mix, setting retail prices, product placement and merchandising, and scheduling hours of operation. Retailers need to know the transactions pattern to determine the best possible combination of these activities.

Solution[1]

Transactions per hour (or any chosen period of time) (TPH) calculates the number of transactions that occur during that time, and is represented by:

$$TPH = \frac{T_{transt}}{T_{ht}}$$

Where

TPH = transactions per hour

T_{transt} = total transactions in time period t

T_{ht} = total hours in time period t

Let's assume your store sells books and you wish to measure TPH. Your store is open from 8am to 9pm every day. You decide to review an entire week's activity to determine TPH. During the week being reviewed, 1,600 transactions occur. We can now calculate TPH:

$$TPH = \frac{1,600}{91}$$

$$= 17.6$$

17.6 transactions occurred in the average hour during the week being measured.

Impact on Decision Making

TPH provides retailers with the flow of business, helping them understand peak times when customer demand is highest. For example, retailers can review transactions in each actual hour to determine which times of day are busiest. This information will enable the retailer to schedule the right number of employees during the busiest times. Equally important, this information will help a retailer determine the best times to run promotions as well, since they would want promotions to be seen by the largest possible number of customers, so as to maximize sales.

Endnote

1 Strategis: Canada's Business and Consumer Site http://strategis.ic.gc.ca/epic/internet/inretra-comde.nsf/en/qn00027e.html

Hourly Customer Traffic

Measurement Need

Retailers seek to measure total customer traffic during a specific period of time.

Solution[1]

$$HCT = \frac{T_{trafft}}{T_{ht}}$$

Where

HCT = hourly customer traffic

T_{trafft} = total customer traffic in time period t

T_{ht} = total hours in time period t

If a retailer has 150 customers during a ten-hour day, then the hourly customer traffic is 15:

$$HCT = \frac{150}{10}$$

$$= 15$$

Impact on Decision Making

Similarly to Chapter 67 (Transactions Per Hour), retailers use HCT information to determine employee scheduling, store hours and even price promotions. The busiest hours warrant the highest staffing levels and may be an opportune time to run a promotion to maximize sales. HCT is different from TPH in one key respect: HCT measures all customer traffic, not just paying customers. Retailers will need more staff during higher customer traffic periods to answer customer questions and handle point of sales cash transactions. Peak customer traffic times are a great opportunity for retailers to focus on improved service since many of those who are merely browsing may return in the future to purchase if their initial service experience was positive.

Endnote

1 Strategis: Canada's Business and Consumer Site http://strategis.ic.gc.ca/epic/internet/inretra-comde.nsf/en/qn00027e.html

Inventory Turnover 69

Measurement Need

In consumer products and retail companies, the marketing effort often includes planning product inventory levels based on forecasts from field sales teams, buyers and internal projections derived from past experience and current conditions. Unless a company is facing rapidly escalating supply prices, then the business's leaders will want to sell through their inventory quickly (a high turnover) to keep their storage, tracking, personnel and warehouse costs down. High inventory levels do occur when prices are rising quickly because companies want to stock up on the supplies before the prices rise further. Marketing management wants to know how quickly the inventory is being sold as it is one indicator of the popularity of the product.

Solution

Turnover measures how quickly total inventory is sold and refilled, usually over the course of a year. It is calculated as follows:

$$Turnover = \frac{S}{I_a}$$

Where

S = sales

I_a = average inventory

Note: average inventory is usually calculated as the sum of each month's beginning-of-month inventory figures (12 in all) plus the last end-of-month inventory amount, then divided by 13.

Suppose a company has a chain of 20 retail outlets and its sales last year were $40 million. The average inventory each month was $4 million. The turnover, then, equals ten, as follows:

$$Turnover = \frac{\$40,000,000}{\$4,000,000}$$

$$= 10$$

Impact on Decision Making

Turnover is a key measure of retail productivity. In effect, turnover is measuring the velocity of inventory change and, since inventory represents money (invested) sitting in a warehouse, the sooner it is sold, the sooner the investment earns returns. Therefore, a high inventory turnover is generally a good sign. For retail accounts, a turnover of ten may sound good, but each business varies, so it is best to compare inventory turnover with that of similar companies or the industry average. Retailers selling perishable goods, such as food, will have higher inventory turnover than those with non-perishable goods, for example, since spoilage from unsold inventory is a very real risk. However, durable goods are also important to turn over quickly since they generate revenues that can then be put to use in newer inventory and for other productive purposes.

A low turnover rate may imply several problems, including poor sales (perhaps from insufficient marketing), underperforming or outdated products, or consumers who have grown weary of the product or category. Poor sales, of course, leads to increasing inventories, which can put pressure on the retailer since the investment in inventory is not producing any return (see Chapter 71 on Gross Margin Return on Inventory Invested for more insight on this). Conversely, a high turnover rate may suggest strong sales performance due to uniquely relevant products that satisfy growing consumer needs. Interestingly, a high inventory turnover may also signal ineffective buying from suppliers, leading a retailer to not having enough inventory to replenish depleted stocks (a concept known as the fill rate). Newer products tend to attract attention and increase purchase frequency, slowing as consumer familiarity and competition grows. Also, expanding retail chains will witness increasing inventories, which will distort the inventory turnover patterns until the new stores gain a consistent operating performance.

Clearly, there are many factors that influence inventory turnover. It is the responsibility of marketers to attract as many consumers as possible, then convert them to buyers so that retail inventories are kept to a manageable level consistent with the particular industry in which their company competes. As referenced periodically in this book, this is accomplished through the marketing mix of product (the right product for the consumer), place (accessibility of products for consumers), promotion (communication that appeals to the consumer), and price (the equivalent of the consumer's cost, which is influenced by perceptions of quality and uniqueness, among many factors). Marketers must pay attention to each of these marketing "levers" to see which ones stimulate consumer purchases most effectively, and maximize profitable sales as a result.

Table 22[1] shows the inventory turnover for several industries and, interestingly, the differences between sole proprietorships and corporations.

Table 22: Inventory Turnover for Sole Proprietorships and Corporations

Sole Proprietorships	Inventory Turnover Ratio
Lumber & Building Materials	7.7
Paint, Glass & Wallpaper	4.5
Hardware Stores	3.0
Retail Nurseries & Garden Supply	5.1
General Merchandise Stores	6.5
Grocery Stores	12.5
New Car Dealers & Brokers	6.2
Used Car Dealers & Brokers	7.6
Gas Stations & Mini-marts	30.2
Auto Parts & Accessories	4.7
Apparel & Accessories	3.2
Furniture & Home Furnishings	5.0
Liquor Stores	6.4
Antiques & Used Merchandise	1.7
Sporting Goods	4.4
Direct Sales Operations	5.9
Gift, Novelty & Souvenir Shops	2.4
Other Retail Stores	3.7
Wholesale—Durable	9.1
Wholesale—Non-durable	20.4

Corporations	Inventory Turnover Ratio
Lumber & Building Materials	5.2
Hardware Stores	3.5
Retail Nurseries & Garden Supply	3.3
General Merchandise Stores	4.7
Grocery Stores	12.7
Other Food Stores	12.2
New & Used Car Dealers	6.8
Gas Stations & Mini-marts	39.3
Auto Parts & Accessories	3.6
Apparel & Accessories	3.5
Furniture & Home Furnishings	4.1
Drug Stores	5.3
Liquor Stores	6.6
Other Retail Stores	4.3
Wholesale—Groceries & Related	17.8
Wholesale—Machinery & Equipment	4.8
Wholesale—Vehicles & Automotive	6.9
Wholesale—Furniture & Fixtures	5.5
Wholesale—Lumber & Construction	9.9
Wholesale—Sporting Goods & Related	4.8
Wholesale—Electrical Goods	6.8
Wholesale—Hardware & Plumbing	5.2
Wholesale—Other Durable Goods	7.0
Wholesale—Paper & Related Products	10.7
Wholesale—Drug Store Items	8.5
Wholesale—Apparel & Related	5.5
Wholesale—Chemical & Related	9.4
Wholesale—Petroleum & Related	42.4
Wholesale—Alcoholic Beverages	8.5
Wholesale—Misc. Non-durable	7.8

However, a word of caution is warranted. While competitive or industry comparisons based on averages may provide insight into a company's own performance, this can be misleading. For example, let's look at Dell and Gateway[2], both of which compete in the PC market. In 2004, their respective inventory turnovers were as follows:

- Gateway = 28.97
- Dell = 107.08

Both companies have inventory turnover rates that are considerably higher than most of the examples in Table 22. Both companies compete in the aggressive direct distribution PC business (among many other businesses in which both compete, including televisions and other household electronics), meaning that they build and ship PCs based on direct customer request from their respective online stores. Despite competing in the same market, Dell's inventory turnover is substantially higher than Gateway's. Dell is quite efficient with its inventory, working directly with its suppliers to acquire the necessary PC parts "just in time" to build the product sought by the customer. Gateway, while certainly having a high inventory turnover, has been struggling since 1999 due to several reorganizations and a failed attempt to develop retail stores. These challenges undoubtedly contributed to a poorer performance on inventory turnover relative to Dell. Gateway's marketing managers would want to research the customer purchase patterns and even survey their customers to gain an in-depth understanding of current customer perceptions. Furthermore, they might also want to examine the differences in the two companies' approaches to the market, including website design, ease of use, product configurations, pricing, supplier quality (and relationships) and similar issues to see if there are areas to fix that would improve their inventory turnover performance.

Endnotes

1 ©2004 BizMiner Industry Reports-BizMiner.com http://www.bizstats.com/inventory.htm

2 http://ocw.mit.edu/NR/rdonlyres/Sloan-School-of-Management/15-511Summer2004/
4B07B1A4-166B-4112-8122-C6EE460670D8/0/lec8.pdf

Percent Inventory Carrying Costs

70

Measurement Need

Retailers regularly adjust inventory levels to service depleted store stocks and not overly burden their storage and warehouse facilities with unsold inventory. Inventory residing in storage incurs carrying costs, which are the costs associated with leasing storage space, insuring the unsold inventory, moving inventory to new locations, shrinkage, and the labor used to periodically count each item. Retail management needs to determine the percentage of net sales attributed to the carrying costs of managing the unsold inventory.

Solution[1]

Percent inventory carrying costs (PICC) is calculated with the following formula:

$$PICC = \frac{I_{cct}}{S_{nt}} \times 100$$

Where

$PICC$ = percent inventory carrying costs

I_{cct} = inventory carrying costs in time period t

S_{nt} = net $ sales in time period t

If your company is a computer retailer with net sales of $100,000 during the month, and your inventory carrying costs were $30,000, then your PICC is 30%:

$$PICC = \frac{\$30,000}{\$100,000} \times 100$$

$$= 30\%$$

Certainly, the lower the PICC, the better for your financial bottom line, since carrying costs eat into margins and reduce profitability.

Impact on Decision Making

Retailers face a daily cost challenge due to labor, shrinkage, facilities maintenance, insurance, rent and product returns. Keeping inventory levels as low as possible while still being able to effectively replenish in-store stocks is a constant struggle. Dell has had an inventory cost advantage for years over rivals like HP, Compaq (now part of HP), IBM and even Gateway. This is due, in part, to Dell's extremely efficient customer-direct focus and just-in-time inventory practices. In 1996, Dell had nearly a 14% cost advantage over Compaq in PCs, with a similar advantage over other rivals as well (working out to a $50 cost advantage per PC)[2]. In more recent years, lower manufacturing costs in emerging markets like China, Thailand, Vietnam and India have created a significantly more attractive wage differential. This has allowed Dell's competitors to reduce their own costs, particularly through using ODMs (original design manufacturers) in those countries to build computers. Nevertheless, Dell maintains a healthy and low PICC, enabling them to garner higher margins compared to rivals and reinforce a competitive advantage they have enjoyed for over a decade.

It is incumbent on retailers to learn more about their customers, develop stronger supplier relationships, implement sophisticated IT solutions, and improve operational controls. Consequently, the best retailers will pay close attention to product and purchase patterns, facilitating a more efficient and effective inventory management system that, ultimately, will help reduce costs and improve profitability.

Endnotes

1 Strategis: Canada's Business and Consumer Site http://strategis.ic.gc.ca/epic/internet/inretra-comde.nsf/en/qn00027e.html

2 Cohan, P. S."Tech Trends-Contracting Profits". *Computer World Magazine*, April 10, 2006

Sources

http://www.logisticsfocus.com/Glossary/glossary-i.asp

http://www.effectiveinventory.com/article38.html

Gross Margin Return on Inventory Investment

71

Measurement Need

Akey source of profits is the investment in inventory. Retail managers want to invest in those products that yield the highest potential return on the amount invested. Retail marketers are interested in this as well since the characteristics of the products in inventory have a direct influence on price, merchandising and, ultimately, marketability. If a retailer's merchandise is more favorably received by customers and can earn a higher profit as well, then their decisions will also favor the products offering the highest investment return potential.

Solution

Gross margin return on inventory investment (GMROII) measures how successfully a retailer has invested its money used for inventory. More simply, it is a measure of an item's gross profitability. It is calculated using this formula:

$$GMROII = \frac{M}{C_{ai}}$$

Where

$GMROII$ = gross margin return on inventory investment

M = gross margin dollars

C_{ai} = average inventory costs in dollars

Let's assume that a sporting goods retail chain is earning gross margins of $3 million. Average inventory at cost is $1 million. Therefore, the GMROII is $3.

$$GMROII = \frac{\$3,000,000}{\$1,000,000}$$

$$= \$3$$

This means that the retailer is making a very healthy 300% gross margin on their originally $1 million inventory investment.

Impact on Decision Making

GMROII is a measure of the productivity of a company's inventory investment. It helps describe the relationship between key retail performance measures: total sales, the gross profit margin earned on sales and the number of dollars invested in inventory. In this example, $1 of investment earned $3 in return. Another way to explain this is that GMROII tells managers how much they have earned back on their original inventory investment during one year.

GMROII is also a useful measure because it applies to any merchandise within the retailer's business. Furthermore, it is a viable management tool for employee performance, especially those responsible for selling. Goals for gross margin, sales targets and team rewards for high-performing departments can all be tied to GMROII, serving as an incentive for employees to focus on the factors that improve this metric. Marketers are advised to take note as well, since the promotional activities they create to attract buyers will have a direct impact on GMROII.

Each retailer's unique mix of business activities affects how marketers develop programs (promotions, pricing, message, point of purchase) to attract customers while also maximizing GMROII. Marketers are keen to satisfy customers and want to know that their customers are receiving what they expect when they expect it—not just that an order left their warehouse on time. However, GMROII poses some challenges for retailers. For example, retail businesses also measure operational efficiency based on the fill rate, which effectively measures the amount of stock available to fill a particular order. If a customer order requires 100 items and the retailer's available stock allows it to ship 95 items, then the fill rate is 95%. Management efficiency would suggest that filling close to 100% of the order is important, both for customer satisfaction and for reputation development for the retailer. A high GMROII may indicate a low fill rate, meaning that the retailer has low inventory (perhaps related to high inventory turnover which could indicate that the dollars invested in inventory are turned into profitable sales) and cannot fill the full order. Increasing the fill rate would compel the retailer to invest more money in advance to increase inventory (and hopefully improve future fill rates, which would satisfy customers) before turning that investment into profitable sales. Yet the return on the inventory investment would be low until sales occur to reduce the inventory.

What is the right fill rate and GMROII? Each retailer must make that decision based on their business needs, operating model, and customer expectations of service, among many considerations. Furthermore, while GMROII may be high, it could be at the expense of shipping the wrong product, the wrong quantities (as referenced above) or using the wrong transportation logistics (which might affect delivery date and final customer price).

A low GMROII may result from a different set of factors. Discounts and dating (special terms offered to customers if a purchase is paid for within a certain time limit) can reduce the GMROII, as can rebates offered at the time of sale. A retailer may have the optimal mix of inventory and fill rate, which would suggest operational efficiency and good customer satisfaction, but a low GMROII due to marketing program discounts that drove demand higher. In this instance, the marketer's programs increased demand, but it affected margins.

The point is that GMROII is useful, but not perfect. Marketers and retail management must recognize the impact of their various programs on costs, gross margins, inventory and customer satisfaction to determine the appropriate mix that yields the proper investment return.

Sources

Davis, J. *Magic Numbers for Consumer Marketing*. Singapore: John Wiley & Sons (Asia) Pte Ltd., 2005: pp.253-255.

http://64.233.167.104/search?q=cache:h1Z_16vAHeUJ:www.dcenter.com/Journal/PDFs/BeyondFill.pdf+retail+fill+rate+definition&hl=en

http://www.cascade.com/gmroi.htm

http://www.businessknowhow.com/manage/inventory.htm

Sales Per Square Foot 72

Measurement Need

Retail space is an expensive solution, whether owned or leased, so retailers need to maximize the sales per square foot of the main customer selling space.

Solution

Sales per square foot measures how productive a retailer is with the use of retail space for merchandising products that generate revenue. It is important to note that selling area refers to the actual selling space, as opposed to window displays (to which consumers have no access), dressing rooms (where no merchandise is displayed for sale) and similar non-selling floor space. Also, vacant space costs money (much like an empty airline seat costs money), so the productive use of existing space is critical to successful sales.

$$SPSF = \frac{S}{S_a}$$

Where

    $SPSF$ = sales per square foot

      S = total sales

      S_a = selling area in square feet

Suppose that a sporting goods retailer has total sales of $20 million and a total selling area across all stores of 100,000 square feet. The sales per square foot is $200, calculated as follows:

$$SPSF = \frac{\$20,000,000}{100,000}$$

$$= \$200$$

Impact on Decision Making

A retailer's selling space is a key productive asset since its business model depends on its effectiveness at utilizing this space to generate profitable sales. Retail space is a form of marketing, and marketers pay close attention to the use of each store's selling space so that it is appealing and even inspiring to customers (assuming the retailer is customer-focused)—hopefully leading to improved sales. Store layout, merchandise mix and general ambience all influence consumer purchase decisions at the store level, and each of these are important to marketers who want to create a positive shopping experience for consumers and develop the proper image for the company. As sales per square foot varies, marketers can and should review the changes to determine the factors that may be influencing sales. Furthermore, any advertising and promotions marketers run to increase customer traffic and sales will have a direct and measurable impact on sales per square foot. Of course, the challenge is determining which specific marketing programs yield financial changes.

Large retail chains will use sales per square foot to assess performance across all stores, looking for those that either under- or over-perform against the chain average. In an effort to maximize buying power from suppliers and develop consistent expectations from the market, large chains often focus on designing selling space with identical layouts and merchandise mixes. However, this assumes that customer expectations and needs are the same everywhere, which is rarely true. In the U.S., for example, there is a wide variety of cultures, regional interests and economic patterns that can penalize retailers who do not pay attention to the unique needs of customers in, for example, southern California versus those in Minnesota. The same logic applies when expanding internationally since cultural differences, language barriers and historical traditions can directly affect merchandise mixes and product acceptance. Retailers ignore these differences at their own peril. The same is true for small retailers as well, albeit on a smaller scale.

Of course, too much variety can undermine efforts to develop a consistent image in the marketplace just as much as rote repetition. Retailers must clearly understand their overall strategic objectives and determine how individual store execution supports company efforts.

Marketers will want to compare sales per square foot for the same period in prior years to understand how their programs affect buying patterns.

Promotions, such as yearly "sales"(discounts), can drive temporary revenue increases and even higher monetary margins on an absolute basis, although they will likely be lower on a percentage basis. Correspondingly, months with low or no marketing promotions may result in lower overall financial performance. The challenge is determining the proper use of aggressive marketing programs since, done too frequently, they can train consumers to wait for promotions before shopping, harming the business pattern during non-promotion periods. Marketers will also want to understand how their performance compares to that of their competitors' and/or the industry in which they compete. Table 23[1] shows sales per square foot for several leading U.S. retailers, providing interesting insight into their relative performances.

Most retailers generate daily sales reports that are consolidated into weekly and monthly financial summaries. Information on each store's square footage should be available in the detailed notes of the company's tangible assets. Marketers merely need to match each store's revenues with its square footage to ensure the correct SPSF total is calculated at the store level. This is usually aggregated to the company level to arrive at an overall average sales per square foot figure.

Table 23: Metrics for Leading U.S. Retailers

Estimated Averages per North American Stores	Average Annual Sales per Store	Average Sales per Sq. Foot	Gross Margin %	Inventory Turnover	Estimated Sq. Feet per Store
Starbucks	755,951	$504	59.1%	5.5	1,500
The Gap (includes Banana Republic & Old Navy)	4,113,870	$482	41.3%	4.8	8,585
Home Depot	44,928,000	$415	29.9%	5.3	132,000
Nordstrom (includes Rack stores)	48,765,318	$342	34.0%	4.2	142,000
Costco	113,115,743	$844	10.1%	11.7	134,000
Wal-Mart (All Stores)	see below	see below	21.4%	6.9	see below
Wal-Mart (Sam's Club only)	54,269,147	$447	see above	see above	121,445
Wal-Mart (All Stores except Sam's Clubs)	43,883,350	$375	see above	see above	117,053
Barnes & Noble	5,711,712	$243	27.6%	2.7	26,000
B Dalton Books (Barnes & Noble)	1,211,459	$299	n/a	n/a	4,130
Babbages (Barnes & Noble)	1,007,447	$659	n/a	n/a	1,534

McDonalds (Stores open over two years)	1,647,000	$549	n/a	n/m	3,000
McDonalds (All Stores as computed by BizStats)	1,409,972	$470	n/a	n/m	3,000
Outback Steak-house	3,409,000	$550	n/a	n/m	6,200
Carrabas Italian Cafe (Outback Steakhouse)	2,909,000	$437	n/a	n/m	6,650

Endnote

1 © 2003 BizStats.com http://www.bizstats.com/realworld.htm

Sources

http://www.lionhrtpub.com/orms/orms-12-97/pyrihmain.html

http://www.investopedia.com/features/industryhandbook/retail.asp

Sales/Profits Per Employee

Measurement Need

Productivity is important in every business. Retailers have high fixed costs in property, plant and equipment, plus additional investments in inventory and marketing. Retail stores with slow or no business must still pay employees to keep the business running during operating hours. Therefore, evaluating the financial contribution (sales!) generated by each employee is an important productivity measure.

Solution[1]

This is a measure of financial performance on an individual employee basis.

$$SPPE = \frac{S \ or \ P}{E}$$

Where

SPPE = sales/profit per employee

S = total sales

P = total profits

E = total number of full-time employees

Let's assume a marketer's product line has $40 million in sales and $4 million in profits and that there are 400 full-time employees working in this particular business. The sales per employee is therefore $100,000, calculated as follows:

$$SPPE = \frac{\$40,000,000}{400}$$

$$= \$100,000$$

Its profits per employee are:

$$SPPE = \frac{\$4,000,000}{400}$$

$$= \$10,000$$

Impact on Decision Making

Sales/profits per employee (SPPE) is an important measure of productivity. It helps a retailer gauge, in effect, the amount generated (either revenues or profits) per employee. A lower figure is an indication that either the company is over-staffed or under-productive with its employees and that, therefore, ways must be found to improve. Training might prove to be a worthwhile investment, for example. Or perhaps new point-of-sale technology that makes operations and consumer tracking more efficient, allowing employees to take better care of customers. Retail management may also include operations staff when measuring productivity since their wages are effectively paid by the sales revenues generated. Of course, this can distort the performance of employees on the selling floor.

A company's sales are likely to be somewhat cyclical during the course of the year, with certain times of the year stronger (from a revenue standpoint) than others. This will affect the SPPE figure differently at each change in the business cycle. For example, the Christmas holiday season in the United States is the busiest time of the year for consumers. A sizable percentage of a retailer's annual revenue is gained in November and December. This is particularly true in the toy industry. Retailers may find that their SPPE numbers are quite strong during this time (relative to the full-time employees), which can distort the overall productivity picture for a company.

SPPE may also be misleading if industry averages are used as performance benchmarks since competitors, while offering similar products, may have very different business models and cost structures. Therefore, marketers and company managers need to consider SPPE in the context of their capabilities and asset utilization first, before comparing it with the competitions. However, if your company's SPPE is dramatically different from industry norms, and you are supplying similar products, then it would be prudent to examine the reasons behind the differences more closely. It may turn out that you have longer-term challenges to correct to remain competitive.

The sales and profit data comes from the company's financial statements; specifically, from the income statement. The employee information is most likely in the human resource files. This example refers only to full-time employees.

Endnote

1 Strategis: Canada's Business and Consumer Site http://strategis.ic.gc.ca/epic/internet/inretra-comde.nsf/en/qn00027e.html

Average Transaction Size 74

Measurement Need

Retail management wants to measure the average value of each transaction.

Solution

This measures the average financial value, in dollars (or whichever currency being used), of each transaction/sale.

$$T_a = \frac{S_t}{T_t}$$

Where

T_a = average transaction size

S_t = total dollar value of sales in time t

T_t = total number of transactions in time t

Let's assume a retail store generates $1 million in sales annually, and the total number of transactions is 50,000. Then the average transaction size is $20 per transaction.

$$T_a = \frac{\$1,000,000}{50,000}$$

$$= \$20$$

Impact on Decision Making

Average transaction size is an important metric because it can help retailers measure their success in making increasingly larger sales from each customer. An important concept to understand in the preceding sentence is "increasingly larger sales". Ideally, the average transaction size should always be increasing since it strongly suggests that the retailer is having not just continued, but increasing success in selling products to its customers.

Retail managers and marketers want to know how much the average customer spends per transaction so that they can develop strategies and programs to cost effectively improve the per-transaction sales amount. Often, this is a matter of persuading customers who are already committed to buying to buy more. Ideally, retailers want to see the average transaction size increase year over year because this is a measure of their productivity, their success at selling products and their ability to regularly attract customers. Furthermore, the transaction size can be an indicator of the types of items that sell well versus those that do not. It may well suggest the profile of their average customer, even by time of day. By understanding this, retailers can also develop a plan that improves their merchandise mix and, over the longer term, more effective in-store product arrangements, point-of-purchase displays and the general attractiveness of the store layout.

Marketers and retail store managers can find the average transaction size a useful indicator of shopping patterns at different times of the day. Savvy retailers will use this information to vary the in-store promotions throughout the day, creatively combining promotions for short durations, knowing that customers buy particular combinations of products and that, with proper incentive, may be inspired to add to their purchase if the item is relevant to their profile.

Technological innovations and pricing algorithms have led to ever more sophisticated ways for studious retailers to maximize the average transaction value. These advance gather detailed, minute-by-minute data of purchase patterns per individual buyer, allowing for greater understanding of the choices customers make throughout the day.

Marketers must be careful to consider the meaning of the average transaction value before reaching conclusions. For example, purchase patterns for cold medicine may increase sharply for a brief period of time when a promotion for that product is run. However, the medicine may have been purchased due to the imminent need by the customer for the product, irrespective of the price promotion. In this instance, the marketer will have effectively decreased the product's margin when the sale would have occurred anyway. Therefore, marketers must exercise sound judgment in determining the reasons behind changes in average transaction value.

The temptation is to infer behavior when the reality is that behavior is very hard to glean from transactions statistics.

Depending on the retailer and the sophistication of its IT systems or the discipline of store management, this data is captured every day. Well-run retailers do their end-of-day totals to review the day's performance and to close the books for that day so that the next day can be measured anew. Point-of-purchase systems will usually measure each transaction individually, by item and selling price. Even manual systems record each sale so, either way, the information should be captured at the store level.

Sources

Davis, J. *Magic Numbers for Consumer Marketing*. Singapore: John Wiley & Sons (Asia) Pte Ltd., 2005: pp.259-260.

http://www.cascade.com/gmroi.htm

Average Items Per Transaction[1]

Measurement Need

Retailers need to know the typical transaction's profile, including the number and types of items purchased, the average transaction's value, and even the time of day. Knowing the average number of items per transaction reveals to the retailer part of the customer's preferences, even if the customer's expanded profile is unknown (age, income, behavior).

Solution

Average items per transaction is a simple formula, represented by:

$$S_{avg} = \frac{S}{T}$$

Where

S_{avg} = average number of items sold per transaction

S = total number of items sold

T = total number of transactions

Let's assume a traditional convenience store in the U.S. (which is about 2,500 square feet in size and offers 500 SKUs (stock keeping units))[2], sells 200 items and averages 50 transactions per day. We calculate the average number of items per transaction as follows:

$$S_{avg} = \frac{200}{50}$$
$$= 4$$

The same formula would apply to online retailers as well.

Impact on Decision Making

In absolute terms, the metric merely measures the average quantity of items purchased. But this data can also provide insight into the basic purchase patterns of their average customer. Depending on the number of items purchased and any increases over time, this metric may suggest to a traditional retailer's management that customers find their merchandise mix and store layout attractive, thereby inspiring additional purchases. Of course, the opposite is true as well. It is also conceivable that some customers prefer to buy items related to a specific category (known as item affinity, which refers to the similarity or "complementarity" between items).

A clever retailer will want to understand the mix of items in each transaction to see if there are interesting patterns or trends to be exploited. But because the metric only measures average items per transaction at the time of sale, the traditional retailer cannot determine which aisles the customers merely visited without purchasing representative products, how long the customer was in the store or where the customer went afterward. They can only speculate. However, if a marketer ran a price promotion campaign for a limited period of time and sales increased during that time, it would be reasonable to infer that the promotion affected the sales increase.

The advantage online retailers have is due partly to the unique software tools (usually called web-analytics or, simply, analytics software) available to measure Internet activity. Online marketers will find that the analytics programs offer more precision in understanding the activities a customer undertook before and after purchase, which can be useful in developing future promotions, marketing programs and merchandise selections. There are software tools for online marketers that "learn" from prior visits from customers. Known as affinity engines[3] or personalization servers, these tools are designed to provide online customers with suggestions of other products the customer might find interesting based on the items they are reviewing while on the Internet. Amazon.com, among many online retailers, illustrates this. Whenever a customer visits Amazon, her selections are remembered and, when a customer visits next, Amazon greets her with a simple reminder of what she purchased (or even merely browsed) before, recommending similar or related items the customer ought to consider. There is a great deal of programming complexity (called business rules) involved in this seemingly simple activity, but it is a capability that is growing in sophistication and it can result in a positive online shopping experience. Marketers, of course, gain important advantages with web-analytics, personalization, and affinity engines since it improves the potential for increasing the number of items per transaction.

Timberland, the outdoor footwear and apparel company, sells its products in traditional retail stores around the world as well as online through its company website. Its online efforts blend web-analytics with human judgment by using the knowledge from employees who have prior traditional in-store experience to review the data from online purchases to explain possible reasons Internet users are buying certain combinations of products. The reason for this blend of software analytics and human judgment is simple: the software alone does not fully reveal how or what customers think, merely what they do. With the insight from employees with prior in-store experience, Timberland is able to develop a richer understanding of its customers, which can be used to directly affect online merchandise selections in the future. For marketers, this is an appealing combination, since it combines hard data with softer insights, allowing them to develop marketing programs that are relevant to target customers.[4]

Marketers may be tempted to over-interpret behavior based on information resulting from this metric. Marketers should be wary of speculating about the reasons behind the actual items per transaction since many factors can affect a consumer's purchase decision. Certainly, price promotions can induce additional purchases of a product beyond a normal selling volume. But it is conceivable that spontaneous decision making may also be a factor. The key takeaway is that the reasons behind the purchase decision are hard to glean without a direct and immediate survey of a large sample of customers. The knowledge gained from such a survey can be useful, but it can be expensive and time consuming as well.

Most traditional retailers capture daily sales totals at the end of each business day. These are increasingly tracked via computerized systems, known as point of purchase systems. Assuming the retailer has an automated point of purchase system, the transactions data is captured with every customer sale, typically from electronic bar-code scanning. The data usually includes item description, quantity, price and any promotional discounts. Each transaction also logs the time of day, which is useful in identifying shopping patterns.

Online retailers have software programs that automatically track each transaction, plus provide data on customer clicking patterns. Analytics programs have been developed that can measure not just the actual item-specific sales activity, but the cross-selling factors that may have influenced the customer's final decision. For example, before a customer buys a product online, other web pages may have been viewed that influenced the customer's final decision. After the transaction is completed, the analytics programs can provide data on which web pages the customer visited next.

Endnotes

1 Davis, J. *Magic Numbers for Consumer Marketing*. Singapore: John Wiley & Sons (Asia) Pte Ltd., 2005: pp.261-263.

2 National Association of Convenience Stores (NACS) website http://www.nacsonline.com/ NR/exeres/00002daajcpwltgfkyhcgdpl/GeneralUse_Resource.asp?NRMODE=Published& NRORIGINALURL=%2fNACS%2fResource%2fIndustryResearch%2fwhat_is_a_cstore% 2ehtm&NRNODEGUID=%7b26411FAF-587F-466D-8968-90799BACDE74%7d&NRQU ERYTERMINATOR=1&cookie%5Ftest=1

3 IBM website, WebSphere Portal http://publib.boulder.ibm.com/infocenter/wpdoc/v510/index. jsp?topic=/com.ibm.wp.zos.doc/pzn/pzn_item_affinity_engine.html

4 Internetretailer.com http://www.internetretailer.com/dailyNews.asp?id=10397

Retail Close Ratio 76

Measurement Need

Retailers want paying customers and not merely window shoppers (those who browse but do not purchase). Both types of customers visit stores, so the retailer wants to know how many of the total customers become paying customers.

Solution

The close ratio measures how many customers convert from shoppers to actual buyers. It is calculated as follows:

$$C_r = \frac{B_t}{T_r}$$

Where

C_r = close ratio

B_t = buyers in time t

T_t = total traffic in time t

Continuing with the convenience store example from Chapter 75, our retailer has 50 total buyers on any given day. If this retailer has total traffic of 500 shoppers in the store, then the close ratio is 10%, computed as follows:

$$C_r = \frac{50}{500}$$

$$= 0.10 \text{ or } 10\%$$

Similarly to Chapters 74 and 75, the data for buyers (transactions) is captured in the end-of-day totals and/or in the point of purchase software. The harder figure to determine is the total number of shoppers, but this can be done either with electronic counters mounted near the entrance to the store, or people can be hired to survey the total number of shoppers who visit each day over a period of several days to determine an average.

Impact on Decision Making

Understanding the close ratio can assist retailers in developing strategies designed to increase the conversion from shoppers to buyers, which will likely lead to increased sales. A useful marketing tool in Figure 20 is derived from the Ansoff Matrix[1] outlining available options.

| | **Products** | |
	Existing	New
Existing	• Sell more of existing products to same customers 1. Increase share of wallet	• Sell new products to same customers 1. Innovate and develop new products
New	• Sell existing products to new customers 1. Expand geographically 2. Win customers from competitors	• Sell new products to new customers 1. Innovate new products 2. Target new customers

Customers is the label for the left side (rows).

Figure 20: Strategic Growth Choices

Each quadrant describes a different customer and product approach. Of course, this framework can be expanded by marketers to outline corresponding marketing programs, including pricing, promotion and placement. The purpose is to determine a strategy or combination of strategies to inspire higher conversion from shoppers to buyers and, thus, increase sales.

Most retailers do not have the time or resources to count shoppers who visit their store on any given day, although there are tools available to assist. Electronic triggers mounted at store entrances can record each shopper that crosses their path, enabling store managers to review the visitor totals when they close the daily books. A more expensive, and arguably less precise, option is to pay someone to count the number of shoppers who enter the store over a period of a few days to develop an average shopper total for those days. Errors are reduced with electronic triggers or even doormat counters that record a shopper every time someone steps on the mat. However, these, too, can be imperfect since shopping carts may be mistakenly counted as shoppers. Furthermore, the electronic method does not distinguish between unique visitors, repeat visitors and buyers; information that is of interest to marketers since they want to understand buyer profiles as deeply as possible to develop marketing programs that maximize purchases.

Endnote

1 The Ansoff Matrix first appeared in the *Harvard Business Review* in 1957 in an article by H. I. Ansoff entitled "Strategies for Diversification". Ansoff discussed it further in his book *Corporate Strategy*, New York: McGraw-Hill, 1965.

Retailer's Margin Percentage

Measurement Need

Retailing is a high-cost business yielding low margins. High capital investment in equipment, plus facilities costs, whether leased or owned, put pressure on the retailer to generate profitable sales. Additional costs include labor and inventory. Each of these costs reduces the retailer's profits, so it is imperative that retail management has a clear understanding of their margin objectives.

Solution

The retailer's margin percentage is the profit margin that retailers realize after purchasing from the wholesaler and then selling to the consumer. It is a measure of how much money the retailer makes. The following formula summarizes the calculation:

$$RMP = \frac{(S_p - P_p)}{S_p}$$

Where

RMP = retailer's margin in percentage terms

S_p = selling price to consumers

P_p = purchase price from wholesalers

Suppose a retailer is selling a consumer product at a retail price of $5 and the price they paid from the wholesaler was $2.50. The retailer margin percentage is 50%.

$$RMP = \frac{(\$5 - \$2.50)}{\$5}$$

$$= 50\%$$

Impact on Decision Making

A retailer's margin percentage objectives have an important impact on product and category profitability, positioning and even image. They reflect the retailer's strategy in attracting the target audience and they are also influenced by the manufacturer's own recommendations. If a retailer selects a premium price position, it is most likely trying to achieve higher margins. However, higher margins are usually not associated with high volume. Conversely, lower margins may signal a more aggressive position to grow demand through volume sales, but then low-price retailers can often face negative returns, especially during slower selling cycles.

The retailer's margin percentage will also influence the retailer's merchandise mix between store brands and national or global brands. Store brands may allow a retailer to increase its margins, even accounting for the in-house production and manufacturing costs, over non-store, national brands, thereby improving the retailer's margin percentage. For non-marketers, store brands are a retailer's own product, typically developed and marketed by them. Store brands are usually lower priced (and sometimes lower quality) versions of better-known branded products. However, many store brands have improved their quality in recent years. Either way, a store brand reduces costs for the retailer since the retailer is not paying the premium prices for the national brands. Part of the higher pricing for national brands is to offset the higher advertising costs, although the higher prices also reflect the fact that national brands are better known and trusted, allowing their companies to charge higher prices. For companies like WalMart, store brands can be a very effective component of their merchandise mix and overall profitability, especially if they do not get the margin concessions they expect from large international brands. A smaller, less well-known retailer may depend on non-store brands simply because it does not have the financial wherewithal to develop its own product line.

Retailers set prices based on several factors including their own per-store expenses, store positioning, product type and customer type. Manufacturers influence retail price expectations by providing guidelines to their retail accounts, depending on their own positioning and margin objectives. In the U.S., laws and regulations prevent manufacturers from dictating a retail selling price. However, they provide a "manufacturer's suggested retail price", which can be a very persuasive guide, depending on the strength (in terms of brand or overall market size and clout) of the company. Manufacturers, such as Nike, want to encourage retailers to properly represent their products and price is one of the key tools in this effort.

The final retail price is also affected by slotting fees (payments a manufacturer pays to a retailer to place the products on store shelves), co-op marketing (a shared advertising or promotional arrangement between manufacturers and retailers to encourage product sales), promotional allowances (additional discounts offered to retailers for performing promotional activities in support of the manufacturer's products) and other similar marketing programs. For manufacturers and retailers, these fees are usually set at the corporate level and are often negotiated. Retailers will have their own set of pricing and profit guidelines for each product they sell, often down to the individual store level (since goals may vary slightly from market to market, even if the store is part of a chain). In some cases, the corporate strategy may include a tacit understanding that each store manager has limited freedom to adjust corporate requirements based on the prevailing market situation in a given area.

The wholesale selling price is usually found on shipping or customer invoices, purchase orders and/or accounting reports. The retail selling price to consumers is influenced by several factors including manufacturers, marketing programs and, of course, consumer response. Ultimately, the retailer will have this information contained in its end of day sales summaries at the store level, by item.

Sources

http://www.oligopolywatch.com/2003/05/08.html

Hurlbut, T. "Gross Margin—The Overlooked Percentage". *Inc. Magazine* online: http://www.inc.com/resources/retail/articles/200509/hurlbut.htmljh

http://www.csgnetwork.com/marginmarkuptable.html

Markdown Goods Percentage 78

Measurement Need

Retailers sell products at both full retail and markdown prices. Markdowns refer to the amount reduced from the original selling price[1]. The markdown goods percentage (MGP) describes the percentage of total net sales attributed to products sold at markdown prices. Markdown goods percentage also helps retailers determine their effectiveness at selling products at full price since the difference between total net sales and sales from markdown prices is full price sales.

Solution[2]

MGP is represented as follows:

$$MGP = \frac{S_{nmt}}{S_{nt}} \times 100$$

Where

MGP = markdown goods percentage

S_{nmt} = net sales at markdown during time period t

S_{nt} = total net sales during time period t

For example, if your store sells $10,000 per day of merchandise, of which $2,500 is attributed to markdowns, then the MGP is 25%.

$$MGP = \frac{\$2,500}{\$10,000} \times 100$$

$$= 25\%$$

Impact on Decision Making

The MGP offers a retailer insight about how its products are selling by showing the percentage of sales attributable to both full retail prices and markdowns. If the markdown percentage is high, then it may signal to the retailer that problems exist in its operation that need to be addressed if the retailer is to improve the ratio of products sold at full price. When the markdown percentage increases, retailers will want to review their merchandise selection and store design, compare their pricing to the competition's, evaluate their advertising efforts, and examine their inventory levels to determine if they have overbought certain items. Each of these factors can contribute to a high MGP. Retail margins are notoriously low, so avoiding a high MGP is a priority for retailers and should be addressed promptly.

Endnotes

1 American Marketing Association (AMA) website http://www. marketingpower.com/mg-dictionary-view1813.php

2 Strategis: Canada's Business and Consumer Site http://strategis.ic.gc.ca/epic/internet/inretra-comde.nsf/en/qn00027e.html

Source

http://www.apparelsearch.com/retail_math.htm#Markdown%20Dollar%20%20%20ApparelSearch.com

Percent Utilization of Discounts

Measurement Need

When retailers buy products from suppliers, the supplier often offers discounts for certain volume levels or as an incentive for the retailer to purchase specific products the supplier is particularly keen on selling. At the end of each business reporting cycle, retailers review the financial results of the time period being measured. This includes measuring the discounts actually taken from suppliers when purchasing merchandise, to determine if the various discount opportunities offered were utilized. Each discount represents the potential for the retailer to improve their margin, hence the importance of understanding this metric.

Solution[1]

Percent utilization of discounts (PUD) measures the total value of discounts taken compared to the total purchases from the supplier:

$$PUD = \frac{V_d}{P_t} \times 100$$

Where

PUD = percent utilization of discounts

V_d = $ value of discounts taken

P_t = total $ purchases

A retailer's buyer or buying team (in the case of large, multi-department retailers such as warehouse stores and department stores) purchase their merchandise from a network of suppliers. The suppliers induce product sales often through the use of buyer discounts, used primarily to increase the placement of new products and/or for volume purchases. If a supplier offers 20% discounts for purchases over $100,000, then a retailer that buys $200,000 of merchandise will pay $160,000:

$$PUD = \frac{\$40,000}{\$200,000} \times 100$$

$$= 20\%$$

Impact on Decision Making

PUD is a simple, yet highly useful measure enabling retailers to see what percentage of their total purchases received a discount. Retailers want to maximize the use of supplier discounts since it can lead to improved retail margins. When the level of supplier discounts utilization is low, then the retailer can review purchases with their buyers to see where and what discounts were missed. The information would also demonstrate to the buyer the bottom line impact of missed supplier discount opportunities.

Endnote

1 Strategis: Canada's Business and Consumer Site http://strategis.ic.gc.ca/epic/internet/inretra-comde.nsf/en/qn00027e.html

Shrinkage to Net Sales 80

Measurement Need

Shrinkage is a retail term used to describe the difference between inventory purchased and officially received at the time of delivery, and the actual value of that same inventory in the stores, warehouses, or other stages in the retailer's distribution channel. Shrinkage results from customer or employee theft, misplaced or careless inventory storage, or administrative errors. Retail management needs to determine the percentage of inventory lost to shrinkage.

Solution[1]

Shrinkage to net sales (SNS) is calculated as follows:

$$SNS = \frac{AI - BI}{S_{nt}} \times 100$$

Where

SNS = shrinkage to net sales

AI = actual inventory in $ (measured at the retailer's cost)

BI = book inventory in $ (measured at the retailer's cost)

S_{nt} = net $ sales in time period t

Retailers regularly confront unaccounted inventory shrinkage. Let's assume a local hardware store that sells tools does a weekly inventory and its most recent results reveal that the actual inventory for its most recent week-ending inventory was valued at $55,000. The managers compare that number with the book inventory (determined by calculating inventory purchases minus sales for the same week) which indicates a value of $62,000. Total net sales for that week were $71,000 (measured at full retail price). The calculation is as follows:

$$SNS = \frac{\$55,000 - \$62,000}{\$71,0000} \times 100$$

$$= -9.9\%$$

Therefore, this retailer has SNS of 9.9%. With low net margins common in retail businesses, a nearly 10% shrinkage has a substantial impact on the bottom line.

Impact on Decision Making

SNS helps retailers understand the direct financial impact of shrinkage, although it does not suggest a cause. Retail management should review its security procedures and inventory tracking systems, compare purchase orders to products shipped, and review the signatures that approved inventory for shipping. Management should also review any records that contain daily inventory levels and identify the times of day when products were shipped to determine any patterns that may exist. Perhaps the same employee is on the job each time actual versus book inventory levels differ and is improperly recording shipments, in which case more training is needed. It is conceivable that when the inventory was first received it was counted incorrectly. Of course, the worst-case scenario is theft and pilferage. The most important action management should take is to reduce shrinkage through a diligent review of every touch point the inventory crossed from its arrival to its shipment (or when it went missing).

Endnote

1 Strategis: Canada's Business and Consumer Site http://strategis.ic.gc.ca/epic/internet/inretra-comde.nsf/en/qn00027e.html

Sources

Stitches Magazine: http://stitches.com/mag/apparel_inventory_shrinkagea_growing/index.html

Retail Industry: http://retailindustry.about.com/cs/lp_retailstore/a/bl_ey051303.htm

III

SALES FORCE

The measures in this section help sales managers set the size of their sales force, establish quotas, evaluate salesperson performance, calculate variances to plan and determine compensation. They are:

Sales force size

- Independent sales representative analysis
- Percent of sales
- Turnover rate
- Recruiting
- Breakdown approach
- Workload approach

Sales force quotas

- Sales performance quotas
- Average sales per call
- Close process and close ratio
- Cost per call
- Break-even sales volume
- Sales productivity
- Four factor model
- Sales variance analysis

Sales variance analysis

- Sales price variance
- Sales volume variance

Sales force compensation

- Straight commission plans
- Profit-based commissions

- Straight salary

- Salary plus commission or bonus

- Salary plus commission and bonus

- Commission plus bonus

- Team selling compensation

Sales forces conducting person-to-person selling remain one of the most effective ways to market products. The costs are higher due to the limited number of customers a salesperson can reach, versus the broad-based reach of integrated marketing communications. But business is still conducted primarily based on relationships between companies and with customers, so salespeople play a critical role.

Salespeople uncover the needs of buyers, whether retail buyers, wholesalers, B2B buying teams or individual consumers in retail stores. The best salespeople excel due to a unique combination of business intelligence, entrepreneurial spirit, strong people skills and an intense desire to win.

Companies have a significant investment in their sales forces and they want to see them succeed by producing a regular stream of sales from new and existing customers. Sales management must plan their sales activities each year based on corporate goals, market conditions and the performance expectations of each salesperson. The challenges are sizable since markets, customers and competitors constantly change. The challenges are compounded by the relentless pressure to produce results. Sales management has to establish the right expectations via quotas and targets, monitor the activities of each salesperson, keep the sales team focused on growing the business, motivate the team to keep working hard, and minimize interference from non-salespeople in the organization.

The measures in this section provide needed quantitative insight. Selling success is a relationship-driven process, however. No matter how elegant or sophisticated the quantitative analysis, closing the sale depends on interpersonal relationships, in which trust is crucial. The Five Ambassadors framework[1], shown in Figure 21, describes the behaviors of top-performing businesspeople, particularly those in sales. It should be given careful consideration by sales and marketing management in the development of their plans since, ultimately, talented people are needed to ensure successful implementation.

Figure 21: Value-Producing Behaviours of Top Performers

The Five Ambassadors framework describes the behaviors of top performers. It has evolved over five years. Initially based on interviews with U.S. CEOs and top sales performers, it has been further developed since, through discussions with CEOs of companies in Asia and Europe, feedback about top sales performers in multiple industries, and student research of over 90 companies in the U.S. and Asia since 2001.

Each of the Five Ambassadors is a specific behavior exhibited by the top performers at different times of their job. Typically, these behaviors were most prominent when the individual was selling a product, service or idea. The top performer effortlessly shifted from one Ambassador role to the next, depending on the specific business conditions they faced at that time. The Five Ambassadors behaviors were also exhibited when the top performers were seeking assistance (funding, budget increase, project help) from another party. These behaviors are rarely conscious. The top performer did not think to him or herself, "Now I must act like a resource ambassador." Rather, the Five Ambassadors were a fluid set of behaviors that ultimately convinced the other party of the merits of the top performer's argument. Each of the Five Ambassadors encompasses multiple behaviors, but the behaviors are similar enough to be grouped into the broader Ambassador designations. Separately, each of the Five Ambassadors is an admirable set of behavior characteristics. Collectively, they are a powerful combination of skills that contributes to the overall success of the enterprise. Finally, the Five Ambassadors are not sequential behaviors. They are often simultaneous.

Brand Ambassador

This describes an individual's efforts to present his or her company, product or department to another person or group (customer, vendor or another internal department), using visual or verbal imagery. Visual imagery is self-explanatory: top performers are adept at using relevant visual examples to complement their presentation, making it memorable and connecting the audience to the initiative being presented. Verbal imagery deals with the words used to paint verbal pictures.

Resource Ambassador

Resource Ambassador describes the top performer's understanding of his or her own company. This is not merely a surface level awareness of the company's products, but an in-depth understanding of its organization: the most influential people, how different departments contribute, and which resources would be most appealing and relevant to the buying or receiving party. It is often exhibited as an explicit description of which departments or functions were part of the solution being sold. For example, in the enterprise software industry, a product sale is far more than just the software. It includes engineering support, customer service, warranties, consulting and more. Once the sale is made, the customer requires that the product works and functions as specified and, if not, wants to know what remedies are available. Top performers understand this and, in the pre-sales effort, they work hard to describe these various resources to convince the customer that the company supports its products and to differentiate themselves from competing products. The bottom line is that the Resource Ambassador behaviors connect a company to the customer beyond the core product purchase by extending the product definition to include the areas that support it. As a result, the customer develops confidence that the company will support the products it sells.

Knowledge Ambassador

The Knowledge Ambassador describes the knowledge that the top performer has and uses to describe for the buyer market conditions, trends in the economic environment and similar information. The top performer then presents this information throughout the sales or persuasion process to help the customer understand outside conditions and influences that could affect his or her business (explaining the "need" to buy the product). This information is gleaned from a wide range of sources (the Internet, magazines, newspapers) and becomes a crucial aspect of the top performer's efforts to win the customer. Top performers frequently update their market knowledge so that they can be an advocate for both the customer and their own company while demonstrating why the customer needs its products to be successful in the challenging environment described. The Knowledge Ambassador behaviors help the customer become smarter about his or her own business and understand why the seller's products are an integral piece of their success.

Relationship Ambassador

The Relationship Ambassador behaviors describe how sellers relate to buyers. A salesperson must have a deep understanding of his or her buyers. Not just the company overall, but the buyers individually, including who they are, what they like and dislike, what their interests are, why they have bought before, and what they have bought before. The Relationship Ambassador behaviors continue even when a sale has been completed, as the seller shifts to a more informal relationship, but never stops contact. The seller wants to be the first person the buyer thinks of when it comes time to purchase again.

Experience Ambassador

The Experience Ambassador behaviors relate to the wisdom that comes from trial and error and the application of that wisdom every day.

Overall, the Five Ambassadors are a seamless pattern of behaviors exhibited by top performers. Rather than approaching each business relationship with a methodical, rigid plan outlining their behavior, the top performers combine spontaneity with thoughtful planning to achieve their objectives.

Sales managers understand the dual needs of quantitative and qualitative measures. The challenge is determining what measures are most important so that a salesperson's performance can be improved.

Endnote

1 Davis, J. *Magic Numbers for Consumer Marketing.* Singapore: John Wiley & Sons (Asia) Pte Ltd., 2005: pp.116-128.

Independent Sales Representative Analysis

81

Measurement Need

A critical need is determining whether to have a dedicated sales force, and the associated higher fixed costs, or an independent sales force, usually from a third-party firm contracted to the company. The question is how to compare these two approaches.

Solution[1]

The analysis begins with setting the cost of a company sales force and an independent sales force equal to each other:

cost of company sales force = cost of independent sales force

Sales management would need to solve for the breakeven level of sales, below which the independent sales force would be more attractive and above which the dedicated sales force is the more sensible approach. To do this, cost comparisons need to be made. Let's assume the company has a total sales cost of $3 million and company-employed salespeople are paid $75,000 plus a 4% commission on each sale. The average independent salesperson is paid a 7% commission, plus an allowance for administrative costs of $25,000 per person. In the formula below, x represents the breakeven level of sales:

$$0.04x + \$3,000,000 = 0.07x + \$25,000$$

$$\$2,975,000 = 0.03x$$

$$\$99,166,667 = x$$

Therefore, break-even sales is \$99,166,667, below which the company should use the independent sales force and above which the company should use a dedicated force.

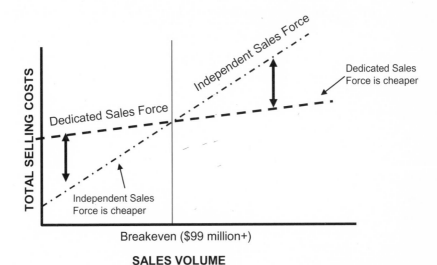

Figure 22: Total Cost—Independent Sales Force vs Dedicated Sales Force[1]

Impact on Decision Making

Cost is not the only consideration for sales management in weighing the pros and cons of a dedicated sales force versus an independent sales force. In the 1990s, Nike's ACG (outdoor products) division used a combination of company salespeople (called "in-line") and an independent sales force. The in-line salespeople knew Nike's strategic retail accounts best (such as Footlocker, FootAction, SportMart), while the contracted independent sales force were experts in the outdoor market and had relationships with leading retailers specializing in outdoor products (hiking shoes, trail shoes, cycling footwear, outdoor sandals). Nike needed the credibility with the outdoor retailers provided by the independent sales force's expertise in that market.

A dedicated sales force is expensive since the company is paying salary and full benefits, even as sales cycles inevitably increase and decrease. But a dedicated sales force is also going to be more loyal and devoted to the company's products, whereas an independent sales force is representing products from multiple companies and may emphasize those products easiest to sell. However, a proven independent sales force provides a significant boost to the company by generating sales at a lower cost. Furthermore, similar to the reward options available to in-house sales forces, company management can create incentives to facilitate better cooperation and performance from the independent team.

There is no clear-cut resolution, nor should this analysis be used to guarantee one. Sales management needs to consider the situation in which their company operates and factor in longer-term strategic goals. Costs will influence the decision, but other harder to control factors, like dedication and loyalty, may dictate which option will be more successful in the long term.

Endnote

1 Adapted from: Cron, W.L., DeCarlo, T.E. and Palrymple, D.J. *Sales Management*. New York: John Wiley & Sons, Inc., 2004: pp.253-254.

Percent of Sales 82

Measurement Need

To help determine the optimal sales force size (and the associated investment), management can base it on a percent of sales. Sales force size and investment, therefore, would be based on the coming period's forecast.

Solution[1]

The percent of sales measurement is calculated using the following steps:

1. Forecast planned revenues
2. Determine percent of sales based on industry standards, the firm's own historical performance, or a combination of both
3. Budget for management and field sales roles

Let's assume that a New York-based food manufacturer of classic New York hot dogs had sales of $50 million last year and anticipates 20% growth next year, to $60 million in sales. It sells to retail chains and individual sidewalk vendors, and the industry average for the cost of the sales force as a percentage of total sales is 3.6%. The company's sales budget is divided into management (20%), field sales (75%) and support staff (5%). Based on this, we can now determine the sales force size by first calculating:

1. Sales force budget
2. Sales force percent
3. Sales force dollars

Sales force budget

$$SFB \ = \ PR \times FSR$$

Where

SFB = sales force budget

PR = projected revenues

FSR = field sales ratio (based on industry average)

$$SFB = \$60,000,000 \times 0.036$$

$$= \$2,160,000$$

Sales force percent

$$SFP = FS + SS$$

Where

SFP = sales force percent

FS = field sales percent of budget dollars

SS = support staff percent of budget dollars

$$SFP = 0.75 + 0.05$$

$$= 0.80$$

Sales force dollars

$$SFD = SFB \times SFP$$

Where

SFD = sales force dollars

SFB = sales force budget

SFP = sales force percent

$$SFD = \$2,160,000 \times 0.80$$

$$= \$1,728,000$$

If the average salesperson in this company (or industry) costs $75,000 (including salary, bonus, commission and benefits—also known as "fully loaded"costs), then we can calculate the number of salespeople the company can afford as follows:

$$SFS = \frac{SFD}{SFC}$$

Where

SFS = sales force size

SFD = sales force dollars

SFC = sales force costs

$$SFS = \frac{\$1,728,000}{\$75,000}$$

$$= 23$$

If it had 20 people last year, then three additional people can be hired for a total sales force size of 23.

Impact on Decision Making

Sales management may find this tool useful for planning purposes and to justify an expansion in its team. However, management should also consider whether the gain in sales can be accomplished by altering compensation incentives of the existing team, realigning territories or shifting responsibilities among the existing team members. Hiring new people adds a sizable potential cost to the sales budget and, if the forecast numbers are not met, then the sales organization's performance will be worse than before since new people were added but no new sales. The pressure will then be on sales management to quickly either increase sales, thereby putting additional stress on the field sales force, or terminate some of their sales reps, potentially hurting morale.

The use of industry standards, as shown in Table 24, is rarely a practical benchmark, attractive though it may be for planning purposes. Industry standards use averages, but often companies within an industry have significantly different operating standards, sizes and financial requirements, distorting the averages. The chart on the following page provides data on the average sales force size across industries. If a company is noticeably different than its industry average, then management would be wise to analyze the possible reasons for the variation, keeping its own context firmly in mind. For example, if traditional PC manufacturers compare their percent of sales with the industry average, they may be in for a shock since the industry average would include figures from low-cost operators like Dell. Yet trying to match Dell's figure would materially harm the company's competitive position since fewer sales people would be used to achieve the same level of sales. In this case, the challenge for Dell's competitors is not related to sales force cost, but instead lies in their operating model, a far more daunting and complex challenge to address.

Table 24[2]: Sales Force Cost as a Percentage of Sales

	Sales Force Total Cost as a Percentage of Sales		Sales Force Total Cost as a Percentage of Sales
Company Size		**Industry**	
Under $5 million	14.7%	Business Services	1.7%
$5-$25 million	10.5%	Chemicals	2.9%
$25-$100 million	7.9%	Communications	9.8%
$100-$250 million	3.5%	Educational Services	47.9%
Over $250 million	6.8%	Electronics	4.2%
		Fabricated Metals	10.8%
Product or Service		Health Services	19.9%
Industrial Products	4.1%	Hotels & Other Lodgings	21.4%
Industrial Services	6.4%	Instruments	2.3%
Office Products	9.4%	Machinery	10.1%
Office Services	8.1%	Manufacturing	13.6%
Consumer Products	5.4%	Office Equipment	9.0%
Consumer Services	7.9%	Paper & Allied Products	6.8%
		Printing & Publishing	12.0%
		Retail	6.1%
		Trucking & Warehousing	12.2%
		Wholesale (Consumer Goods)	3.7%
		Wholesale (Industrial Goods)	9.5%
		Average	6.9%

Endnotes

1 Adapted from: Cron, W.L., DeCarlo, T.E. and Palrymple, D.J. *Sales Management*. New York: John Wiley & Sons, Inc., 2004: pp.114-115.

2 Ibid., p.115.

Source

Cron, W. L., De Carlo, T. E. and Palrymple, D. J. *Sales Management*. New York: John Wiley & Sons, Inc., 2004: p.115.

Turnover Rate

Measurement Need

Departures of salespeople can be expensive since management invests time and money into recruiting, training and retaining salespeople. When salespeople leave, especially top performers, they take knowledge (about the company, its products and its strategy, as well as insight into their own territories about customers and market dynamics) to another firm. Therefore, reducing turnover is an important need for sales management.

Solution[1]

The turnover rate calculates the number of salesperson departures relative to the total sales force size, multiplied by 100 (to convert it to a percentage):

$$TR = \frac{D}{F} \times 100$$

Where

TR = turnover rate

D = number of departures annually

F = total sales force size (annual average)

If a company has 1,000 sales people worldwide and 75 depart, then the turnover rate is 7.5%.

$$TR = \frac{75}{1,000} \times 100$$

$$= 7.5\%$$

Impact on Decision Making

Turnover is inevitable as organizations change. The turnover rate should be reviewed in light of your company's strategic objectives to determine if your results are "acceptable". Industry and competitor comparisons may be part of your company's sales review, but be cautious because these statistics are based on averages and may offer little practical guidance given the unique circumstances of your company. A low turnover percentage may sound great from the HR and expense perspectives, but it may also signal that your company is overly generous with its compensation, loose with its performance standards, or that sales management has a hard time identifying and replacing under-performing people.

Turnover is comprised of several components:

- Death

- Involuntary departure (i.e. termination)

- Voluntary departure (i.e. recruitment by another company)

- Retirement

- Internal transfer

Death, of course, is a form of involuntary departure. As the least controllable factor, it should not be a key management concern. Termination results from poor performance, poor sales rep/company fit, illegal or unethical salesperson behavior, or job loss due to company-wide cutbacks. Sales management can minimize turnover from termination if their recruiting and candidate selection criteria are clear, the interview process involves managers and colleagues from several departments, and a thorough background check is conducted. Voluntary departure may be within management's control if it is familiar with its salespeople and can identify sources of dissatisfaction before they grow into problems. Sales management may decide to respond by improving financial compensation, promoting staff, changing responsibilities or offering other non-financial benefits (more days of paid vacation, for example). Any of these decisions will be weighted against the potential future value expected from the sales reps most likely to depart. Retirement is less likely to be a significant challenge for savvy sales management since they will have anticipated replacing those retiring for months or even years, allowing time for recruiting of new salespeople and for succession planning. However, early retirement may occasionally surprise sales management, perhaps due to personal reasons from the sales rep.

In each of these instances, sales management must decide whether replacement is warranted or if the departing person's responsibilities can be reassigned to other members of the sales team.

Turnover's impact can cost your company money in other ways. A 2004 report by Better Jobs Better Care, a U.S.-based program funded by the Atlantic Philanthropies and The Robert Wood Johnson Foundation, outlined additional costs related to turnover[2]:

Direct costs include

- Cost of separation from the company
- Cost of vacancy
- Cost of replacement
- Cost of training and orientation
- Cost of increased injured workers

Indirect costs include

- Lost productivity until replacement is trained
- Cost due to reduced service quality
- Lost clients to other agencies due to deterioration in agency image, etc
- Cost due to deterioration in organizational culture and employee morale adversely impacting reputation, service quality and further increasing turnover

Costs at service delivery level include
- Consumer/Clients

    o Reduction in quality of care and quality of life
    o Care hours not provided
- Workers

    o Increased worker injuries
    o Increased physical and emotional stress
    o Deterioration in working conditions leading to increased likelihood of quitting

Third-party payer costs include

- Under-funding of care services due to financial drain of turnover
- Increased downstream medical costs due to illnesses and injuries attributable to reduced service quality
- Illnesses and injuries attributable to reduced service quality
- Higher levels of institutionalization of clients due to insufficient community based staffing & quality of care

Given the expense related to turnover, sales managers should conduct diligent and thorough evaluations of the causes of their organization's turnover to determine areas for improvement.

Endnotes

1 http://www.tutor2u.net/business/people/workforce_turnover.asp

2 Adapted from: http://www.bjbc.org/content/docs/TOCostReport.pdf

For additional insight and formulas about turnover, visit:

http://www.uwex.edu/ces/cced/publicat/turn.html#calc

Recruiting 84

Measurement Need

With salespeople filling a vital role (growing revenues, profits and customers), identifying and recruiting the best talent is one of sales management's most important tasks. Sales management may lead its own recruiting effort or, more likely, they will work with the human resources department to coordinate the recruiting efforts. Since successfully recruiting the right talent is rarely a 1:1 ratio (one applicant leads to one hire), there is a need to determine the number of applicants required to ultimately fill the vacant positions.

Solution[1]

The following formula can be used to determine the scope of the recruiting effort:

$$R = \frac{H}{S \times A}$$

Where

R = recruiting

H = new hires required

S = percentage of recruits selected

A = percentage who accept

An illustration will help:

- Company X needs 25 new salespeople

- Past experience indicates 20% of those who apply will be offered positions

- HR statistics suggest that 75% of those offered a new position will accept

Simply plug in the data:

$$R = \frac{25}{(0.20) \times (0.75)}$$

$$= 167$$

Based on these statistics, a minimum of 167 people would need to apply if the company wants to fill the 25 positions.

Impact on Decision Making

Recruiting is an important activity and sales management must carefully plan the time and people resources required to do an effective job. In this basic example, 167 applicants may be a large number of applicants to review if your organization is small or medium-sized. On the other hand, if you are IBM, then the number of people available from HR and field sales is large enough that the responsibilities can be distributed with lower disruption from regular work activities. No matter how large the organization, recruiting requires a keen sense of the following:

- the company's culture
- the personalities that would fit your company's culture
- the skills of recruits sought
- a clear process for the recruit that is explained upfront
- a thoughtful description of the job
- a set of interview questions designed to identify the best possible candidates for your company
- the professional will to stick to your overall recruiting standards and not settle on talent less qualified than you need

Endnote

1 Adapted from: Cron, W.L., DeCarlo, T.E. and Palrymple, D.J. *Sales Management*. New York: John Wiley & Sons, Inc., 2004: p.324.

Breakdown Approach

85

Measurement Need

As a company's business grows, successfully servicing existing and new customers is both a responsibility and ongoing challenge for the field sales force. Every company is different, and tailors their sales planning based on corporate sales objectives (volume or profit-oriented, customer loyalty or new customer acquisition) and market conditions (customer needs, competitor tactics, economic and demographic trends). Sales managers design their tactical go-to-market plans around maximizing the potential financial returns from their targeted customer base. They must determine how many salespeople are needed to service existing customers and also attract new customers. Given these factors, companies need to determine sales force size, and the breakdown approach is useful when the primary information available to a company's decision makers, aside from its own baseline sales, is market growth (economic and/or demographic).

Solution

To determine sales force size using the breakdown approach, a different formula is used than the one introduced in Chapter 82. Sales professionals must know their previous sales history, projections of their own new sales for the upcoming year, and market forecasts.[1] It is calculated using this formula[2]:

$$SFS = \frac{FS}{SPP}$$

Where

SFS = sales force size

FS = forecasted sales

SPP = average sales per person

To determine sales force size, sales management must first develop total forecast sales for the year. To illustrate[3], let's assume that a herbal beverage company had sales of $100 million last year, and management wants to know the sales force size needed to succeed in the current year. Due to the nature of the company's contracts with its distributors, all existing business will be renewed for the coming year. Furthermore, the company has confirmed a new distributor contract for $5 million. Research indicates the overall market in herbal beverages will grow 15% this year. To summarize:

Sales previous year $= \$100,000,000$

New distributor contracts current year $= \$5,000,000$

Preliminary sales forecast current year $= \$105,000,000$

Projected total market growth $= 15\%$

The company's current year's sales forecast is the sum of last year's sales plus this year's expected new contracts plus projected market growth:

$$FS = FS_p + MG \text{ (in dollars)}$$

Where

FS = current year's forecasted sales

FS_p = current year preliminary sales forecast

MG = market growth in dollars

Therefore,

$$FS_p = \$105,000,000 + \$15,750,000$$

$$= \$120,750,000$$

At this stage, the company can determine whether its existing sales force is the right size or if it needs to adjust it (increase or decrease) based on the total forecast sales. Last year, the herbal beverage company had 100 salespeople. The average salesperson generated sales of $1 million ($100,000,000 / 100). To maintain $1 million of sales per person, this company must have 121 sales people, a 21% increase in sales force size:

Average sales per person $= \$1,000,000$

Sales force size $= \dfrac{\$120,750,000}{\$1,000,000}$

$= 121$ salespeople needed

Impact on Decision Making

The breakdown approach is useful for determining sales force size, but sales professionals must be careful not to depend only on last year's average sales per person as a benchmark for future sales needs. As business grows, companies seek to improve both efficiency and effectiveness, which includes establishing growth targets for existing salespeople. The example in this chapter simplifies a common sales management challenge: how to inspire the sales force to achieve these new growth targets yet not demotivate them by being overly aggressive. The breakdown approach might lure sales management into the comfortable world of maintaining existing sales standards ($1 million of sales per person in this case). While the field sales force may find the new goals a relief, since they only have to maintain the same level of sales as last year's (it is the number of new representatives hired that drives growth in this case), it offers little long-term challenge, and the risk of complacency grows over time. Conversely, if the same 100 salespeople are asked to achieve the new $120.75 million target, then the 21% sales increase required may be too formidable, leading to reduced motivation.

Sales management must look at the factors contributing to the projected sales increase. Sales data for the previous year's sales is found in the annual report. Expected market growth can be obtained from economic forecasts for the given company's specific industry. And projected customer growth can be learned from market research data including customer survey information. Each of these will affect the sales management's decision on the right balance between sales force size requirements and projected sales growth.

Endnotes

1 http://www.busmgt.ulst.ac.uk/h_mifflin/glossary/glossary.html

2 http://futrell-www.tamu.edu/SM_OUTLINE_CHAPTER6.doc

3 http://www.va-interactive.com/inbusiness/editorial/sales/ibt/sales_fo.html

Sources

http://www.allbusiness.com/periodicals/article/123857-1.html

Evetts, J. *Seven Pillars of Sales Success*. Sterling Publishing Co., 1990.

Bangs, Jr., D.H. *The Start Up Guide*. Upstart Publishing Co., 1989.

Leza, R.L. and Placencia, J. *Develop Your Business Plan*. The Oasis Press, 1988.

Bangs, Jr., D.H. *The Market Planning Guide*. Upstart Publishing Co., 1998.

Burstiner, I. *The Small Business Handbook*. New York: Simon & Schuster Inc., 1997.

Resnik, P. *The Small Business Bible*. New York: John Wiley & Sons, Inc., 1988.

http://futrell-www.tamu.edu/fos%20chapter%2016.doc

http://highered.mcgraw-hill.com/sites/0072398868/student_view0/chapter16/chapter_outline.html

Workload Approach

86

Measurement Need

Sales plans usually include a projection of the total work required to achieve a goal. The challenge lies in the cost of reaching the goal: salespeople are expensive. A business' leaders want to keep costs low to maximize profits while also maintaining good relations with customers. It can be a vexing challenge. The need, therefore, is determining the right size for the sales force given the amount of work to be done.

Solution

The workload approach organizes customers into common groups, usually based on account size. Management then determines how many sales people are required to call on the various customer groups[1]. There are three workload approaches that will be discussed here.

Approach 1[2]

The workload approach calculates sales force size as follows:

$$SFS = \frac{SE}{SE_{aps}}$$

Where

SFS = sales force size

SE = total selling effort needed (total calls to be made)

SE_{aps} = average selling effort per salesperson (average total calls made per salesperson)

Network marketing companies (such as Amway and Mary Kay) offer a useful illustration of this workload approach. Networked marketing companies generate sales through large networks of independent sales representatives. Each sales representative generates their income from a combination of product sales and the sales from other representatives they have recruited into their organization (this recruited organization is also known as the downstream sales team). Let's assume that a hypothetical sales representative named Barbara has identified 3,000 new customers in her territory that she wants to reach in the next 30 days to achieve her sales objectives. She must now determine the number of salespeople required.

First, Barbara would outline the facts as she knows them:

$$\text{Total number of customers} = 3,000$$

$$\text{Duration (in days)} = 30$$

Next, she needs to determine the denominator (average selling effort per prospective salesperson) by dividing the number of customers to be reached by the number of days required:

$$\frac{\text{Total selling effort needed}}{\text{Number of days required}}$$

$$= \frac{3,000}{30}$$

$$= 100 \text{ calls}$$

Finally, Barbara can now determine the number of salespeople she needs by dividing the total selling effort needed by the average calls made per salesperson:

$$= \frac{3,000}{30}$$

$$= \frac{3,000}{100}$$

$$= 30 \text{ sales persons}$$

From a practical point of view, it is likely that not all of Barbara's new hires will stay the entire 30 days (perhaps due to the type of work, challenges with customers or finding another job). She should factor in a turnover rate to ensure she can get the equivalent of 30 salespersons' work for 30 days. Each industry turnover rate differs, but Barbara determines that 20% is normal for network marketing. Therefore, her calculation is refined:

$$= 30 \times 0.20$$

$$= 6 \text{ (added to the original forecast of 30 people)}$$

$$= 36 \text{ total sales people required}$$

Approach 2[3]

A slight variation on the first approach is outlined in the sequential steps below:

a. Identify the total number of calls needed or customers to be reached (3,000, in Barbara's case)

b. Determine time needed per call (roughly 1.6 hours per call in this case, derived from 100 calls per salesperson divided by 20 days in a working month, assuming an 8 hour day)

c. Determine total working time (a × b) (4,800 hours in this case)

d. Determine actual selling time available per salesperson (160 hours based on 8 hours per day × 20 days)

e. Determine number of salespeople (c / d) (4,800 / 160 = 30)

Once again, Barbara would want to consider a turnover rate.

Approach 3[4]

An alternative workload method is known as reach-frequency, and it is represented by the following:

$$FTE = \frac{reach \times frequency}{capacity}$$

Where

FTE = full time employees

$reach$ = how many customers need to be reached

$frequency$ = customer visits during the sales period

$capacity$ = total number of calls per sales representative per time period

Let's assume that Barbara and her team have identified 10,000 potential customers in four different segments:

Customers	Reach	Frequency	Calls
Segment 1	3,000	2	6,000
Segment 2	2,500	2	5,000
Segment 3	2,500	1	2,500
Segment 4	2,000	1	2,000
Total	10,000		**15,500**

The average sales representative has a total sales capacity of 100 calls (20 selling days × 5 calls per day).

Sales representative capacity	100 calls

Using the formula, we can then determine the needed sales force:

$$FTE = \frac{15,500}{100}$$

= 155 sales reps needed.

Clearly, Barbara's sales force needs have changed, but so too have the assumptions. The first two approaches assumed one call per potential customer, but not all customers will buy on the first contact. In fact, most will not. The reach-frequency method provides more guidance when the assumed number of customer visits before a sale is made is larger than one. Of course, the numbers from the previous two approaches can certainly be used to illustrate Approach 3:

Customers	Reach	Frequency	Calls
Segment 1 Total	3,000	1	**3,000**

$$FTE = \frac{3,000}{100}$$

= 30 sales reps needed

Impact on Decision Making

The workload approach is useful, particularly with less complex, higher-volume products such as consumer goods, since established practices and expectations exist between product manufacturers, sales reps and customers (whether consumers, in the case of network marketing businesses; or channel accounts, in the case of traditional consumer products distribution). The reason is that metrics exist from years of industry practice and management can approximate the number of customers they need to reach to achieve a certain level of dollar sales. The workload approach becomes more challenging with more complex products (industrial machinery and software technologies, for example) since achieving the sales objective depends on qualitative factors such as the depth of the relationship with the customers and the amount of customization required to complete a sale. These variables are hard to pin down numerically but are nevertheless important in this type of sale. Also, the workload approach focuses only on the costs (or investment) made, and not the return. More complex management issues such as pricing, marketing communications and promotion programs, market share goals, and training expenses are ignored. Sales management must also consider these factors when determining sales force sizing.

Endnotes

1 Adapted from http://grader.prenhall.com/BB_CGI/BB_Grader/1,1002,,.html

2 Adapted from http://www.business.txstate.edu/users/ds60/296,36,Sales Force Size: Analytical Tools

3 http://classwork.busadm.mu.edu/Andrews/MARK%20140/PPTch16.ppt

4 http://www.bayser.com/SalesForceStrategy.htm

Sources

http://nsslha.org/about/continuing-ed/ASHA-courses/SSA/SSA6710.htm

www.embarcadero.com/ resources/tech_ papers/managing_ sql_server_ performance _with_ performance_ analyst. pdf

http://www-rohan.sdsu.edu/~renglish/377/notes/chapt16/

Sales Performance Quotas 87

Measurement Need

Sales management establishes quotas that serve as revenue targets for each sales representative. The quotas apply to one or more growth objectives: geographic territories, product sales and/or number of customers, and are measured in dollars or units.

Sales volume quotas are a common tool for companies of all sizes because they guide salespeople on where to apply their effort, motivate them to perform, and serve as benchmark standards for performance evaluation.

Solution[1]

The following methods are useful guidelines for establishing sales volume quotas:

1. Last year's total company or territory sales numbers by product or customer

2. Last year's salesperson's sales numbers by product or customer

3. Sales costs times a multiplier (x 3, for example)

4. Corporate general administrative costs plus a gross margin

5. Revenue goals committed to industry analysts or shareholders

6. Total of the sales team's goals (by territory, product or customer) divided by the number of salespeople

7. Estimated income potential provided to the salesperson if he/she achieves 100% of their quota

8. Analyst's projected annual growth rate for this industry for this year (for example, if the analyst forecasts industry growth of 20%, then quotas are up 20%)

9. Vice President of Sales' experiences at other companies

10. A percentage of the top salesperson's performance in their territory

To illustrate the first method listed on the previous page, let's look at the sales revenues by quarter for Procter & Gamble in 2005[2], as shown in Table 25.

Table 25: Sales Revenues for Procter & Gamble

PERIOD ENDING 2005	31-Dec-05	30-Sep-05	30-Jun-05	31-Mar-05
Total Revenue	18,337,000	14,793,000	14,258,000	14,287,000

If Procter & Gamble were to use volume quotas to guide its salespeople, then these quarterly revenue figures would be further divided by region and/or product group and/or customer type. The sales representatives would receive a quota for 2006 based on these figures from 2005, plus percentage increases described by the company's growth plan for 2006. This example uses dollars as the standard measure.

Impact on Decision Making

The sales management plan flows directly from the corporate strategic plan and key marketing objectives. For example, the corporate strategic plan may set product innovation as the primary objective. Marketing would develop its customer development plans based on the corporate objective. In this case, marketing would target early adopter customers who find innovative products appealing. Sales would then identify specific customers who are the closest fit to the corporate and marketing profiles. When the targets are achieved, sales representatives receive compensation above and beyond their base salary.

Planning assumptions are important when developing sales volume quotas. Reflecting on the Procter & Gamble example, if the company does set future quotas based on last year's sales plus percentage increases based on the company growth plan, then it assumes that the salesperson has maximized the potential of his/her market the previous year. In Table 26, the salesperson exceeded their one-year target of $1.2 million by $150,000, achieving 113% of their quota.

Table 26: Sales Representative Activity Quotas—Target and Actual

Quota	1 year target	Actual	Quota % achieved
Sales Volume ($)	$1,200,000	$1,350,000	113%

However, the salesperson may be an underperformer in a territory with significant potential. Therefore, using last year's performance plus expected growth may still not realize the full potential of the territory. Sales management must work directly with the sales representative to develop quotas based on the territory's true potential.

Sales quotas are most effective when salespeople are directly involved with sales management in their own goal development. Setting goals with management allows the salesperson to provide and receive direct feedback on their past performances, and provide their insights to sales management about the unique characteristics of their territory.

Individual sales quotas are less effective in team selling situations since cooperation may be hindered by each salesperson's individual performance goals. Team volume quotas are feasible, but require a clear agreement among the sales team members that success is based on their combined effort, irrespective of imbalances in individual contribution. However, contribution imbalances are likely in team situations since each person has a different point of view on how best to achieve an objective, and therefore team volume quotas may be short-lived since one or more members of the team may feel they were under-compensated for their contribution. Sales volume quotas are less effective with large-scale industrial sales such as heavy equipment or complex enterprise software because the sales cycles are unpredictable and quite long. Products with extreme pricing variation are harder to measure using sales volume quotas since market conditions may make early planning assumptions invalid at the time of the actual sale. Finally, sales volume quotas reward activities related to selling. Non-selling activities such as planning, proposal development and customer support programs are usually ignored.

Addendum 1—The Unit Volume Quota

The performance expectations of sales representatives selling high cost products such as computer hardware, complex enterprise software or products with significant pricing variation are measured more effectively with a unit volume quota.

For example, if a salesperson sells 50 units of a product priced at $10,000 per unit, then $500,000 is the total sales figure. But if the price increases 20% to $12,000 per unit (perhaps due to materials price increases or similar sources of supply price changes), then only 42 units are sold at the same dollar volume as shown in Table 27.

Table 27: Sales Representative Activity Quotas—Target and Actual

Quota	1 year target	Actual	Quota % achieved
Unit Volume	50	42	84%

If the objective of the salesperson is to sell 50 units, then his/her challenge is to achieve that target irrespective of price. A unit volume quota shifts the emphasis to features and benefits that solve the customer's problem so that price becomes secondary. It also forces a change in the salesperson's behavior. Addendum 4 at the end of this chapter discusses activity quotas which establish performance goals for activities related to improved performance in revenues, profits, market share, product volume, territory development or customer acquisition, and retention.

Addendum 2—The Point Quota System

Point quota systems set targets based on accumulating a certain number of points and not dollars or units. Point quotas reward sales representatives for selling certain combinations of products, dollar volumes or units. For example, sales management may award five points for new products, three points for upgrades and two points for legacy products to encourage new product placement. Management may also award points for certain levels of dollar or unit sales achieved. Or, management might convert new product, dollar and unit sales into points.

Point systems are useful when management wants to change the behavior of sales representatives that are meeting their quotas through the sale of one or two key products that are easier to sell, downplaying other products as a result. Senior management would assign more points to products that need greater placement in the market. Alternatively, if profitability needs to be improved, then points can be assigned to those products with higher relative profitability.

To illustrate, let's look at a variation of the tables used earlier and assume that Procter & Gamble's management wishes to improve sales of products A and B because they are more profitable than products C and D, which are less profitable but easier to sell.

Furthermore, Procter & Gamble management decides to award 1 bonus point for any sales over quota. Tables 28 and 29 show the respective performances of two different sales reps:

Table 28: Sales Rep 1

Quota	1 year point target	Actual	Quota % achieved	Bonus points
Product A	5	6	120%	1
Product B	4	5	125%	1
Product C	3	4	133%	1
Product D	3	3	100%	0
			119.5%	3

Table 29: Sales Rep 2

Quota	1 year point target	Actual	Quota % achieved	Bonus points
Product A	5	4	80%	0
Product B	4	2	50%	0
Product C	3	9	300%	1
Product D	3	6	200%	1
			157.5%	2

In the point system, senior management will reward the first sales rep more favorably than the second sales rep, even though the second sales rep achieved 157.5% of quota versus the first sales rep's 119.5%. The first sales rep earned her bonus by beating her quota with the harder-to-sell products that are also more profitable.

Point quota systems have the advantage of forcing sales team attention to focus on products management seeks to sell, but the disadvantage of growing complexity as a company's product offering expands into multiple lines and product pricing levels.

Addendum 3—The Profit Quota

Whereas the point quota system helps focus sales attention on management's product mix priorities, the profit quota pushes sales representatives to achieve pre-determined profits for each product's sales volume. Profits are defined on either a gross margin or contribution margin basis. Gross margin is the difference between net sales (gross sales less returns, discounts and allowances) and the cost of goods sold (expenses associated with producing the product, including labor, raw material, overhead). Contribution margin is defined as the sales price minus the variable costs. The profit quota approach works best when sales representatives have some influence over final pricing. Procter & Gamble's actual 2005 gross margin was over 52%, so the profit quota would set a gross margin target of at least 52% for each product. In our earlier table, products A and B have higher profits; therefore management might set a gross margin target of 60%. Products C and D might have a gross margin target of 48%. The goal is to meet or exceed each gross margin target. If this is done, then a bonus is paid.

Addendum 4—The Activity Quota

A firm's senior management sets performance targets that include specific financial, market, and product objectives. These objectives are translated by the next level of management into specific targets for their respective areas of responsibility. Each salesperson is rewarded based on achieving the specific targets set for them. Senior management needs a tool that motivates salespeople to pursue the right activities so that the goals are reached. Activity quotas are a good tool for motivating salespeople to plan the specific activities that will lead to improved performance in their territory.

Sales management must establish activity quotas that set proper expectations for their sales team. Activity quotas include:

- Total number of calls to new and existing customers per period of time
- Total number of letters sent to prospective customers
- New account calls
- Product displays
- Account meetings with loyal customers
- Additional product and support services presentations to customers
- Internal account update meetings
- Coordinating product installations
- Account coordination meetings with strategic partners
- New proposals

Activity quotas are intended to guide specific behaviors that will ensure the performance targets are met. Sales management must define the most important activities their sales representatives perform, from which specific activity targets are then set. If the right behaviors and activities are identified and measured, then salespeople should have a clear picture of senior management's expectations and an equally clear sense of those activities that do not conform to senior management's expectations and, therefore, should be avoided.

In Table 26, the rep achieved 113% of their quota based on sales volume quota setting. Table 30 illustrates how activity quotas can provide a clearer picture of the sales representative's performance:

Table 30: Sales Representative Activity Quotas—Target and Actual

Quota	1 year target	Actual	Quota % achieved
Sales Volume	$1,200,000	$1,350,000	113%
Product demonstrations	24	18	75%
Average calls per week	30	24	80%
New accounts per month	5	4	80%
		Average	87%

Sales management would review this performance with the rep to improve the weaker activity areas. Since the sales volume quota was exceeded while the other activity areas underperformed, sales management would want to establish more aggressive sales volume targets as well.

Activity quota achievement is determined from the sales call reports of each sales representative, which places responsibility on the salesperson to accurately record the results of customer meetings. Sales management may occasionally audit the data from these reports by calling the customers directly to verify the information. However, audits can send a demotivating signal that conveys a lack of trust between sales management and the sales representatives.

Each quota system in this chapter provides management with a method for achieving a particular result. However, setting quotas is complex since most businesses do not face uniform markets with consistent customer demands and clearly delineated competitor offerings. Therefore, companies may employ multiple quota methods even for the same product simply due to differences across territories. Each sales rep's territory is likely to differ on multiple dimensions:

- Maturity of the local market

- Popularity and reputation of your products versus those of the competition

- Number of qualified customers

- Economic characteristics of each market

- Sales potential of each territory

- Financial targets for each territory

Finally, even with sound quota systems, sales representative performance also depends on softer abilities like motivation, confidence and desire. Setting quotas for these intangibles is not possible, but their influence in successful selling is well researched and should be carefully factored into each reps' individual performance plan by sales management.

Endnotes

1 Adapted from http://www.derbymanagement.com/knowledge/pages/tactics/setting1.html

2 http://finance.yahoo.com/q/is?s=PG

Sources

http://www.buseco.monash.edu.au/depts/mkt/dictionary/uuu.php

http://en.mimi.hu/marketingweb/unit_volume_quota.html

http://rcw.raifoundation.org/management/mba/saleanddistributionmgmt/lecture-notes/lecture-19.pdf

http://www.marketingpower.com/mdictionary.php?Searched=1&SearchFor=quota&Term_ID=3805&SearchDefinitionsAlso=ON

Average Sales Per Call

88

Measurement Need

Sales management wants to know how much each salesperson generates in dollars per call.

Solution[1]

Average sales per call measures the value in dollar sales arising from each sales call. The formula is:

$$SPC_{avg} = \frac{T_{salest}}{T_{callst}} \times 100$$

Where

SPC_{avg} = average sales per call

T_{salest} = total sales in time period t

T_{callst} = total calls in time period t

Woodside Hotels is a small, upscale hotel company based in northern California. The sales team consists of two salespeople per property for each of the five properties belonging to the company. Each salesperson is responsible for group business (ten or more rooms for each group). Most of the salespeople conduct their own customer research and cold calling (there is no telemarketing or third party market research firm to help). The average number of sales calls (cold calls included) in a five-day work week is 75, and the average total group sales per sales rep per week is $20,000. Therefore, the average sales per call is $266.

$$SPC_{avg} = \frac{\$20,000}{75} \times 100$$

$$= \$267$$

Each call generates $267 in revenue.

Impact on Decision Making

A quick review of these numbers will suggest that not every sales call on behalf of Woodside Hotels results in revenue being generated. Instead, only a few of each week's 75 calls lead to group books, usually four to five. Assuming five bookings is the average number of bookings per week, then the average sales per booking call is $4,000, a more reasonable result given the price of rooms, length of stay and size of groups.

Average sales per call helps sales management understand each salesperson's performance, both individually and compared with other salespeople's. Over time and repeated measuring, performance patterns will emerge that will guide future sales management decisions on customer account management, territory structure, pricing latitude and target segments. Knowing the average sales per call will also help sales management understand the strengths and weaknesses of each salesperson with respect to the kinds of customers being contacted, thereby aligning account assignments more effectively in the future.

As a stand-alone measure, average sales per call is less revealing than if it is applied in conjunction with other productivity measures, based on company goals.

Sources

http://www.referenceforbusiness.com/encyclopedia/res-sec/sales-management.html

http://www.exinfm.com/workshop_files/sales_customer_measures.doc

Close Process and Close Ratio

89

Measurement Need

In pursuing sales, the salesperson is interested in closing (concluding) sales as quickly as possible and with maximum financial benefit to himself and the company (see Chapters 82-87 on sales compensation for more information on different incentive structures to reward specific performance objectives). Sales management also wants to evaluate each salesperson's performance.

Solution

Two tools are useful in measuring the sales close:

1. The close process
2. The close ratio

The Close Process

Historically, there are several known variations on the typical sales cycle process, including AICP (awareness, interest, conviction, purchase) and AICTR (awareness, interest, conviction, trial, repeat).

As sales has grown in sophistication, so too has the close process and, consequently, the steps involved in the time to close. It is represented by Figure 23[1].

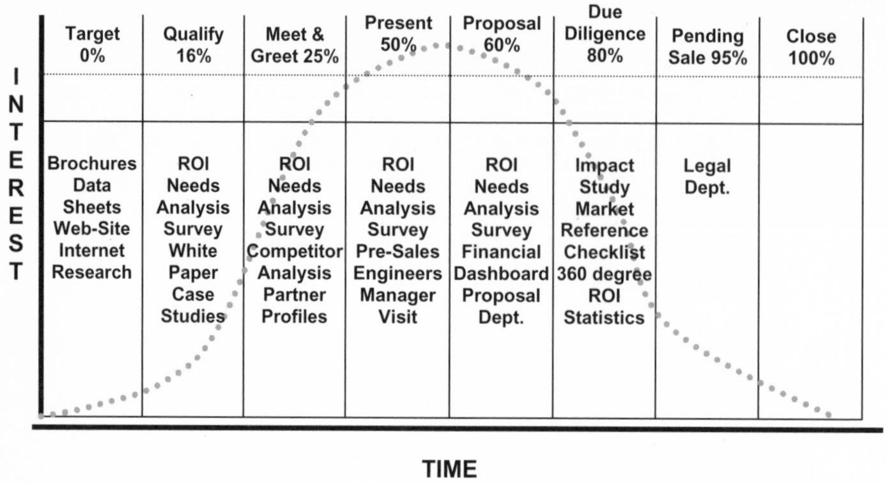
INTEREST
Target 0%
Qualify 16%
Meet & Greet 25%
Present 50%
Proposal 60%
Due Diligence 80%
Pending Sale 95%
Close 100%
Brochures Data Sheets Web-Site Internet Research
ROI Needs Analysis Survey White Paper Case Studies
ROI Needs Analysis Survey Competitor Analysis Partner Profiles
ROI Needs Analysis Survey Pre-Sales Engineers Manager Visit
ROI Needs Analysis Survey Financial Dashboard Proposal Dept.
Impact Study Market Reference Checklist 360 degree ROI Statistics
Legal Dept.
TIME

Figure 23: Sales Process—Resources and Close Percentages

The chart graphically portrays common steps in the sales process, from initial targeting to close. Each step is labeled across the top and the accompanying percentage indicates the likelihood of the sale being concluded at that stage. Within each step are many of the probable activities that occur in that stage. The percentages and activities listed are purely for illustration and each sales management team and rep will have a better understanding of each stage's needs for their own situation. The bell curve illustrates the intensity of effort, which reaches its peak in the presentation and proposal stages, where a great deal of effort has gone into preparing these critical phases. Assuming the customer remains interested, the sales effort shifts toward concluding the sale (and minimizing any last minute obstacles). The chart is not meant to imply that the salesperson loses interest as the sale approaches the close phase. Instead, it merely reflects the changing intensity of effort and not a diminishing of interest.

The Close Ratio

At any given time a salesperson will have multiple customers, each at different stages of the close process. As the salesperson and customers move through the stages, each increases their commitment to the effort and reduces the chances of canceling before the close. To get to this stage, salespeople either directly cold call customers themselves, or cold calls are conducted on their behalf by a telemarketing team. Either of these identifies and separates those customers worthy of pursuing from those no longer of interest. As the salesperson and their customers enter this cycle, not all customers will complete it. Therefore, the salesperson and sales management are interested in the percentage of customers that close once they enter the close process cycle. This is expressed as follows:

$$CR_t = \frac{C_{at}}{C_{pt}} \times 100$$

Where

CR_t = close ratio in time period t

C_{at} = actual sales closed in time period t

C_{pt} = potential sales to close in time period t

Let's assume that a salesperson for a medical devices company has 12 potential customers per month over the course of a year. On average, seven customers per month complete the process to close. This salesperson's close ratio is 58%.

$$CR_t = \frac{84}{144} \times 100$$
$$= 58\%$$

Impact on Decision Making

The close process is important to understand as it helps the salesperson plan their progress toward the close and, psychologically, it helps them see the progress, providing a form of motivation. For those sales reps who are experts in their industry and understand their customers, they are quite likely able to estimate the probable length of time of each stage as well. It also enables them to know where each of their customers currently stands in the process, helping the salesperson organize their work effort more effectively, including mapping out which buyers need to be contacted at a particular stage of the process (B2B sales efforts usually involve buying teams, with each person having a different interest). The best salespeople keep detailed notes of each meeting with the customer, so they can identify gaps in their selling efforts to be addressed at the next meeting.

The close ratio ultimately measures their success in the close process. Returning to the earlier example, if the salesperson was able to improve the close ratio to eight out of 12 potentials each month, the improvement in their close ratio is significant, plus they have gained 12 additional customers during that same time period, which will improve their future repeat sales business:

$$CR_t = \frac{96}{144} \times 100$$
$$= 67\%$$

By using the close process and close ratio together the sales rep can more easily identify stages where potentials are lost, and use this information to improve their own future sales results, income and the company's business.

Endnote

1 Koenig, K. M. and Nick, M. J. *ROI Selling.* Dearborn Trade Books, 2004: p.250.

Sources

Doyle, C. *Collins Internet-Linked Dictionary of Marketing.* Harper Collins, 2003, 2006: p.70.

Imber, J. and Toffler, B.A. *Dictionary of Marketing Terms.* Barron's Educational Series, 2000: p.108.

Cron, W.L., DeCarlo, T.E. and Palrymple, D.J. *Sales Management.* New York: John Wiley & Sons, Inc., 2004: pp.215-218.

Cost Per Call 90

Measurement Need

Sales professionals must grow the business by finding new customers and getting existing customers to buy more products. Therefore, they must allocate their limited time toward the best customer prospects. However, salespeople need to know how much their time is worth and the expense of making each customer contact, so they need to calculate their cost per call.

Solution

To determine cost per call, the salesperson needs three pieces of data:

- Sales expenses per time period (usually one year)
- Total selling days per time period (same time period)
- Average number of calls per day

According to *Sales & Marketing Management* magazine, the average compensation (base salary plus bonus and commissions) for all salespeople in the U.S. in 2003 was US$111,135[1]. This figure is only part of the total sales expense, however. Salespeople incur additional expenses in the course of their annual selling activities, including transportation, entertainment and support materials expenses. The number of actual selling days is affected by non-selling demands on their time, including training, meetings, vacations and weekends. A sales professional must budget for each of these components when forecasting his total selling expenses if he wants to accurately estimate his cost per call. Table 31 captures these additional figures[2] and shows that this salesperson's cost per call is $270.80.

Table 31: Sales Representative Cost Per Call Analysis

COMPENSATION		
Salary, commissions, bonus	$111,135	
Fringe benefits (insurance and other)	$15,225	$126,360
DIRECT SELLING EXPENSES		
Automobile	$12,636	
Lodging and meals	$9,856	
Entertainment	$5,181	
Communications	$7,076	
Samples, promotional materials	$2,780	
Miscellaneous	$2,654	$40,183
Total Direct Exepenses		$166,543
CALLS PER YEAR		
Total available days		260 days
Less:		
Vacation	10 days	
Holidays	10 days	
Sickness	5 days	
Meetings	18 days	
Training	12 days	55 days
Net selling days		205 days
Average calls per day		3 calls
Total calls per year (205 x 3)	615 calls	
Average cost per call ($166,543/615)		$270.80

Impact on Decision Making

Top sales performers succeed because they rigorously plan their activities to maximize selling time to the right customers. Measuring cost per call enables salespeople to determine the costs incurred to make each sales call. Cost per call is a useful tool in the beginning of any sales plan because it forces the salesperson to think carefully about the many expenses incurred on behalf of each customer sale. However, cost per call is one of several key planning steps. The next several chapters add depth to the sales planning effort.

Endnotes

1 Galea, C. "2004 Salary Survey". *Sales & Marketing Management*, May 2004: p.28.

2 Adapted from: Cron, W.L., DeCarlo, T.E. and Palrymple, D.J. *Sales Management*. New York: John Wiley & Sons, Inc., 2004: p.127.

Break-Even Sales Volume 91

Measurement Need

Chapter 90 describes cost per call, a calculation that measures the costs of making each sales call based on projected expenses, selling days and the average number of calls per day. The example in Chapter 90 calculated the cost per call to be $270.80. However, cost per call does not factor in the number of calls required to make a sale. Figuring the break-even sales volume helps salespeople determine the best customer or sales size (by dollars). As implied, the break-even point is the minimum customer size needed—any customer sale below break-even should be avoided.

Solution[1]

The formula for break-even sales volume is common across industries, although the formula's variables will vary, sometimes dramatically, by industry and even within an industry.

$$BE_{sv} = \frac{CPC \times NCC}{C_s}$$

Where

BE_{sv} = break-even sales volume

CPC = cost per call

NCC = number of calls to close

C_s = sales costs, expressed as a percentage of sales

There are no universal rules governing the number of calls to close a sale. Selling consumer perishables, such as canned foods, is very different from selling mainframe computers. The canned foods salesperson may be able to close a sale in two or three calls since the buyer regularly needs to replenish inventory on store shelves. The mainframe computer salesperson may have five to six meetings, or more, over several months with their buyers before a sale is concluded. Salespeople should be familiar with the performance standards of their industry. Their own experience with customers also serves as a relevant guideline for the number of calls typically needed to close a sale. Even with industries where practices tend to be similar overall, each company within the industry quite likely allocates percentages differently for each expense category, including direct selling expenses. Salespeople must learn management's expectations and factor those into their break-even analysis. Table 32 shows these percentages by industry[2].

Table 32: Select Sales Performance Statistics for Closing a Sale—By Industry

Industry	Cost per call (in $)	Number of calls needed to close a sale	Sales costs as a percentage of total sales
Business Services	46.00	4.6	10.3%
Chemicals	165.80	2.8	3.4
Construction	111.20	2.8	7.1
Electronics	133.30	3.9	12.6
Food Products	131.60	4.8	2.7
Instruments	226.00	5.3	14.8
Machinery	68.50	3.0	11.3
Office Equipment	25.00	3.7	2.4
Printing/Publishing	70.10	4.5	22.2
Rubber/Plastic	248.20	4.7	3.6

Using the chart, each industry's break-even sales volume can be calculated. To illustrate, let's look at food products:

$$BE_{sv} = \frac{\$131.60 \times 4.8}{0.027}$$

$$= \$23,396$$

The food products salesperson now has a minimum performance benchmark that helps him or her target customers more effectively, reallocating time and resources away from customers who do not meet the standard.

Impact on Decision Making

Successful sales planning requires sales managers and their team members to carefully evaluate their customers. The minimum performance benchmarks are not hard and fast rules, since an underperforming customer may have potential to be brought above break-even.

The break-even sales volume provides a minimum acceptable standard for determining the attractiveness of a customer account. The measure helps salespeople focus on those businesses that represent the best potential, reducing the number of less-attractive customers. Salespeople can then begin the more rigorous phases of their account planning, including profiling each customer account in greater detail and the main buyers within. However, business decisions are usually more complex than this simple illustration. A customer may be below the break-even threshold, yet if their business is growing at an attractive rate (for example, ahead of the pace of their competitors), then management should consider the longer-term potential before dropping them. There may also be inefficiencies in the company's sales force system that, upon correction, may change the break-even calculation and allow more customers to survive. New products may also change the relationship with customers since they may find the new offerings attractive. Even though the break-even threshold is not met due to a product's newness, the customer's previously profitable loyalty may suggest that the overall relationship should be nurtured, despite the initially unattractive break-even volumes.

Sales professionals have many factors to consider when reviewing their customers. Break-even sales volume is a logical step since it helps focus the sales effort, improving efficiency (since the wrong accounts won't be pursued) and effectiveness (since the salesperson now knows the sales amount required to break-even). The challenge arises from the complexity of other factors that cannot be easily measured, such as long-term potential and ease of account service, yet can have a significant impact on success over the long term.

Endnotes

1 Adapted from: Cron, W.L., DeCarlo, T.E. and Palrymple, D.J. *Sales Management*. New York: John Wiley & Sons, Inc., 2004: pp.126-127.

2 From Table 3-2, Cron, W.L, DeCarlo, T.E. and Palrymple, D.J. *Sales Management*. New York: John Wiley & Sons, Inc., 2004: p.128.

Sources

Doyle, C. *Collins Internet-Linked Dictionary of Marketing*. Harper Collins, 2003, 2006: pp.45-47.

Imber, J. and Toffler, B.A. *Dictionary of Marketing Terms*. Barron's Educational Series, 2000: p.71.

http://www.toolkit.cch.com/text/P06_7530.asp

http://www.ces.purdue.edu/extmedia/EC/EC-725.pdf

Sales Productivity 92

Measurement Need

Sales management needs to know how productive its salespeople are. Productivity can be measured in the following ways:

- sales (revenues) per person (measured in dollars)
- profits per person (measured in dollars)
- volume sold per person (in units)

Most sales productivity measures focus on revenues per person.

Solution

The following formula calculates sales productivity:

$$SP = \frac{\sum S_t}{\sum S_p}$$

Where

SP = sales productivity

$\sum S_t$ = sum of total sales for all salespeople

$\sum S_p$ = total number of salespeople

In the late 1990s, Transamerica Intellitech was a small U.S.-based company that sold real estate data and software to title companies, real estate firms, appraisers and financial institutions. In 1996, the company's revenues were $11 million, generated by 33 salespeople. Sales productivity was as follows:

$$SP = \frac{\$11,000,000}{33}$$

$$= \$333,334 \text{ per person}$$

Competitive data on field sales performance was hard to verify, but management's evaluation suggested that the competition's average sales productivity was nearly 80% higher.

The senior management team embarked on an aggressive growth plan that included new products, acquisitions and advanced sales force training. By 1999, revenues had grown to $42 million and the sales team numbered 60. Sales productivity changed as well:

$$SP = \frac{\$42,000,000}{60}$$

$$= \$700,000 \text{ per person}$$

Sales productivity per person improved during that period of time. This provided a key performance measure enabling Transamerica Intellitech to more effectively evaluate its progress.

Impact on Decision Making

Sales productivity is a simple measure as used here. The results of this analysis will affect decisions at the company, team and individual level. Since every company's needs differ, measures of productivity will vary accordingly. Every company's leadership should develop its own productivity measures, derived from the business plan goals. Sales productivity measurement should inspire deeper analysis into the underlying causes of the performance (whether good or bad). Management decision making will focus more on the questions raised by the detailed sales productivity results which, in turn, are influenced by overall company goals, sales targets, sales territory definition, and segment and account strategies.

Company-level decisions are complicated by hard-to-control factors. Assuming sales managers are familiar with their teams, they may conclude that a poor performance as revealed by sales productivity analysis could be due to other, less controllable factors such as unrealistic goals, a weak correlation between pay and performance, or shifting market conditions that affected the assumptions that supported the original sales plan. These must be weighed against sales management's future compensation plans, sales targets, account objectives and, ultimately, changes in personnel.

Sales management will use productivity to understand a sales representative's individual performance as compared with that of colleagues or competitors. Marketing can use the results to advise under-performers about more effective segmentation or new segment opportunities. Sales management can also use the results to counsel poor performers in better account selection, time management and selling strategies for each customer. More specifically, sales managers can use the productivity results to develop a step by step plan for improved individual performance.

Finally, sales management must be careful not to misinterpret sales productivity data. A handful of top performers may disguise the under-performance of the rest of the team. Therefore, the sales productivity results will need to be viewed across the sales force and at the individual salesperson level. High performers will certainly generate substantial revenues, but if those results were partly secured by offering customers generous, low-cost support contracts, then the financial impact on the rest of the company could be severe. Perhaps the high performers generated strong sales, but also had higher returns due to a less thoughtful selling effort. Or, their significant sales volumes may strain the production and delivery capabilities of your firm, particularly if the revenue growth is sudden and sharp. The outcome could be unhappy customers, which is certainly counter to the purpose of selling and marketing in the first place.

Sources

http://hbswk.hbs.edu/item.jhtml?id=3952&t=dispatch

http://www.entrepreneur.com/article/0,4621,324059,00.html

http://www.exinfm.com/workshop_files/sales_customer_measures.doc

Cron, W. L., DeCarlo, T. E. and Palrymple, D. J. *Sales Management*. New York: John Wiley & Sons, Inc., 2004: p.356.

Four Factor Model 93

Measurement Need

Performance appraisal of salespeople is complex. Qualitative influences like attitude, emotional resiliency and persistence play an important role in selling success, but are difficult to objectively evaluate. While achieving consistently successful sales results is never assured, certain tasks performed by sales people are clear and measurable since they are developed with a specific eye toward growth in revenues, profits, units sold and number of customers. These tasks are part of the selling routine and include setting personal goals, identifying customer targets, organizing the sales tactics for each customer, scheduling sales calls, closing sales and, finally, following up with the customer after the sale is complete. Since each of these activities yields a clear result, sales management needs a way to measure them.

Solution[1]

The Four Factor Model evaluates the salesperson's efforts in four specific areas:

- Days worked
- Calls/days worked
- Orders/calls
- Sales $/orders

The formula used is:

$$Sales\$ = Days\ worked \times \frac{Calls}{Days\ worked} \times \frac{Orders}{Calls} \times \frac{Sales\$}{Orders}$$

Let's look at NWR[2], a hospitality company that owns one resort, plus works in partnership with six regional hotels and resorts, representing a total of 900 hotel rooms. Salespeople are compensated for booking group business, defined as ten or more rooms per night plus one group meal and two coffee breaks during the day (minimum), each day. Table 33 outlines the performance of three salespeople:

Table 33: Four Factor Sales Representative Performance Comparison

Criteria	Sales Rep 1	Sales Rep 2	Sales Rep 3
Annual sales	$622,200	$1,567,125	$931,139
Days worked	230	225	231
Total calls*	2,760	3,375	3,696
Group bookings	100	90	112
Avg. length of stay (# of nights)	2	3.5	3
Avg. daily rate per person per group	$148	$134	$90
Avg. daily F&B per person per group	$35	$65	$42
Avg. # of rooms	17	25	21
Total calls/total days worked	12	15	16
Bookings/call	3.6%	2.7%	3%
Sales $/booking	$6,222	$17,413	$8,313
Sales expense (non-wage)	$6,500	$17,200	$9,000
Sales expense per call	$2.35	$5.16	$2.43
Sales expense per booking	$65.	$191.11	$80.36
Sales expense as % of total sales	1.04%	1.1%	.97%
FOUR FACTOR TOTAL**	**$618,218**	**$1,586,760**	**$921,745**

*calls defined as: telephone, client tours of hotels, visits to client sites. Most calls were by telephone.
**Sales Rep 1 = 230 x 12 x .036 x $6,222 = $618,218
   Sales Rep 2 = 225 x 15 x .027 x $17,413 = $1,586,760
   Sales Rep 3 = 231 x 16 x .030 x $8,313 = $921,745

Impact on Decision Making

The Four Factor calculations show dollar sales totals nearly the same as the total annual sales for each salesperson. The numbers are interesting, given the sizable differences between sales reps, but sales management will want to review the performances and their underlying causes with greater scrutiny. For example, Sales Rep 2's Four Factor results are higher than her annual sales. The most obvious factor is her sales dollars per booking average. Her total dollar per group is larger because the number of rooms her groups book is substantially higher, as is the average length of stay for her groups. Before concluding she is superior, sales management should review her territory, because the customers in her territory may be substantially larger than those of Sales Reps 1 and 3. So Sales Rep 2's customers may simply book more rooms per group as a result of being larger. Her typical customer's average length of stay is also longer, which may signal she is more effective at selling hotel space, perhaps by emphasizing unique features that business groups find attractive (such as few distractions and more business services), hence the customers decide that their productivity will be improved by staying one night longer. An examination of each sales rep will be required to determine if changes are warranted, particularly given Sales Rep 2's performance, or if each is already maximizing their potential given the kind of territory each has. The Four Factor Model provides direction for sales management on where to look next to improve performance.

Industrial selling cycles are longer and more complex than their consumer selling counterparts, so each of the Four Factors will have a different baseline performance than that shown in the illustration. But the impact on decision making will be similar since sales management will compare the results to other salespeople on their team, or against competitors and/or industry standards.

Endnotes

1 Cron, W.L., DeCarlo, T.E. and Palrymple, D.J. *Sales Management*. New York: John Wiley & Sons, Inc., 2004: pp. 545.

2 Adapted from information provided by Northwest Resorts, Inc.

Source

http://faculty.bus.olemiss.edu/dvorhies/Sales%20Management/Powerpoint%20Slides/ch13.ppt.ppt

Sales Variance Analysis 94

Measurement Need

Sales managers develop budgets for their business plans that outline how the department's money is going to be allocated between revenues and costs for a specific period of time, usually for the forthcoming year. Once the year has been completed, the actual financial performance is compared to the original budget. Sales management needs to measure the differences and see where the deviations occurred. Sales variance analysis is the methodology used.

Solutions[1]

There are several formulas used to calculate sales variances:

1. *Sales value variance*

2. *Sales price variance*

3. *Sales volume variance*

4. Sales mix variance

The formulas for each will be outlined below, but for illustration purposes, the focus will be on sales price variance, sales volume variance and sales value variance (italicized above), since these are three of the most common variables used to assess sales performance. The sales mix variance is best applied to companies with multiple products within several product lines. Readers are encouraged to visit the resources listed for this chapter should they want more detailed treatments of these formulas.

1. Sales value variance

This measures the difference in monetary value between actual sales and budgeted sales (in monetary terms) in time period t (usually one year).

$$SV_{al}V_t = S_a - S_b$$

Where

$SV_{al}V_t$ = sales value variance during time t

S_a = actual sales

S_b = budgeted sales

If actual sales are more than budgeted sales, then this formula will return a favorable variance. Whether positive or negative, sales managers will want to determine the source of this variance. If the variance is positive, then it is due either to higher actual prices compared to budget, or higher actual volume compared to budget. The converse would be true if the variance were negative. With price as one of the determinants, sales management would now want to measure the sales price variance.

2. Sales price variance*

The sales price variance explains the difference between actual price received and the price budgeted at the beginning of period t.

$$SPV_t = Q_a(P_a - P_b)$$

Where

SPV_t = sales price variance during time t

Q_a = actual quantity sold during time t

P_a = actual price per unit

P_b = budgeted price per unit

Actual price differences result from promotional or volume discounts, allowances, giveaways, or bundled offerings (such as two-for-one deals), all of which are tools used by salespeople to gain a buyer's commitment. Correspondingly, their use affects the final price received.

*Note: Chapter 95 provides a more detailed example of calculating sales price variance.

3. Sales volume variance*

Sales volume variance measures the difference in actual quantity sold during time t versus the budgeted quantity, multiplied by the budgeted price per unit.

$$SVV_t = P_b(Q_a - Q_b)$$

Where

SVV_t = sales volume variance during time t

P_b = budgeted price per unit

Q_a = actual quantity sold during time t

Q_b = budgeted quantity sold during time t

Sales volume variances are caused by several factors. Changes in price or quality, delivery delays, shifting market trends and competitor promotions are among the key influences. Marketers and sales management must review sales results closely to understand the source of the variances.

***Note:** Chapter 96 describes another approach to evaluating sales volume variance.

Illustration

To illustrate sales value variance, sales price variance, and sales volume variance, let's assume that Company A sells three products, known as X, Y and Z, respectively. Company A budgeted the following sales for 2005:

Sales Budgeted for 2005

Product X: 100,000 units sold at $25 each	= $2,500,000
Product Y: 50,000 units sold at $30 each	= $1,500,000
Product Z: 25,000 units sold at $35 each	= $875,000
Budgeted sales	**$4,875,000**

Sales Actual for 2005

Product X: 90,000 units sold at $28 each	= $2,520,000
Product Y: 45,000 units sold at $32 each	= $1,440,000
Product Z: 30,000 units sold at $34 each	= $1,020,000
Actual sales	**$4,980,000**

The next steps are to examine the sales value, sales price and sales volume variances.

Company A had a favorable sales value variance. In this case, the actual sales of all three products exceeded the budgeted amount by $105,000, shown as follows:

$$SV_{al}V_t = S_a - S_b$$
$$SV_{al}V_t = \$4,980,000 - \$4,875,000$$

Sales value variance = $105,000

The sales price variance for each product shows the following:

Product X = 90,000(28–25)	= $270,000
Product Y = 45,000(32–30)	= $90,000
Product Z = 30,000 (34–35)	= ($30,000)
Sales price variance	**$330,000**

The overall SPV was favorable, but whereas Products X and Y had favorable individual SPVs, Product Z had an unfavorable variance.

The sales volume variance for each product shows the following:

Product X= $25(90,000–100,000)	= ($250,000)
Product Y= $30(45,000–50,000)	= ($150,000)
Product Z = $35(30,000–25,000)	= $175,000
Sales volume variance	**($225,000)**

The overall SVV was unfavorable. Products X and Y both had unfavorable SVVs, but Product Z had a favorable variance.

A quick check of the sales price variance and sales volume variance should verify the sales value variance figure:

Quick Check	
Sales price variance	$330,000
Sales volume variance	($225,000)
Total variance	**$105,000**

The quick check agreed!

4. Sales mix variance

Sales mix variance measures the impact of different mixes of product sold. This is useful for companies with multiple products and product lines where management needs to understand the financial implications to the company of the actual product mix sold versus the budgeted product mix.

$$SMV_t = Q_t \, (A\% - B\%) \, CM_b$$

Where

SMV_t = sales mix variance during time t

Q_t = actual quantity (in units) of all products sold in time t

$A\%$ = actual sales mix percentage

$B\%$ = budgeted sales mix percentage

CM_b = budgeted contribution margin per unit

Impact on Decision Making

Sales variance analysis enables company management to identify the impact of specific variables on overall sales performance. If management reviewed only total sales results, then it would conclude that the business performed better than plan (using this chapter's example). But the sales variance analysis sheds light on the performance of individual products. Interestingly, Products X and Y had favorable sales price variances, but unfavorable sales volume variances (the actual prices for which the products sold more than offset the lower than expected unit sales). Conversely, Product Z had an unfavorable sales price variance due to the lower actual price for which products were sold versus budget, but it also had a favorable sales volume variance.

Company management would want to carefully review the reasons for these performance swings. All three products are somewhat price elastic, meaning that customers are sensitive to price changes. Perhaps the competition offers equivalent products to X and Y, but at better prices. Therefore management might consider either improving product quality or finding ways to reduce costs. The small price decrease for Product Z (less than 3%) led to a 20% increase in units sold (30,000 actual versus 25,000 budgeted) and a positive sales volume variance of $175,000. Furthermore, Product Z actual sales were $145,000 higher than budgeted ($1,020,000 actual vs. $875,000 budgeted), a 16.6% increase in sales. For Product Z, the 3% price decrease resulted in a disproportionate, positive percentage increase in sales volume variance and actual sales. Sales management would want to analyze these results more closely to better understand why Product Z's results were superior to those of Products X and Y and determine whether similar results might be replicated in the future.

There are many reasons for these results beyond the simple explanations offered here. Sales variance analysis provides meaningful insight into your businesses performance. While it raises more questions for management, it also offers guidance on where to look for the answers.

Endnotes

1 http://www.rcw.raifoundation.org/management/mba/Financial&ManagementAccounting/lecture-notes/lecture-28.pdf

2 http://rcw.raifoundation.org/management/mba/Financial&ManagementAccounting/lecture-notes/lecture-29.pdf

Sources

http://www.google.com/search?q=%22sales+volume+variance%22+definition&hl=en&lr=&start=10&sa=N

http://www.freeworldacademy.com/newbizzadviser/fw29.htm

http://www.maaw.info/Chapter13.htm#Part%20I.%20Alternative%20Four%20Variance%20with%20Sales%20Mix

http://www.prenticehall.ca/horngren/horngren_cost_3/ppt/teall_cost_3_ch16.ppt#259,6,Sales-Mix and Sales-Quantity Variance

Sales Price Variance 95

Measurement Need

This chapter expands on the sales price variance methodology introduced in Chapter 94. Actual selling prices usually vary from the retail or recommended price due to specific customer situations, market conditions and competitor actions. Sales and marketing management want to know the resulting sales price variance.

Solution[1]

The sales price variance formula is:

$$SPV_t = Q_a (P_a - P_b)$$

Where

SPV_t = sales price variance in time period t

Q_a = actual units sold in time period t

P_a = actual price during time period t

P_b = retail or recommended price

To illustrate, Glob Toys (hypothetical) sells a product called "BlobSlob" which is a shiny, clay-like substance that kids mold into monster shapes. The company sold 100,000 units last year at an actual price of $4 each. Suggested retail was $5.

$$SPV = 100,000 \times (\$4 - \$5)$$
$$= -\$100,000$$

The calculation shows that Glob Toys had an SPV of $100,000, meaning that actual sales were lower than projected sales by that amount. Let's look at a more sophisticated treatment: Glob Toys has two products, BlobSlob and SlobberChops (a toy dog that perpetually drools). Glob planned their expected results as shown in Tables 34 and 35.

Table 34: Projected Performance

	BlobSlob	SlobberChops
Unit sales (projected)	100,000	50,000
Unit price (recommended)	$5	$10
Unit cost (projected)	$3	$6

Table 35: Actual Performance

	BlobSlob	SlobberChops
Unit sales (actual)	120,000	60,000
Unit price (actual)	$4	$8.50
Unit cost (actual)	$3	$6

In this case, costs remain the same because Glob Toys had locked in supplier prices and production costs in advance. We can now compare:

Projected revenue	(100,000 × $5) + (50,000 × $10)	= $1,000,000
Actual revenue	(120,000 × $4) + (60,000 × $8.50)	= $990,000
Projected profit	(100,000 × $2) + (50,000 × $4)	= $400,000
Actual profit	(120,000 × $1) + (60,000 × $1.50)	= $210,000
	Total sales variance	−$190,000

The next step is to calculate the SPV:

$$SPV = \{120,000 \times (\$4-\$5)\} + \{60,000 \times (\$8.50-\$10.00)\}$$
$$= -\$210,000$$

Therefore, Glob Toys' sales price variance shows the effect of price changes from projected to actual, resulting in this case in $210,000 less in total sales versus plan.

Impact on Decision Making

While it is clear that price changes have an impact on actual financial performance versus projected, it is less obvious how to fix it in the future. The marketer could mandate a strict "no discounting" policy, with the CEO and CFO's blessings, no doubt. Some consumers would likely pay the full amount, but many more would simply shift to a competitor product or delay purchase to a later time period. This would exacerbate the sales variance problem since there would now be a smaller customer base *and* lower sales, not to mention a probable negative perception of Glob Toys' image, particularly from retailers who want to sell the inventory quickly. They may reduce their future purchases of Glob Toys' products, knowing that the firm is inflexible and insensitive to their needs and the market conditions that created them. Marketers in this situation have several options:

1. Hold firm on price and risk reduced overall sales and a smaller customer base

2. Allow pricing deviations to attract more customers, but recognize the lower sales as a result, plus reduced margins. This may increase market share for a short period of time, but it may also lock in a more permanent lower-margin performance

3. Reduce costs to allow for greater pricing flexibility without eroding margins

4. Increase the value-add of the products, perhaps by offering a unique loyalty program or a clear explanation for why their product is superior and why it is relevant to the customer.

None of these are easy choices and a marketer may try each of these in an effort to find the best combination that maximizes sales and profits, and attracts the largest number of customers.

Endnote

1 Gilligan, C. and Wilson, R.M.S. *Strategic Marketing Management: Planning, Implementation & Control.* Richard M.S. Wilson and Colin Gilligan, Elsevier Butterworth-Heinemann, 2005: p.781.

Sales Volume Variance 96

Measurement Need

Chapter 94 introduced sales variance analysis, including an alternative to sales volume variance. Chapter 95 discussed sales price variance, which helps marketers understand how price changes impact actual sales. In this chapter, we provide a modified approach to sales volume variance. This approach uses sales quantity variance and sales mix variances as the two variables (whereas Chapter 94 used budgeted price, actual quantity and budgeted quantity as the variables). Readers will note the factors that determine sales mix variance (projected and expected profits from actual sales) and sales quantity variance (projected profit based on projected sales and expected profit from actual sales) are similar, although not identical, measures.

Solution[1]

Sales volume variance is calculated by:

$$SVV_t = SQV_t + SMV_t$$

Where

SVV_t = sales volume variance in time period t

SQV_t = sales quantity variance in time period t

SMV_t = sales mix variance in time period t

To solve, the marketer first needs to solve for SQV and SMV. These are calculated as follows:

$$SQV_t = PPPS_t - EPAS_t$$

Where

SQV_t = sales quantity variance in time period t

$PPPS_t$ = projected profit based on projected sales in time time period t

$EPAS_t$ = expected profit from actual sales in time period t*

*calculated as though profit increases or decreases proportionately with changes in the level of sales[2]

$$SMV_t = EPAS_t - PPAS_t$$

Where

SMV_t = sales mix variance in time period t

$EPAS_t$ = expected profit from actual sales in time period t

$PPAS_t$ = projected profit from actual sales in time period t**

**sum of projected profit for all units sold[3]

Returning to Glob Toys from Chapter 95, we can now compute the results:

$$SQV_t = \$400,000 - (\$990,000 / \$1,000,000 \times \$400,000)$$
$$= \$4,000$$
$$SMV_t = \$400,000 - \{(120,000 \times \$2) + (50,000 \times (\$4)$$
$$= -\$40,000$$

Solving for the sales volume variance:

$$SVV_t = \$4,000 + (-\$40,000)$$
$$= -\$36,000$$

Total sales variance

Using the results from Chapter 95, the marketer can now calculate their total sales variance:

$$TSV_t = SPV_t + SVV_t$$
$$= -\$190,000 + (-\$36,000)$$
$$= -\$226,000$$

Impact on Decision Making

Several factors affect sales volume variance:

1. Customer needs changed, resulting in an increase/decrease in quantity ordered

2. Unexpected cost increases forced an increase in price during time period t

3. Competitors introduced a new product that attracted customers away

4. Production delays forced competitors to cancel commitments

The implications differ for each of these factors and marketers will need to adjust their plans accordingly to ensure their products perform closer to expectations.

Endnotes

1 Gilligan, C. and Wilson, R.M.S. *Strategic Marketing Management: Planning, Implementation & Control.* Richard M.S. Wilson and Colin Gilligan, 2005: p.781-783.

2 Ibid.

3 Ibid.

Straight Commission Plans

Measurement Need

The management teams of most companies set specific targets for revenues, profits or units sold. These are divided into smaller goals across the sales team, weighted according to their company's needs, the size of each salesperson's territory, the dynamics of the market and the "stretch goals" set by sales management (stretch goals are designed to challenge each salesperson to improve their performance over the preceding year, yet not be unachievable). The challenge is choosing a compensation system that is aligned with company objectives.

It is helpful to visualize the sales process using a familiar tool: the product lifecycle S curve (called this due to the S-shape of the curve) as shown in Figure 24. Each product tends to follow a multi-stage development and growth sequence. This sequence describes how products grow over time. Most business literature on this topic identifies the stages as: introduction, growth, maturity and decline. The product lifecycle is not limited to products, however. It is a useful mechanism to describe a company's evolution, marketing stages and even changing customer dynamics. In the early stages (particularly the introduction stage) salespeople are working hard to attract new customers.

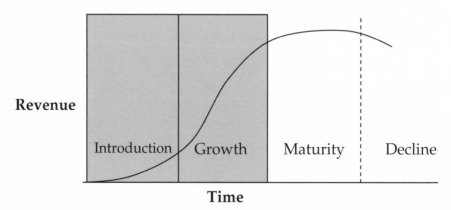

Figure 24: Company Lifecycle—Early Stage Straight Commission Plans

Convincing customers to buy new products is time consuming and hard work, even if the company is already established. Salespeople thrive on success and expect to be rewarded for their efforts. Straight commission rewards the salesperson's specific achievements.

Solution

A commission is simply a percentage of either the final sales price of a specific product or total dollar sales by an individual salesperson. Commission percentages will vary by industry and company. Furthermore, commissions are not fixed and can vary based on the goals set by management. Successful commission sales depend on the effort and energy of each salesperson. Attitude, relentless drive, the proverbial "thick skin", high achievement drive and energy are typical characteristics of commission-based salespeople.

Impact on Decision Making

Sales management needs to be clear about how commissions are determined. Commissions paid at the close of sale will likely be different (and higher, costing the company more) than when the final product is delivered because there may be additional costs (post-sale discounts, payment terms) that can erode the initial price agreed upon with the customer. There are additional pros and cons.

Pros

- Straight commission inspires rapid growth since salespeople are motivated to find new customers because the alternative is no income

- Straight commission will attract salespeople with high ambition and aggressiveness

- Commission salespeople are risk takers and expect to be compensated for their hard work. They thrive on rewards and, conceivably, commissions have unlimited potential—as long as the salesperson keeps finding new customers, he or she will earn more money

- Commission salespeople are highly individualistic and need little direction. This allows management to focus more on strategic and operational issues

- Straight commission can keep costs lower during a downturn since less compensation is paid due to fewer or smaller customer orders

- Commissions are correlated with goals, so sales management can set specific quantitative targets against which performance can be easily measured

- Commissioned salespeople in many companies do not receive benefits (medical, dental, life insurance, profit sharing), therefore employee expenses are lower

Cons

- While commissions can be as simple as a straight percentage of total sales, companies will often vary commission percentages based on strategic objectives and product position needs. This can lead to a complex compensation plan that is challenging to accurately track and administer

- Commission salespeople may be less of a team player and more of a hired gun: moving jobs, companies or industries as commissions change

- Commission salespeople are less likely to perform non-sales tasks and may be unwilling to do basic administrative account record keeping

Sources

http://www.eridlc.com/onlinetextbook/index.cfm?fuseaction=textbook.chpt19

http://www.marketingpower.com/mg- dictionary.php?Searched=1&SearchFor=straight%20commission%20plan

Cron, W.L., DeCarlo, T.E. and Palrymple, D.J. *Sales Management.* New York: John Wiley & Sons, Inc., 2004: p.501.

Doyle, C. *Collins Internet-Linked Dictionary of Marketing.* Harper Collins, 2003, 2006: p.72.

Profit-Based Commission

Measurement Need

Straight commission sales as discussed in Chapter 97 serve to increase sales volume and market share. Over time, management will want to shift to rewards for achieving specific profit levels on each sale. This will be particularly true as a company transitions from rapid growth (often generated by aggressive volume selling to gain share) to a greater emphasis on higher margins on each sale, essentially a progression into the mature stage of the product lifecycle. This occurs as competitors move into the market after seeing the success earned by current entrants, leading to a decline in prices in their efforts to steal share. Companies are forced to look for ways to improve their profitability, through a combination of cost controls, value-added changes to the product and a sales approach that motivates the salesperson to sell differently if they are to earn commissions. Figure 25 shows profit-based commission in the product lifecycle.

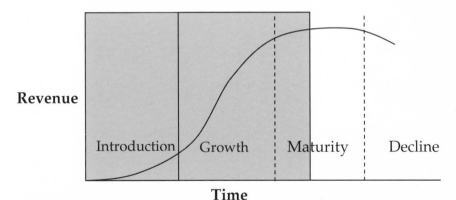

Figure 25: Company Lifecycle—Growth Stage Profit-based Commission Compensation

Solution

A profit-based commission rewards the salesperson for generating sales at a specific profit level (or higher). Volume selling quickly disappears as a sales approach as a result (assuming the salesperson wishes to continue earning a living). As with any business, commission percentages will be based on each company's unique needs and performance objectives.

Impact on Decision Making

A salesperson will alter his or her behavior, assuming there is reward in it for his or her and the objectives are clear. Sales management can mandate a flat profit level across all products, or set specific profit levels to be achieved on each product individually. The challenge in tracking profit-based commissions is allowing the salesperson access to cost information so they can determine the kind of selling required to ensure the overall profit objective is achieved. Without cost information, the salesperson will struggle in conforming final prices to each customer's unique needs.

Endnote

1 Cron, W.L., DeCarlo, T.E. and Palrymple, D.J. *Sales Management*. New York: John Wiley & Sons, Inc., 2004: p.507-509.

Straight Salary

Measurement Need

As businesses grow, so does the complexity of their product lines and the markets they serve. Products are very likely to be at different points along the classic S-shaped product lifecycle curve, as shown in Figure 26. Each stage's unique dynamics require different marketing approaches to meet the needs of customers, which are changing throughout this cycle.

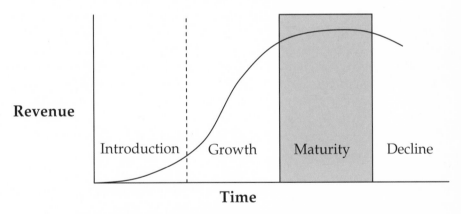

Figure 26: Company Lifecycle—Maturity Stage Straight Salary Compensation

While aggressive selling approaches are useful for attracting customers in the introduction and growth stages (and incentive-laden compensation schemes support this type of selling), customers in the maturity stage are unlikely to respond favorably to these earlier stage sales tactics. Maturity stage customers are more devoted and want their loyalty rewarded through better understanding of their needs and more personal communication. Often, salespeople at the maturity stage are a separate account management team with different skills than the more aggressive, early stage sales team. Consequently, the account manager's compensation should reward their ability to manage the customer relationship over the long-term, and a straight salary is a more useful method to accomplish this.

As the preceding chapters describe, incentive-based plans motivate salespeople to seek only the best customers. But sales management may seek complete coverage of all potential customers in a territory, and not just the top ones. Straight salary is a viable compensation approach to satisfy this need as well.

Solution

Straight salary is not a formula. It is a flat wage paid over a specified period of time, usually in the form of an annual salary paid on a regular schedule, although it could also be a flat-rate contract over a certain number of hours, weeks or months.

Impact on Decision Making

Sales compensation will vary depending on the stage of the lifecycle for the company, its products and its customers, each requiring a different sales approach. Straight salary is particularly useful when the business' intent is to nurture relationships with its most loyal customers. Sales management sets targets for the sales force in the annual sales plan. Straight salary is useful when the targets are more qualitative ("keep the customer happy") versus quantitative ("increase volume 15%") because the individual's impact on sales volume is harder to measure and, therefore, does not lend itself to commission-based rewards.

There are additional pros and cons with straight salary as a compensation scheme.

Pros

- Customers will expect service to be better since the salaried salesperson is focused on the relationship and not the next sale

- Straight salary systems can serve to attract salespeople with better service and relationship development skills, supporting a valuable recruiting need since more aggressive salespeople who prefer higher risk/higher reward commission systems will find straight salary unattractive

- Salaried salespeople are comforted by having a steady income, since their next paycheck is not dependent on generating revenues from new customers (assuming a downturn does not lead to their termination or forced salary reductions)

- Salaried salespeople are compensated more like non-sales management and, therefore, will likely be more willing to perform non-sales activities

- Straight salary is easier for business and financial planning purposes since there is less complexity in the compensation structure. Sales cycles can be volatile and incentive-laden compensation plans can create uneven cash flow needs. straight salary helps management keep expenses at a more constant level, with fewer surprises.

Cons

- Salary expense remains constant even when sales levels decline, reducing margins more than a commission-based salesperson's compensation would, which tends to mirror changes in sales revenues

- Salaried salespeople may be less motivated, whereas incentive-based salespeople are driven to make the next sale. Sales management's challenge is motivating salaried salespeople to keep loyal customers happy, even though the rewards are less tangible. Sales management must clearly describe to each salaried salesperson how their role contributes to customer success and why it is important to the salesperson

- Performance standards, especially the more qualitative and intangible objectives, must be clearly articulated by sales management to the salaried salespeople. This is not easy due to the imprecision of measuring behavior; perhaps requiring sales management to be more hands-on

Final Note:

Since we have examined both straight commission and straight salary in the previous two chapters, let's compare the compensation plans. The following figure[1] assumes a commission rate of 10% versus a straight salary of $40,000. The commission costs the company less than the salary until a certain sales level per person is achieved—$400,000 in this example. Comparing this result with the example of the classic S-curve—whereby it was asserted that a more aggressive sales approach is often needed in the introduction and growth stages, and a more service-oriented account management approach is needed in the maturity stage—we see that a similar result occurs. As sales grow in Figure 27, the company is transitioning from the earlier stages toward maturity, where a straight salary becomes more cost effective.

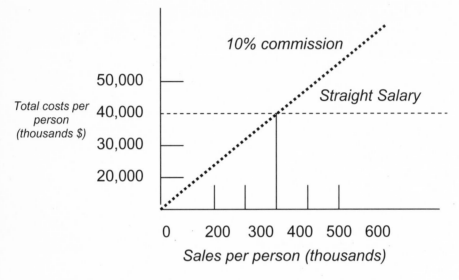

Figure 27: Comparison of Salary and Commission Plans

Endnote

1 Cron, W.L., DeCarlo, T.E. and Palrymple, D.J. *Sales Management.* New York: John Wiley & Sons, Inc., 2004: p.502.

Sources

http://www.marketingpower.com/mg-dictionary-view3054.php

http://www.eridlc.com/onlinetextbook/index.cfm?fuseaction=textbook.chpt19

http://www.econ.jku.at/Winter/lazear/Lecture5.pdf

Cron, W. L., DeCarlo, T. E. and Palrymple, D. J. *Sales Management.* New York: John Wiley & Sons, Inc., 2004: pp.499-501.

Salary Plus Commission or Bonus 100

Measurement Need

As Chapter 99 discussed, an important disadvantage of straight salary compensation is the lack of reward for extraordinary performance. Salespeople on straight salary are unlikely to be motivated to achieve specific targets since there is no corresponding reward. Sales management may decide to set more specific goals, and will need a compensation plan that rewards achievement accordingly. As a company grows and matures, the number of products increases, as does the number of customers and markets served. Straight commission as described in Chapter 97 is no longer adequate to address the competing strategic objectives of the company and its evolving customer base. A more diverse sales compensation plan may be needed to address the different demands of each product at each stage, such as that shown in Figure 28.

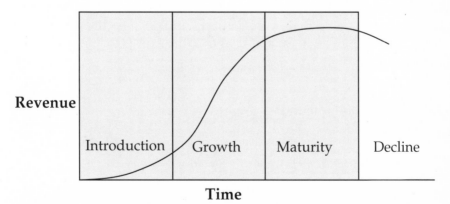

Figure 28: Company Lifecycle—Salary Plus Commission or Bonus Compensation

Solution[1]

Salary plus commission (SPC) or bonus offers management an important tool to motivate behavior since rewards are tied to accomplishments beyond the basic management expectations covered by straight salary. SPC and salary plus bonus (SPB) will be discussed individually, along with the respective impact on decision making of each.

SPC

The logic behind SPC is simply to help sales management motivate salespeople—particularly B2B sellers involved in lengthy sales cycles—to achieve specific targets by paying them a commission if the goal is reached. B2B salespeople receive salary as a base level of income to compensate for the longer time between each sale. If and when the sale occurs, a commission is paid, although it is smaller than a straight commission due to the added benefit of the stable salary. This affords a fair amount of compensation flexibility to management as it can set different commission percentages based on the importance of the strategic need.

For example, let's look at an enterprise software company selling a range of applications in three categories: databases, financial applications and sales force automation software. Its salespeople receive a base salary, which helps offset income declines during business down cycles. The company's management decides that the performance of its sales force automation business can be improved, so it sets a commission of 5% per for monthly sales increases up to $100,000. If a salesperson sells an additional $100,001 to $124,999, then the commission increases to 7.5% on the sales in this range. And if the target is exceeded by more than $125,000, then the salesperson receives a 10% commission for any sales over the $125,000 amount.

Impact on Decision Making[2]

Pros

- SPC can help a company achieve important, short-term goals (sell more soft candy to retail accounts)

- SPC can improve the performance of specific products or services since salespeople will be rewarded for focusing their effort on the selected areas of need

- Commissions paid regularly are a great source of motivation because the salesperson gets almost immediate financial benefit as well as recognition for achievement

Cons

- Similarly to straight commission sales, SPC can become complex, particularly with large product lines

- Commissions are like marketing promotions and can be expensive in the short-term since the company will pay out more in additional financial reward as more sales are generated. It raises the strategic question of whether there is a long-term benefit, such as increased customer loyalty, or if the commission incentive merely spikes revenue only for the length of the program

- Commissions tend to reward volume at the expense of profits, so they should be designed carefully

SPB

SPB programs are typically structured around quotas. Quotas are specific targets derived from company goals. Whereas commissions may be related to individual products and individual sales, quotas are more often tied to growth objectives for customers (both new customers and/or share of customer increases) or total product sales (units or dollars). If the quotas are achieved, then a bonus is paid on a quarterly, semi-annual or annual basis.

For example, let's look at the enterprise software company again. The company's management decides to increase market share in the next year, as measured by units sold. Furthermore, management determines that it wants to grow its market share in the banking sector by 3%. Sales management would establish quotas for each rep, based on their territory, with the aggregate total quotas equaling or exceeding the 3% market share improvement goal. If a sales rep meets their quota, which is known as "achieving quota", then they receive a bonus at the end of the pay period. Many companies will reward for performances that exceed quota, increasing the bonus as the situation warrants.

Impact on Decision Making[3]

Pros

- SPB helps align a salesperson's efforts with longer-term company strategic objectives (increase market share by 3% this year; increase profits per sale by 5%)

- SPB may inspire a more complete, business-oriented approach since rewards will be based on a combination of sales, profits, and customer growth, versus the one-sided volume emphasis of commission compensation

- SPB rewards longer-term behavior, so it can encourage better sales force retention

- SPB provides a more controlled outflow of funds than commission-based sales since bonuses are usually paid on an annual basis, versus the sale-by-sale basis of commissions. This provides more predictable and stable financial control

Cons

- Companies usually allocate a finite pool of money for bonuses, and a percentage payout range that limits rewards. A percentage payout range is issued by senior management, setting limits on bonuses, based on performance. For example, the range might be 3% to 6%, with top performers earning 6%. In this situation, top performing salespeople may be insufficiently rewarded for extraordinary achievement, therefore a company risks losing its best talent while retaining average or even poor performers

- Bonuses are less precise. Whereas a commission is tied directly to an increase in sales, it is harder to correlate a bonus payout to the more complete business approach of revenues, profits and customer growth

- Bonuses are paid less often than commissions. Since salespeople thrive on reward, the longer wait to receive a bonus may be demotivating

Endnotes

1 Adapted from the article, "Sales Compensation: Creating Performance Clarity" by John F. Tallitsch, Managing Director for TOPMARK LLC http://www.ezinearticles.com/?Sales-Compensation:-Creating-Performance-Clarity&id=151492

2 Adapted from: Cron, W.L., DeCarlo. T.E. and Palrymple. D.J. *Sales Management*. New York: John Wiley & Sons, Inc., 2004: pp.502-503.

3 Ibid., pp.503-504.

Source

http://waternet.com/article.asp?IndexID=6634018

Salary Plus
Commission and Bonus 101

Measurement Need

Chapter 100, Salary Plus Commission or Bonus, discussed the value of a more sophisticated sales compensation plan that gives sales management the choice of adding a commission or bonus to base salary. Many companies, particularly large multi-nationals, operate in multiple environments, each at different stages of market development and with correspondingly varied product financial performance objectives. If this is the case, sales management can offer compensation that combines salary, commission and bonus to effectively target the varied business environments (and their sales requirements) in which they operate. Figure 29 illustrates this scheme.

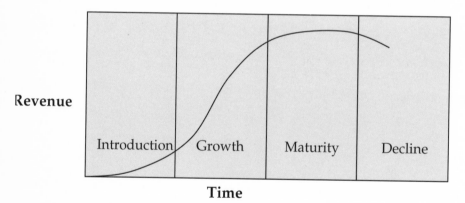

Revenue

Introduction | Growth | Maturity | Decline

Time

Figure 29: Company Lifecycle—All Salary Plus Commission and Bonus Compensation

Solution[1]

Salary plus commission and bonus allows management to compensate salespeople with a steady salary plus commissions to inspire individual performance behaviors and bonuses, usually based on the achievement of company performance milestones. Alternatively, management may choose to vary the structure to a combination of salary, commissions for accomplishing specific individual and team goals, and bonuses paid annually for company performance and customer satisfaction scores.

Impact on Decision Making

The advantages to commissions and bonuses are enumerated in greater depth in Chapter 100. The most attractive element is the maximum flexibility afforded sales management to structure rewards to achieve multiple corporate objectives. This also allows the field salesperson to adopt a sales approach best suited to their abilities. Conversely, the risk is that companies with multiple products, customers and markets also have varied, and often quite complex, performance objectives, making this type of compensation challenging for management to administrate and for salespeople to understand. An unfortunate side effect may be a sub-optimal effort by the salesperson who, instead of trying to master the complexity of the compensation plan to maximize rewards, opts instead to pursue a "low-hanging fruit" approach to sales—working on those goals that involve the least hassle for them, and sacrificing some of the company's overall objectives.

Endnote

1 Adapted from: Cron, W.L., DeCarlo, T.E. and Palrymple, D.J. *Sales Management*. New York: John Wiley & Sons, Inc., 2004: pp.504-505.

Commission Plus Bonus 102

Measurement Need

Companies with a sales force composed of mostly contracted third-party (independent) sales reps, such as real estate firms or industries that rely on part-time help, do not want the overhead expense of fixed salaries. Yet, these companies still need to attract and reward salespeople. Brokerage firms, multi-level marketing companies and even high-tech start-ups often utilize the commission plus bonus form of compensation as it can apply to any stage in the product lifecycle. It is illustrated in Figure 30.

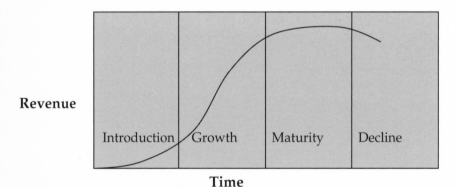

Figure 30: Company Lifecycle—All Stages Commission Plus Bonus Compensation

Solution

Commission sales inspire salespeople because they are paid when the sale is complete, tying reward directly and immediately to accomplishment. The bonus component, as discussed in Chapters 100-101, motivates a longer-term behavior by paying the reward after a specific period of time, usually for company, division or team goals that have been achieved. If the longer-term goals are not met, then the bonus is not paid and the salesperson is paid from commission-based sales alone.

Impact on Decision Making

Like straight commission (Chapter 97), this is a Darwinian approach. It has the benefit to the company of reducing expenses since no salaries are paid, but it can also create cash flow volatility since commissions are paid as sales come in. To survive, the salesperson must sell. To thrive, the salesperson must sell plus achieve certain longer-term goals that are often tied to overall company performance. Commission plus bonus attracts a specific kind of salesperson who is highly independent and self-sufficient, and may also not enjoy structured reporting relationships. In most companies, non-salaried people usually do not receive benefits (Starbucks being a rare exception), so the salesperson is responsible for arranging their own medical and other insurance needs, which are paid out of their earnings. These salespeople tend to be entrepreneurial and find the risks exhilarating because the rewards, if they come, can be high. If an organization simply seeks aggressive sales growth, then this approach can work well. But if the company seeks more loyalty from their sales team, then this form of compensation will not attract the right talent.

Endnote

1 Adapted from: Cron, W.L., DeCarlo, T.E. and Palrymple, D.J. *Sales Management*. New York: John Wiley & Sons, Inc., 2004: p.505.

Team Selling Compensation 103

Measurement Need

Companies with a large sales force will find that sales territories will often overlap. Customer operations may be spread across multiple sales territories, for example. Or a customer may seek a product represented by another salesperson in a different market. Sales management needs a way to motivate the salespeople involved to coordinate their expertise for the benefit of the customer and to close the sale.

Team selling is unlikely to be needed at the introduction stage of the product lifecycle since, as a matter of survival, the company is emphasizing sales to as many customers as possible. Team selling would pull valuable resources from multiple segments and customers to concentrate on a few, reducing the odds for succeeding past this early stage. Even in the growth stage, team selling is less likely because the company is still building its customer base, solidifying its market share gains and trying to satisfy growing demand for its initial group of products.

The shift into late growth and maturity, and perhaps even decline, is when team selling may be necessary as the company looks toward new ways to satisfy existing customers and expands its product and solution offering. The company's customers have been growing as well, with changing needs and increasingly dispersed operations, so the momentum toward overlapping territories and combined sales efforts will grow as well. Figure 31 illustrates team selling compensation.

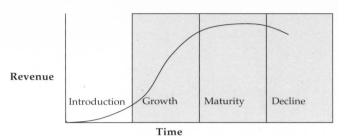

Figure 31: Company Lifecycle—Team Selling Compensation

David Steitz, president of Characters Inc., a multimillion-dollar computer typesetting business in Houston, uses the team sales and planning approach to win over clients during particularly tough presentations.[1]

"[We once] had a large catalog to do for a customer, and we had never dealt with them before. So we developed a team of six people in our company from various disciplines," says Steitz. "The team included myself, the sales representative from my company, the customer service rep, the technical computer specialist, the trainer, and the software specialist meeting with our client."

The sales rep and Steitz were only there to facilitate the discussion and to introduce the other team members. During the sales presentation, which was conducted more like a planning session than a sales meeting, each team member gave a presentation explaining his or her role in the project, as if they were already doing the job.

"I wish I could tell you that this was all done intentionally, but it just happened that way," Steitz says. "My other team members were not salespeople—they were just folks who do the work and do it well. This fact came across brilliantly, and we ended up going from what was supposed to be a typical sales presentation, to a planning meeting, to scheduling with the prospects when we could actually start the project. It was magical."

Solution

A team selling compensation program can address this issue. Two or more salespeople (it is conceivable that a selling team may contain non-sales people, particularly with industrial and high-tech businesses) combine efforts to maximize a customer sale, improve the financial outcome for their company and deliver a solution that could not have been completed in the absence of the team.

Impact on Decision Making

The decision to create a team selling plan presents sales management with a challenge since salespeople are predisposed toward individual achievement. The structure of the compensation plan must be able to satisfy the needs of multiple parties: the individuals, the team and, most importantly, the customer.

A sales manager will want to weigh the opportunity costs of supporting a team for the benefit of one customer versus continuing independent selling by each salesperson. Sales management needs to have a clear understanding of what is expected in each of the following areas:

- Team work
  - Who will be on the team?
  - How is the team's work to be allocated?
  - Is this designed to enhance collaboration for the long-term?
- Objectives
  - Is the proposed team satisfying a one-time need, or is it part of a more significant company restructuring to encourage more cohesive sales objectives?
  - Is the company's customer base changing, requiring expansion of the team selling effort and a move away from individual achievement?
  - How will productivity be measured?
  - How will financial success be measured? Through improved revenues, profits or units sold? Will there be an emphasis on different products?
  - How will this affect recruiting?
- Individual performance
  - How will individual contribution to the team be evaluated?
- Managerial support
  - Will management support the team's efforts?

o Will management support team bonuses?

o How will management review performance?

- Reward fairness

    o Can contribution imbalances be addressed fairly?

    o How is reward size determined? By team? By individual?

    o Will the bonus sufficiently reward the team effort?

- Employee input

    o How much input will each team member have toward the group effort?

    o Will individual inputs be considered by management before the team plan is completed?

    o Will team members have input on quality issues?

Endnote

Source: Kennedy, D. "Dream Teams-Team Buying and Selling". *Entrepreneur Magazine,* September 1997.

Sources

http://www.coba.unt.edu/MGMT/Johnson/courses/366,17,Gainsharing

http://www.findarticles.com/p/articles/mi_m0DTI/is_n9_v25/ai_19892331

Adapted from: Cron, W.L., DeCarlo. T.E. and Palrymple. D.J. *Sales Management.* New York: John Wiley & Sons, Inc., 2004: pp.507.

Index